CHICAGO PUBLIC LIBRARY
SULZER REGIONAL
R0016222490

DISCARD

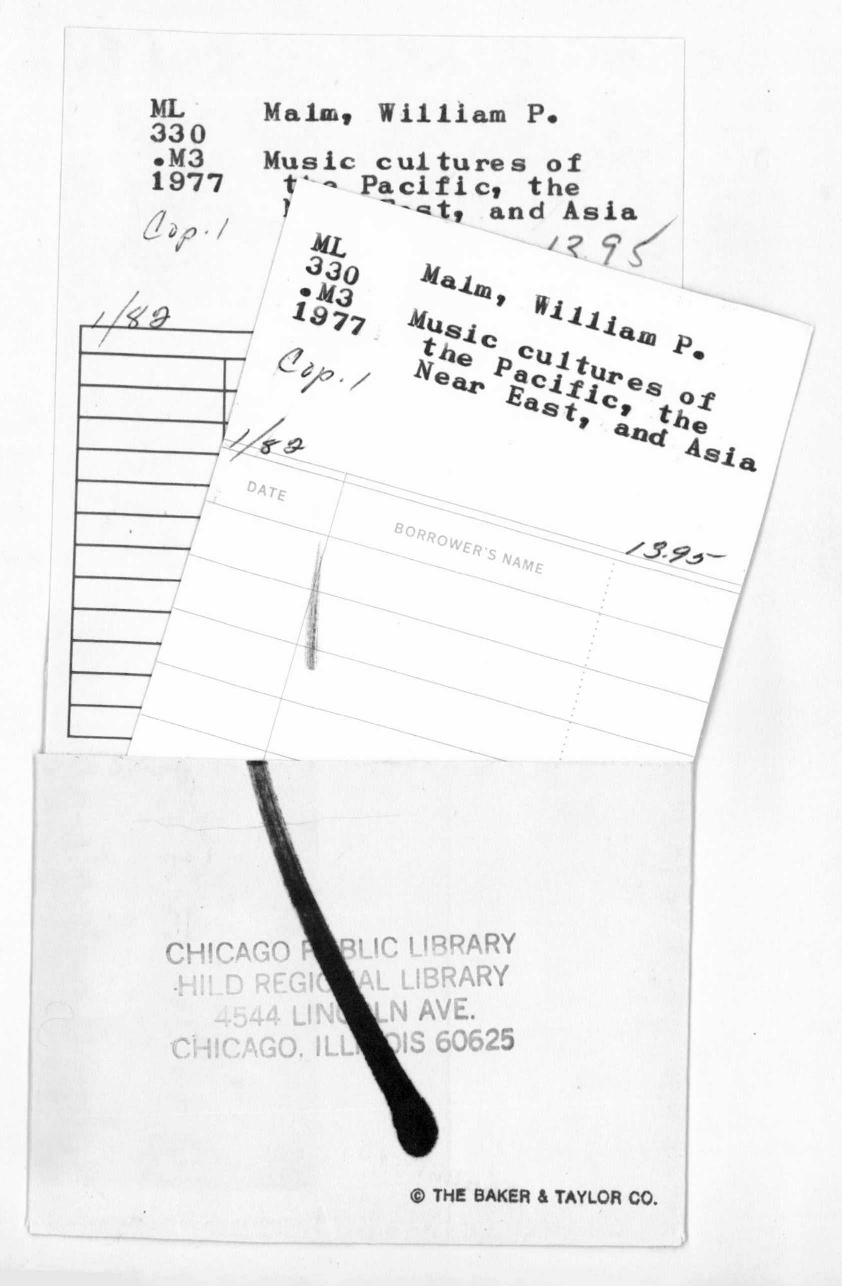
ML
330
.M3
1977
Malm, William P.
Music cultures of
the Pacific, the
Near East, and Asia
Cop. 1
13.95
1/82
DATE
BORROWER'S NAME
CHICAGO PUBLIC LIBRARY
HILD REGIONAL LIBRARY
4544 LINCOLN AVE.
CHICAGO, ILLINOIS 60625
© THE BAKER & TAYLOR CO.

PRENTICE-HALL
HISTORY OF MUSIC SERIES
H. WILEY HITCHCOCK, editor

MUSIC IN THE MEDIEVAL WORLD, 2ND ED., *Albert Seay*
MUSIC IN THE RENAISSANCE, 2ND ED., *Howard Mayer Brown*
BAROQUE MUSIC, *Claude V. Palisca*
MUSIC IN THE CLASSIC PERIOD, 2ND ED., *Reinhard G. Pauly*
NINETEENTH-CENTURY ROMANTICISM IN MUSIC, 2ND ED., *Rey M. Longyear*
TWENTIETH-CENTURY MUSIC: AN INTRODUCTION, 2ND ED., *Eric Salzman*
FOLK AND TRADITIONAL MUSIC OF THE WESTERN CONTINENTS, 2ND ED., *Bruno Nettl*
MUSIC CULTURES OF THE PACIFIC, THE NEAR EAST, AND ASIA, 2ND ED., *William P. Malm*
MUSIC IN THE UNITED STATES: A HISTORICAL INTRODUCTION, 2ND ED., *H. Wiley Hitchcock*
MUSIC OF LATIN AMERICA, *Gerard Béhague*

second edition

MUSIC CULTURES OF THE PACIFIC, THE NEAR EAST, AND ASIA

WILLIAM P. MALM
School of Music
The University of Michigan

PRENTICE-HALL, INC., ENGLEWOOD CLIFFS, NEW JERSEY 07632

Library of Congress Cataloging in Publication Data

MALM, WILLIAM P.
Music cultures of the Pacific, the Near East, and Asia.

(Prentice-Hall history of music series)
Includes bibliographies, discographies, and index.
1. Music, Oriental—History and criticism.
I. Title.
ML330.M3 1977 780'.95 76-44027
ISBN 0-13-608000-6
ISBN 0-13-607994-6 pbk.

Printed in the United States of America

10 9 8 7 6 5 4 3 2 1

PRENTICE-HALL INTERNATIONAL, INC., *London*
PRENTICE-HALL OF AUSTRALIA, PTY. LIMITED, *Sydney*
PRENTICE-HALL OF CANADA, LTD., *Toronto*
PRENTICE-HALL OF INDIA PRIVATE LIMITED, *New Delhi*
PRENTICE-HALL OF JAPAN, INC., *Tokyo*
PRENTICE-HALL OF SOUTHEAST ASIA PTE. LTD., *Singapore*
WHITEHALL BOOKS LIMITED, *Wellington, New Zealand*

CONTENTS

FOREWORD v

PREFACE vii

LIST OF PLATES xi

LIST OF MUSICAL EXAMPLES AND TABLES xiv

1 OCEANIA 1
Australia 1 — Rudiments of Ethnomusicological Music Analysis 7
Melanesia 9 — Polynesia 18 — Micronesia 24

2 THE PHILIPPINES, BORNEO, AND INDONESIA 28
The Philippines 28 — Borneo 33
Indonesia–A Historical Introduction 34 — The Gamelan 34
Javanese Music Theory and Practice 38
Balinese Music 48 — Conclusion 49

3 MOSLEM AFRICA, ETHIOPIA, AND THE NEAR EAST 52
Moslem and Black Africa 53 Ethiopia 55
The Pan-Islamic Tradition 58 Folk Music 58
Classical Music 67 Classical and Modern Instruments 67
Classical Music Theory 69 Classical Music Performance Practice 76
Musical Forms 79 Popular Music 80
A Historical Interlude—The Ancient World of the Near East 81
Jewish Music in the Near East 83

4 CENTRAL AND SOUTHERN ASIA 88
Music of the Soviet Central Asian Republics 88 Afghanistan 92
South Asia—A Historical Introduction 93 Ancient Indian Music 94
Indian Music Theory 95 Indian Music Practice 102
Basic Indian Instruments 107
Some Indian Folk, Popular, and Theatrical Music Traditions 114
A Theoretical Postscript 116

5 SOUTHEAST ASIA 118
Southeast Asian Tonal Systems 119 Instrumental Ensembles 123
Percussion-dominated Ensembles 123
String-dominated Ensembles 128
Wind Ensembles and Instruments 129
String Music—Solo, Accompanimental, and Chamber 130
Sacred and Secular Vocal Music 133 Folk and Tribal Music 134
Theatrical, Rural, and Popular Music 135

6 EAST ASIA 138
Tibet 138 Mongolia 143 China 144
The Formative Period 145 The International Period 153
The National Period 156 The World Music Period 167

7 NORTHEAST ASIA AND THE ISLAND COUNTRIES 176
Manchuria and Korea 176 Taiwan and the Ryukyu Islands 183
Japan 185 Folk Music 185
Japanese Art Music—Ancient Traditions 188
Early Japanese Narrative and Theatrical Traditions 197
Music During Japan's Edo Period 201 Music in Modern Japan 204
The Northern Islands and Beyond 208

EPILOGUE 213

INDEX 217

FOREWORD

Students and informed amateurs of the history of music have long needed a series of books that are comprehensive, authoritative, and engagingly written. They have needed books written by specialists—but specialists interested in communicating vividly. The Prentice-Hall History of Music Series aims at filling these needs.

Six books in the series present a panoramic view of the history of Western music, divided among the major historical periods—Medieval, Renaissance, Baroque, Classic, Romantic, and Contemporary. The musical culture of the United States, viewed historically as an independent development within the larger western tradition, is discussed in another book, and forthcoming will be similar books on the music of Latin America and Russia. In yet another pair, the rich yet neglected folk and traditional music of both hemispheres is treated. Taken together, the eleven volumes of the series will be a distinctive and, we hope, distinguished contribution to the history of the music of the world's peoples. Each

Foreword, continued

volume, moreover, may be read singly as a substantial account of the music of its period or area.

The authors of the series are scholars of national and international repute—musicologists, critics, and teachers of acknowledged stature in their respective fields of specialization. In their contributions to the Prentice-Hall History of Music Series their goal has been to present works of solid scholarship that are eminently readable, with significant insights into music as a part of the general intellectual and cultural life of man.

H. WILEY HITCHCOCK, *Editor*

PREFACE

The purpose of this book is to survey the basic kinds of music and musical instruments found in the major oriental civilizations and in the island cultures of the Eastern Hemisphere. It also is intended as an introduction to the basic attitudes, techniques, and nomenclature of the discipline of ethnomusicology. These two goals are commingled, so that reading a given chapter provides preliminary information about the musical ways of one part of the world, whereas reading the entire book gives one an overview of the continuities and uniqueness in non-Western music, as well as a basic vocabulary with which to discuss music from any part of the world. Those general concepts not discussed in this book appear in Bruno Nettl's companion volume, *Folk and Traditional Music of the Western Continents,* in this series.

Many musics from dozens of cultures and countries have been crowded into the following seven chapters. The chapters themselves are based primarily on geographic areas, but cultural cross-references are found both in the text and the index. The selected list of recordings at the end of each chapter will provide the reader with a channel to some of the sounds of the sonic events discussed, but it must be remembered that only a small part of the total musical effect can be ascertained by listening to the music alone. Where possible, background information has been provided so that the reader may place his listening in a proper cultural matrix. It should be noted that the field of ethnomusicology has grown so rapidly in the ten years since the first edition of this book that even these brief area surveys and materials lists have had to be done over almost completely. Nevertheless, the basic goals of the book remain the same.

Four basic approaches are used in this book: the anthropological, historical, organological, and musical. The anthropologist or behavioral musicologist looks at the place of music in culture, at the values a society attaches to it, and at the people who practice it. Historical musicology will be applied most often in literate societies such as those of India and China where historical periods and theoretical constructs were well established long before the monkish scholars of Europe "invented" the bases of Western art music. Archaeology will also help us in the reconstruction of historical data from destroyed civilizations as well as nonliterate societies. However, although the legends of the ancient and tribal worlds have some use to musicology, potsherds and burial mounds do not give the historical musicologist much to work with. They may prove useful, nevertheless, to the organologist, the student of the history and development of musical instruments.

Organology is important to this book, for many times the only information available in an area is a description of its instruments. Such details tell us only a little about the actual music. When coupled with similar information from other areas, however, they can prove useful for studying possible diffusions of musics throughout the world. They also prepare the reader for what he should expect should he visit a given area in search of traditional music. The excellent line drawings of Masakazu Kuwata were of great help in furthering these organological goals in the first edition. The new drawings (Figures 1, 5, 13, 14, 21, 22, 23, 26, 27, 35, 54, 57, and 64) were done by Ms. Elizabeth McGregor. They are added not only to improve our presentations of specific cultures but also to provide examples for more basic categories of musical instruments and to illustrate certain crucial playing positions.

Whenever and wherever possible, we have been product musicologists; that is, we have looked directly at the musical sounds and tried to find out where they come from, how they make sense, and how one can learn to appreciate them. It is axiomatic that all musics do make sense, for they always consist of the disciplining of tones according to the aesthetic criteria of their particular time and culture. An understanding of such musical logics is the basic goal of this book.

Two major problems in preparing this book were transliteration and transcription. Most of the indigenous terms and instrument names mentioned are derived from languages which have more than one form of romanization. I have tried to choose that spelling for each term which is likely to be pronounced most closely to the original by the nonspecialist; I do not claim any linguistic consistency in my choices. Common alternate spellings are shown in parentheses. Transcription of non-Western music in Western-style notation always creates some form of distortion. To aid the reader in evoking the proper non-Western sounds I have, whenever possible, chosen my examples from recordings commercially available in the United States. Thus, the reader may use the transcriptions as guide lines and correct their inadequacies with his own ear. Special notational symbols are: (↑) a pitch higher than notated; (↓) a pitch lower than notated; (◡̇) a time slightly shorter than notated; (⁄) or (⁊) a sliding entrance to or exit from a note; and (♫) a series of pitches, with a slide from one to another. A note in parentheses is one that is barely heard. If the transcription is transposed, the approximate original pitch is shown at the beginning in parentheses. Any special symbols beyond these are explained in the examples using them. The examples are meant not only to illustrate specific points in the text but also to provide a variety of types for further analysis or discussion. In this context the second edition has provided a *gamelan* piece (Example 2–1) based on an actual recording as well as a non-Western canon (Example 1–3). Unless otherwise noted, the transcriptions are the author's own. Changes in the second-edition versions of earlier examples are based on constructive criticisms from my colleagues and students, ten additional years of listening and transcription experience, and the use of a tape machine with a more accurate speed. I wish to thank the many recording companies, publishers, and individual field collectors who have given their permission to make these transcriptions of their products. Full citations and credits are given with each example. Updated discographies and bibliographies appear at the end of each chapter. A map has been provided to help the reader locate unfamiliar places mentioned in the text.

Each area surveyed in this book is, of course, worthy of a separate study of equal or greater length. Until such books are written, this author must depend on his friends and his critics. Each chapter was sent to at least one regional expert for advice before a final draft was made. Special thanks are due to Shigeo Kishibe, Tajore Viswanathan, Rulan Chao Pian, Hormoz Farhat, Barbara Smith, Mantle Hood, Robert Brown, William Hu, Ernest McCarus, and Mark Slobin for invaluable information and criticism. For the second edition I wish to thank in particular Judith Becker, Jon Higgins, Nazir Jairazbhoy, Ricardo Trimillos, Ivan Vandor, and Ella Zonis for their help. H. Wiley Hitchcock, Ms. Jamie Fuller, and Ms. Geneviev Libin were of special value in guiding my style of presentation. Thanks go also to the Centers for Japanese, South and Southeast Asia, and Russian Studies of the University of Michigan for their cooperation in so many ways. I also wish to thank the Institute for Cultural Learning of the East-West Center in Hawaii and the Villa Serbelloni Center of The Rockefeller Foundation for both providing the time and support that allowed me to complete the second edition. Finally, I thank those scholars who were willing to give advice but preferred not to have their names connected with a book in which one author attempts to cover such a vast area in so few pages. The information and judgments of this book are the author's own responsibility and do not necessarily reflect those of advisors, assistants, or supporting institutions named or unnamed. My hope is that the reader may find in this book a means to a broader understanding of music as a beautiful but often very different worldwide phenomenon.

W.P.M.
May, 1976

LIST OF PLATES

I AUSTRALIAN ABORIGINAL INSTRUMENTS xviii

Figure 1. Rhythm sticks and a *dijeridoo*

II ISLAND INSTRUMENTS 17

Figure 2. New Guinea drum Figure 3. Oceanic nose flute
Figure 4. *Valiha* (tube zither from Madagascar)

III DIFFUSION EXAMPLES FROM SOUTHEAST ASIA 32

Figure 5. *Kudyapi* from the Philippines
Figure 6. *Kachapi* from Borneo Figure 7. *Kacapi* from Java
Figure 8. *Mi gyaun* from Burma

IV JAVA 36

Figure 9. *Rebab* Figure 10. *Saron* Figure 11. *Bonang*
Figure 12. *Gender*

V ETHIOPIA 57

Figure 13. *Tsenatsil* Figure 14. *Krar*

VI THE NEAR EAST 63

Figure 15. *Amzhad* Figure 16. *Yarul*
Figure 17. A *tombak, zarb,* or *darbukka*

VII THE NEAR EAST 65

Figure 18. *Ud* Figure 19. *Tambur* Figure 20. *Tar*

VIII NEAR EASTERN BOWED LUTES 68

Figure 21. *Kamanchay* Figure 22. *Keman*
Figure 23. *Rabab*

IX THE NEAR EAST 77

Figure 24. *Zurna* Figure 25. *Qanun*

X INDIAN DRUMS 109

Figure 26. *Mridanga* Figure 27. *Tabla*
Figure 28. *Baya*

XI INDIAN PLUCKED CHORDOPHONES 111

Figure 29. *Bin* Figure 30. *Bin sitar* Figure 31. *Vina*
Figure 32. *Sitar*

XII INDIAN BOWED AND PLUCKED LUTES 112

Figure 33. *Sarangi* Figure 34. *Sarinda* Figure 35. *Sarod*

XIII SOUTHEAST ASIAN IDIOPHONES 124

Figure 36. *Ranak ek* Figure 37. *Khong wong yai*

XIV SOUTHEAST ASIAN AEROPHONES 125

Figure 38. *Pi nai* Figure 39. *Quadruple reed*
Figure 40. *Khaen*

XV SOUTHEAST ASIAN CHORDOPHONES 131

Figure 41. *Saung kauk* from Burma
Figure 42. *Chakay* from Thailand
Figure 43. A chest resonated monochord

XVI CHINA 151

Figure 44. *Ch'in* Figure 45. *P'ip'a* Figure 46. *Sheng*

XVII CHINA 157

Figure 47. *Hu ch'in* Figure 48. *San hsien*
Figure 49. *Yueh ch'in* Figure 50. *Pan ku*

XVIII KOREA 178

Figure 51. *Kayakeum* Figure 52. *Komungo*
Figure 53. *Changko*

XIX KOREA 179

Figure 54. *Haekeum* Figure 55. *O* or *yu*

XX JAPANESE SHOSO-IN TREASURE 192

Figure 56. Figures on the face of a *biwa*

XXI JAPANESE SHOSO-IN TREASURE 193

Figure 57. The *kugo* harp

XXII JAPANESE CHORDOPHONES 196

Figure 58. *Shamisen* Figure 59. *Koto* Figure 60. *Biwa*

XXIII JAPANESE MEMBRANOPHONES 198

Figure 61. *Ko tsuzumi* Figure 62. *O tsuzumi*
Figure 63. *Taiko*

XXIV CIRCUMBOREAL MEMBRANOPHONE 210

Figure 64. Eskimo pan drums

LIST OF MUSICAL EXAMPLES AND TABLES

1-1 Two Australian aboriginal songs 6

1-2 New Guinea polyphony 11

1-3 A New Guinean *kawari* canonic chant 13

1-4 A Maori *haka* dance song in graph notation 19

1-5 An *oli* and *hula* chant from Hawaii 23

2-1 One Javanese *gongan* in *ketawang* form 39

2-2 The *ketawang* temporal cycle 44

2-3 The Javanese tone system 46

2-4 Balinese resultant melodies 49

3-1 A heterophonic Tuareg love song 60

3-2 A Druse song 61

3-3 Three versions of the mode *ramal maia* 72

3-4 One abstraction of the Persian dastgah system 73

3-5 Two versions of the rhythmic pattern *remel* 75

3-6 A Persian *gushé* 78

3-7 A Yemenite Jewish chant 84

4-1 A *komuz* song from Kirghizstan 90

4-2 A Rig Veda hymn 94

4-3 The Indian theoretical system in outline 96

4-4 The theoretical *sa* and *ma grama* 97

4-5 Two Indian *tala* cycles 101

4-6 Karnatic flute variations 104

5-1 A Burmese orchestral melody 120

5-2 A Cambodian wind ensemble piece 121

5-3 A Malayan gendang keling excerpt 127

5-4 A Thai kheen piece 129

6-1 Two Tibetan folk dance examples 142

6-2 The Chinese *lü* system 147

6-3 The basic Chinese scale system 148

6-4 Two Peking opera excerpts 164

6-5 The national anthem of China 168

7-1 One interpretation of the Korean mode system 181

7-2 A Korean ballad song 182

7-3 A Korean entertainment song 182

7-4 Ryukyu *umui* songs 184

7-5 An Okinawan song "MoAshibi" 185

7-6 The *matsuri bayashi* piece "Yatai" 186

7-7 A Japanese folk song, "Sado Okesa" 187

7-8 Four basic Japanese scales 188

7-9 A *noh* drama excerpt 200

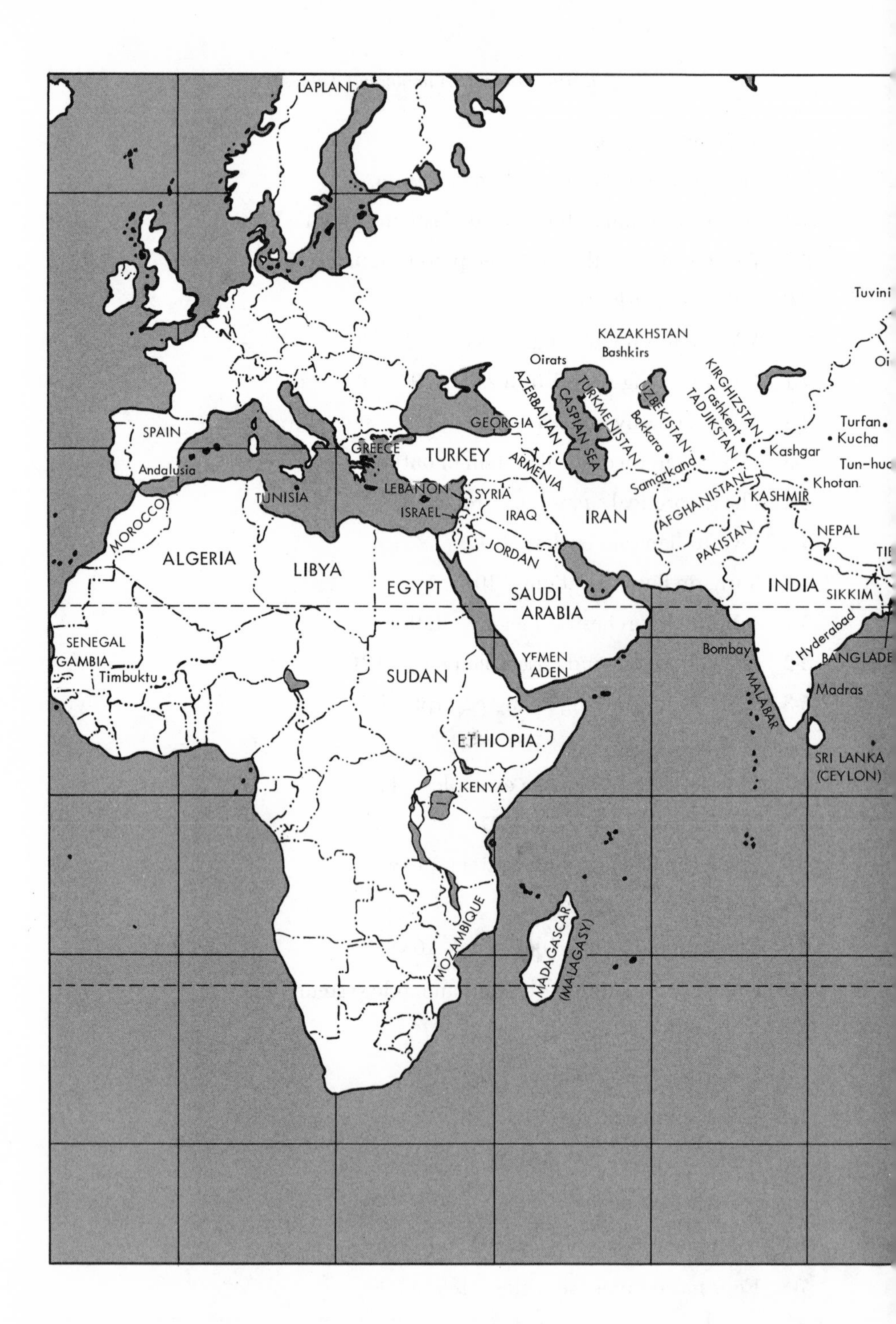
LAPLAND
KAZAKHSTAN
Bashkirs
Oirats
AZERBAIJAN
TURKMENISTAN
CASPIAN SEA
UZBEKISTAN
Bokkara
KIRGHIZSTAN
Tashkent
TADJIKSTAN
Turfan
Kucha
Kashgar
Khotan
GEORGIA
SPAIN
Andalusia
GREECE
TURKEY
ARMENIA
Samarkand
TUNISIA
LEBANON
SYRIA
ISRAEL
IRAQ
IRAN
AFGHANISTAN
KASHMIR
NEPAL
MOROCCO
ALGERIA
LIBYA
EGYPT
JORDAN
SAUDI ARABIA
PAKISTAN
INDIA
SIKKIM
SENEGAL
GAMBIA
Timbuktu
SUDAN
YEMEN
ADEN
Bombay
Hyderabad
MALABAR
Madras
ETHIOPIA
SRI LANKA
(CEYLON)
KENYA
MOZAMBIQUE
MADAGASCAR
(MALAGASY)

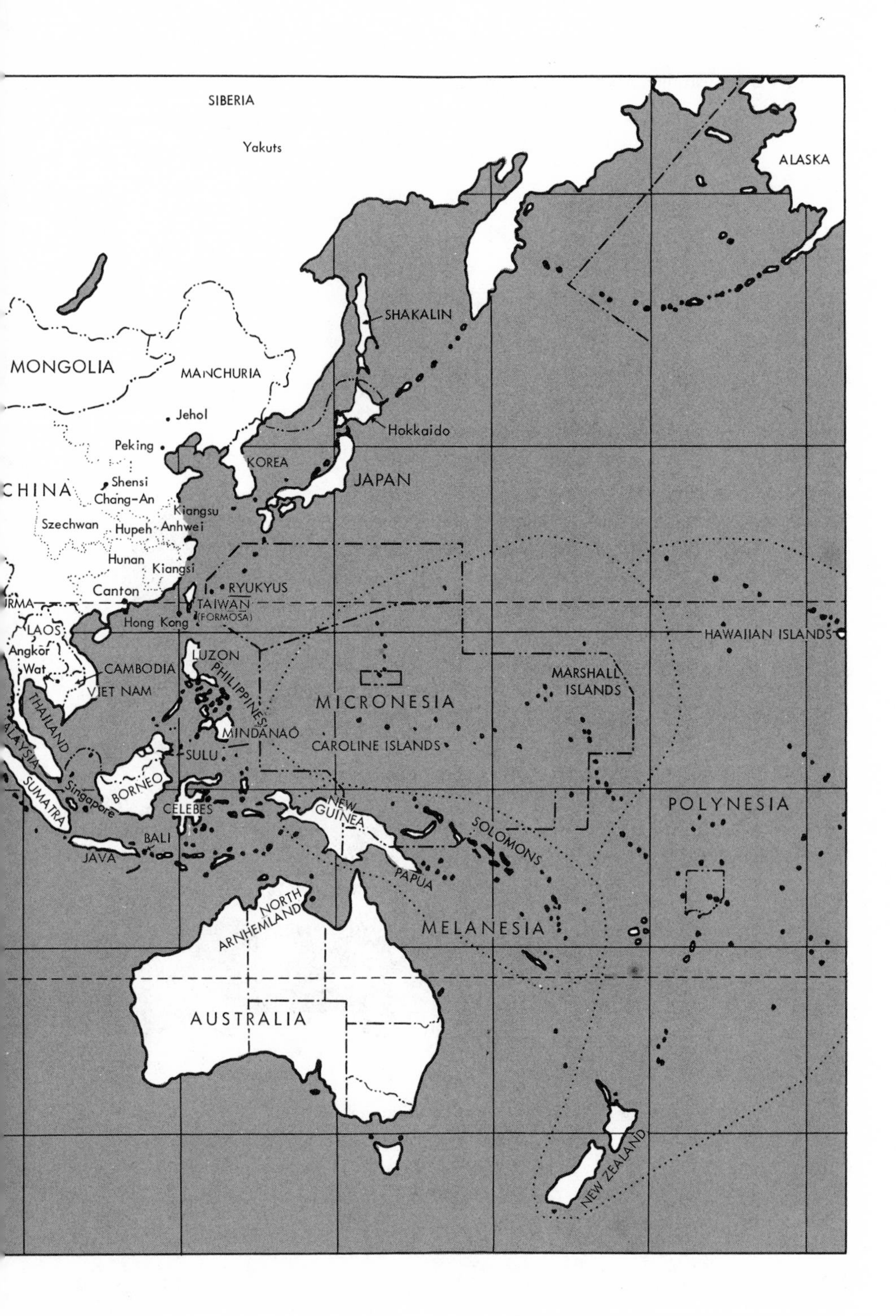
SIBERIA
Yakuts
ALASKA
SHAKALIN
MONGOLIA
MANCHURIA
Jehol
Hokkaido
Peking
KOREA
JAPAN
CHINA
Shensi
Chang-An
Kiangsu
Szechwan
Hupeh
Anhwei
Hunan
Kiangsi
RYUKYUS
Canton
TAIWAN
(FORMOSA)
Hong Kong
LAOS
HAWAIIAN ISLANDS
Angkor
Wat
LUZON
CAMBODIA
PHILIPPINES
VIET NAM
MARSHALL
ISLANDS
MICRONESIA
THAILAND
MINDANAO
CAROLINE ISLANDS
SULU
BORNEO
Singapore
SUMATRA
CELEBES
NEW
GUINEA
POLYNESIA
SOLOMONS
BALI
JAVA
PAPUA
NORTH
ARNHEMLAND
MELANESIA
AUSTRALIA
NEW ZEALAND

PLATE I. Australian Aboriginal Instruments

FIGURE 1. Rhythm sticks and a *dijeridoo.*

ONE
OCEANIA

Oceania is a collective term for all the islands and cultures of the Pacific Ocean. As shown on the map in this book, Oceania is usually divided into four sections: Australia, Melanesia, Polynesia, and Micronesia. Although the Ryukyu Islands are technically part of Micronesia, and the Malay archipelago from Indonesia to the Philippines is also sometimes considered to be a section of Oceania, the music of these areas will be dealt with in later chapters. This chapter will survey the music from the four traditional areas of Oceania in the order listed above. At the same time certain basic concepts and terminologies will be introduced that have been found useful in the study of music on a world-wide basis.

AUSTRALIA

A musical field trip to the towns and farms of Australia would soon uncover there a rich crop of old ballads and dances which were brought to the continent by Anglo-European settlers. There is also a host of folk songs and music-hall pieces that deal with the history of Australia from the resettlement of convicts through gold rushes, hunting, and herding to service in Commonwealth armies. As in the United States and Canada, there are in Australia enclaves preserving many European traditions, such as Greek and Italian, as well as groups from India. Fortunately, the universities and national archives of Australia as well as its recording industry have shown a growing interest in encouraging both the original and the imported Anglo-European musics. In addition, Australian government and research personnel have increased their concern for the traditions of the aboriginal tribes that first possessed this continent.

The music of these Australian aboriginals is an excellent and impressive base for an introduction to the study of the structure and meaning of music in world cultures. Imagine, for example, a group of short, dark men painted with sacred markings of ostrich down and blood; they dance in a circle, holding each others' thighs, and leap like kangaroos while uttering animalistic shouts. What descriptive words come to mind? Stone Age, primitive, savage? All have been applied to the peoples of the Arnhem Land Aboriginal Reserve, which is located on the northern tip of Australia between the city of Darwin and the Gulf of Carpentaria. Among the most archaic cultures still in existence, they are organized in bands, the simplest political units. Their society reflects a dual structure; that is, every creature must belong to one or the other of two basic groups called moieties. Aboriginal material culture seems minimal, for these peoples survive today primarily on government-subsidized reservations or through forms of hunting, fishing, and food gathering that often involve moving with the wandering game. "Common sense" would lead one to expect that their music would be rather pallid, yet field workers are unanimous in their praise of aboriginal songs. What is there to admire?

One of the first notable aspects of Arnhem Land music is its meaningfulness to the culture. Music is used throughout an aboriginal's life to teach him what he must know about his culture, about his place in it, and about its place in the world of nature and supernature. As a baby he is encouraged to dance and sing about everyday tasks. At puberty he learns his first lineage songs—about the totemic plants and animals of his clan and the history and mythology of the group—which belong to his lineage and have specific melodic formulas and modes that distinguish them from other groups' songs. In the bachelors' camp he learns more light-hearted songs which are the basic entertainment media for the band. When he marries and enters further into group responsibilities, however, it is the clan songs that are the central part of his education and his source of strength in times of trouble. His maturation can be measured in the esoteric knowledge he has acquired through song, and as an old man he knows that his honor is based partly on his mastery of the secret sacred songs of the band.

The music of nonliterate peoples in general shares this direct functionality with that of the Australian aboriginals. Literate civilizations, by contrast, tend to increase the separation of music from life. For example, a Western college student must learn to "understand" a Beethoven symphony. The aboriginal understands his music naturally. The Westerner can understand aboriginal music also, if he is willing to learn its language and laws and listen to it in terms of itself. It cannot be compared with a Beethoven symphony because it has nothing to do with it. Both, however, can be enjoyed once one knows what to listen for in each. Thus our first cultural example demonstrates clearly the primary rule motivating and directing the structure of this book: music is *not* an international language. It consists of a whole series of equally logical but different systems. As we look briefly at selected examples of such systems in Oceania and Asia, we will be able to see only a few of the ethnological or musical factors which comprise their basic units. Even such brief views, however, will display some of the wondrous results of man's combinations of culture and sonic events and will help us realize the ingenuity and potential artistry of the human mind. We have already implied some of the cultural functions of music in Australian aboriginal societies. Let us see next what their members can do with an ant-eaten tree branch.

One of the very few—if also best-known—Australian aboriginal musical instruments is the *dijeridoo* (or *digeridoo*), seen in Figure 1. This hollow eucalyptus branch is blown in such a manner that, by nasal breathing and back pressure in the pipe, constant tone is maintained. The pipe end may be placed in a large shell or can to aid the back pressure and the resonance. The instrument is stored in a stream or in mud to keep it moist and soft-toned. Some nine different tone qualities can be produced by a skilled player.[1] The actual pitches played are usually two, a tenth apart. By alternating the tone qualities and pitches, the drone player produces a varied rhythmic and coloristic background for a singer, who often works his melodic line against the drone in a manner reminiscent of Indian classical music. Some *dijeridoo* today are made from modern materials such as cans or plastic tubes. Good tones can still be produced from these instruments.

A skilled drone player is highly respected and may travel with a professional songman to enhance trade meetings or other interband assemblies. In all but a few compositions, the songman himself or some

[1] The basic tones, patterns, and sonic joys of the instrument are found in Trevor Jones' record *The Art of the Dijeridoo* (Wattle Ethnic Series, no. 3).

other performer plays rhythm sticks like those shown in Figure 1. In almost all compositions the songman or another person either maintains with such "time sticks" an accurate beat or creates a rhythmic ostinato characteristic of the style of the kind of piece being performed. There are several different regional styles within Arnhem Land itself as well as among the peoples in other parts of Australia, as in the York peninsula and on the distant western coast. Handclaps instead of rhythm sticks are preferred by some groups, whereas clashing boomerangs or sticks beaten on the ground are characteristic of many of the central desert tribes far south of Arnhem Land.[2] Beating on log drums or on the side of the drone pipe is found among some northern coastal groups, perhaps reflecting their comparative proximity to New Guinea. Notched wooden scrapers appear in some northwest and western tribes, and the so-called bull-roarer can be found in a few northeastern cultures and in one from the central desert. The bull-roarer is an oblong wooden board that is spun overhead on the end of a string. Strictly speaking, it is not necessarily a musical instrument, for its sounds in secret rituals are not considered as independent sonic events but rather are thought to be the sounds of the supernatural itself. Women are forbidden to approach the ceremonial area when the whirl of the bull-roarer is heard.

If the sound of the bull-roarer is not technically music, a logical but somewhat disconcerting general question arises: what is music? In the context of world music two answers are possible. One is purely intracultural and the other is potentially universal. The first is that a sonic event can be called music only if the knowledgeable carriers of the culture in which it appears call it music themselves. This definition depends on the opinion of the people actually living in the culture and ignores what an outside listener may feel about the sounds. The second definition is that any sonic event may be considered and studied as though it were music if it combines the elements of pitch, rhythm, and dynamics so as to communicate emotionally, aesthetically, or functionally in a manner that either transcends or is unrelated to speech communication. Under this definition, one could "analyze" bull-roarer sounds to find their "musical" characteristics without considering how the native performer or listener may view or react to them.

To our earlier remarks about the functionality of music in many societies we must add that the study of music in world cultures may choose to ignore the sonic events altogether, or at least to link them

[2] An excellent map of the distribution of musical instruments in aboriginal culture is found in Alice Moyle's companion booklet (p. 73) for the recording *Songs from the Northern Territory* (Canberra: Australian Institute of Aboriginal Studies, 1967), cat. no. I.A.S. M-001/5. This booklet also summarizes regional musical styles.

primarily with their reasons for existence within a culture. Such a broad, flexible approach to the study of music is found in the discipline called *ethnomusicology,* which may be defined as the scientific study of music in any world culture or subculture in terms of its actual sounds and performance practice, in its relation to the specific culture, or in comparison with other cultures.[3]

We have spoken briefly of the power of Australian aboriginal music in some of its cultural contexts and in its instrumental performance practice. Let us turn now to the actual music. Australian aboriginal music is sometimes classified in three categories: secular, sacred, and secret. These categories are generally more functional than musical. Most secret pieces are also sacred, but a sacred song may appear in a secular situation (like hymns at the Grand Old Opry in the United States), and specific songs may have a variety of sacred or secular texts (like, in the United States, "John Brown's Body," "Mine Eyes Have Seen the Glory," and "Little Peter Rabbit"). There are many sacred songs (such as Example 1–1B) which have solemnity and texts of great meaning. Quite often such a melody may be turned into a secret piece by the place where it is performed or by an "inside" meaning of the text which only the initiated can understand correctly. The texts of secular songs are often topical, with references to events or people of significance to the group at the time.

Example 1-1 illustrates the preliminary steps that can be taken in the transcription of a recording. Such transcriptions are necessary first steps for anyone interested in sonic events in the context of ethnomusicological research. These transcriptions often are not derived from personal field recordings, and the detailed notes of the original field worker are also not normally available. Thus the meaning of the text and the cultural context in which the music was performed are seldom known. This is the case in Example 1–1, which consists of extracts from longer pieces. Thus the texts are not included and only the opening patterns of the drone pipe are shown. In the context of the entire piece, any one of the various elements of the music may be helpful in identifying the particular genre into which a song fits. Example 1–1A is a well-known secular dance piece, "Djanbagari," frequently heard at *corroboree* meetings,[4] whereas 1–1B is a song from an "all-souls" religious ceremony. Fortunately, even these

[3] This definition is the author's; see also Bruno Nettl's *Folk and Traditional Music of the Western Continents,* 2nd ed., in this series (Englewood Cliffs, N.J.: Prentice-Hall, Inc., 1973), 1–15 and 28–29.

[4] It is generally believed that terms like *corroboree* and *dijeridoo* are English distortions of indigenous explanations, though they are commonly used today. The word *dijeridoo* is heard today as an onomatopoeic memory aid (a mnemonic) that represents some of the mouth movements one must make to produce the correct sounds. Listen to examples on the record cited in footnote 1.

short excerpts are able to show how different the melodic styles can be in various genres of aboriginal music. The basic function here of these examples, however, is to provide materials with which we can demonstrate the rudiments of non-ethnocentric musical analysis—that is, an analysis in terms of the music itself rather than in terms of the ideals of one culture alone. These rudiments will be useful in our discussion of music from almost any music culture.

EXAMPLE 1–1. Two Australian aboriginal songs transcribed from the recording *Tribal Music of Australia* (New York: Folkways Record P 439), side 1, band 2 (second version) and side 2, band 6. By permission of Folkways Records and Service Corporation.

RUDIMENTS OF ETHNOMUSICOLOGICAL MUSIC ANALYSIS

One simple but important observation that must be made concerns *performance practice.* Example 1–1A is performed by a singer with rhythm sticks plus a drone (shown here by only its first patterns). Example 1–1B is for singer and rhythm sticks alone. Both pieces use a solo singer. Whatever the mixture of singers and/or instrumentalists may be, it should be mentioned as a first step in describing a music.

Another observation has to do with *time.* Besides showing *tempo* in metronome marks (the number of beats per minute) and notating the rhythm of the sticks and its relation to the vocal part, one can note *meter* —that is, a scheme of time in music that allows one to perceive the basic pulse (*tact*) as being organized in units with implied "first" beats and perhaps other accented beats. Such units are called *measures*; their implied beats need not be those of the accents of the music itself. The apparent caution of this ethnomusicological definition of meter and measure reflects the fact that a major part of the world's music is oral, and thus one's interpretation of the metric structure of a music is often rather subjective and based on one's own cultural rhythmic experience.

If its measure time-units seem to be the same length, as in Example 1–1, a piece can be described as *isometric.* If the units are of equal length, but the individual unit is not a multiple of two or three (such as 5/4 or 11/4, as opposed to 3/4 or 4/4), the music is sometimes described as being in an *asymmetrical isometer.* We should note, however, that this convenient term is somewhat ethnocentric, since a measure that may seem asymmetrical to a Central European or American is quite "even" to someone in the native population of a culture in which such meters are common (as in East European dance music). The term asymmetrical is used here since it is part of common professional parlance; it implies no specific interpretation by a given listener. If the length of the measure units keeps changing (as in Example 4–1), a common description of the piece would include the term *heterometric.*

The first few measures of both pieces in Example 1–1 seem to repeat a rhythm pattern. Since rhythm is not the same as meter, this phenomenon is known as *isorhythm.* It is very common in songs of nonliterate cultures as well as in Western art music. If there is no sense of a basic even pulse, the piece is said to be in *free* rhythm. If the rhythms tend to follow freely those of speech, the piece is in *parlando-rubato* style. A steady tempo is called *tempo giusto.*

The effect of emphasis created by a change in the length of notes (for instance, the shift from short to long in Example 1–1B) is called an *agogic* accent. Finally, observations dealing with the general increase or decrease in the number of notes have to do with *rhythmic density*.

Several characteristics should be considered when *melody* is being described. Among these are: (1) *scale*, (2) *pitch center*, (3) *range*, (4) *frequency* of notes, (5) prevalent *intervals*, (6) *cadence* patterns, (7) melodic *formulas*, and (8) *contour*. The first four observations can be made quickly by writing out the scale with all the notes used, including octave duplications if any, and assigning a large time value to the pitch center and progressively smaller time values to notes according to their frequency of appearance. The scales shown at the end of each piece in Example 1–1 exemplify this technique: the numbers beneath the notes represent the number of occurrences in the melody; this *weighted scale* method also shows the range. In describing scales, octave duplications are discounted (there are none in Example 1–1). The total number of different pitches in a scale is often described by Greek-derived terms: thus Example 1–1A is based on a *pentatonic* (five-tone) scale and 1–1B is *hexatonic* (six tones).

The frequency of intervals in the excerpts of Example 1–1 can be shown in the following manner:

	Maj. 2nd	Min. 2nd	Maj. 3rd	Min. 3rd	P 5th
Ex. 1–1A	5	1	0	3	1
Ex. 1–1B	15	9	1	0	0

The cadence pattern for 1–1A consists of the notes D D C, whereas that of 1–1B is a group of repeated C's. The examples are too short for us to speak significantly about melodic formulas, though extended patterns on one note are important in each excerpt.

Contour can be described as ascending, descending, pendulous, or terraced, or it may be shown by graphic lines. Both pieces in Example 1–1 have basically descending contours. A study of the contour and the actual distribution of intervals (like those listed above) allows one to describe the melodic style as primarily *conjunct* (as in Examples 1–1 and 4–1, p. 90) or *disjunct* (as in Examples 3–1, p. 60, and 6–1, p. 142). The style or the contour of a melody can be said to be *static* if its movements and intervals are quite limited (as in Example 1–4, p. 19, or 4–2, p. 94).

Form cannot be analyzed in Example 1–1 because it contains incomplete pieces. However, in formal analysis of relatively short, repetitive pieces a few descriptive terms have been found to be most useful (although they lose their usefulness when one deals with more complex musical structures). The term *iterative* can be used to describe the form of a piece in which one small melodic formula tends to be repeated throughout (as in the Anglo-American children's chant "Rain, rain, go away"). If a piece returns to its first phrase after a digression, the form is *reverting* ("Swanee River" is an example). If in either of these forms the same large formal unit is used for new text, the form is called, in addition, *strophic* (like "Oh! Susanna" or "Au Clair de la Lune"). If a form continues to add new melodic material, it is called *progressive.*

In vocal music, another important characteristic is the relation of music to text. When one note is used for each syllable of the text, the style is *syllabic.* If one syllable is used with many notes, the style is *melismatic.* The study of text also offers opportunities for finding relations between language accents and music accents as well as musical reactions to important or colorful words in the poem.

While there is much more that one can do with music analysis,[5] these basic tools will help the researcher or the musically curious layman to understand a given music in terms of itself rather than in terms of only one musical subculture of the Western world. We must add that only an innate musicality and an enthusiasm for finding beauty in sound will turn this knowledge into positive music appreciation.

Looking once again at the pieces in Example 1–1, we can see that analysis reveals their similarities and differences. They share an isometer, an isorhythmic tendency, a descending contour, a related range (a sixth), and a conjunct melodic style. They differ in performance practice, tempo, scale, and cadences. Though the texts are not shown, Example 1–1A is syllabic, and 1–1B is syllabic in the first half of each measure and melismatic in the second half. Space will not permit such lengthy analyses of each example in this book, but the format used here may prove useful in the reader's own efforts at analysis.

Two excerpts from only two aboriginal genres show marked differences in style. What of the rest of the music? It is axiomatic of every culture mentioned in this book that if one took time to look further behind the musical aphorisms of our survey, a deeper degree of sophistication and variety of style could be found. The field worker's admiration of Australian aboriginal music mentioned earlier is based upon such detailed studies plus personal experience. In this book we can hope to add only "armchair" exploration and intellectual appreciation and skill as we move further into Oceania.

MELANESIA

North of Arnhem Land is New Guinea, the largest island in the world. The great varieties of peoples who inhabit its mountains, jungles,

[5] See Nettl, *Folk and Traditional Music of the Western Continents.*

and coastal plains range from Negroid Melanesians to Papuans and small-statured Negritos. Its musical cartography has yet to be drawn, but already the music has revealed a vast and colorful range of styles.

One common performance practice in New Guinea is group singing in unison or octaves; such music is called *monophonic,* as is solo melodic music. Sometimes one singer will sing a line that is answered by another singer or a group using the same or a different melody; this is *call-and-response* or *responsorial* style, and it too is common in New Guinea. If one group sings the call and another group sings the response, the performance practice is called *antiphonal.* But regardless of the number of people involved, if only one melody is heard at a time the music is monophonic.

When many people are involved in a performance, the possibility is great that various notes will appear at the same time. Whether this is deliberate or accidental, the result is many-voiced or *polyphonic* music. The term polyphony is often thought of primarily in terms of European art music, but in this book it is used in its literal meaning, "many sounds," in a world context,[6] to distinguish such music from monophony. There seem to be three basic kinds of polyphony in the world. If the different parts are performing different notes but in the same basic rhythm, this may be called harmony or, to keep with our "-phony" series, *homophony* (see Example 5–4, p. 129). If the different parts are performing different notes but are relatively independent rhythmically, we might call the result "counterpoint," but this term seems too heavily loaded with Western historical meanings; the neutral Latin-Greek combination *disphony* (separate sounds) has been suggested, since it is our ability to recognize as separate the various parts which distinguish such multi-sounds from *homophony.*[7] The disphonic style has subdivisions: if the melodies of the various parts are quite similar, the style may be called *imitational disphony;* if they are basically the same tune but are begun at different times, it is *canonic disphony* (as is seen in Example 1–3, p. 13). Finally we come to the most nebulous multi-part term, *heterophony.* This is applied to music in which the different parts are performing the same tune at the same time, but each part is making its own melodic or rhythmic variants of it (as seen in Example 3–1, p. 90).[8]

[6] Mieczyslaw Kolinski has suggested creating a newer, more ethnically neutral term like "multisonance." See *Ethnomusicology,* XVII/2 (1973), 279.

[7] The author explains the invention of this term in *Ethnomusicology,* XVI/2 (1972), 247–249. Professor Fredric Lieberman has suggested in private correspondence the term "paraphony" ("sounds alongside"), but to us this term implies too strongly that the musical lines are parallel.

[8] In all these definitions the word "part" is used (rather than "voice"), since it may be applied to any music, instrumental or vocal.

Putting the whole sonic conceptual vocabulary together, we have the following: (1) monophony—unison or octave sounds; and (2) polyphony—two or more sounds, with their rhythmic relationships being differentiated as homophonic, disphonic, or heterophonic. These attempts at ethnically neutral terms seem potentially useful in describing music from any area of the world. It must be remembered, however, that in any given piece the various "-phonies" cannot always be clearly separated. Example 1–2, for instance, begins monophonically with a caller (sometimes termed the precentor) to whom the chorus responds in a manner that might be considered either heterophony or a short moment of imitational disphony. The process is repeated in m. 4, while m. 6 clearly illustrates indigenous homophony.

Although all kinds of polyphony are found in New Guinea, the dominant style seems to be monophony. Vocal music predominates, often accompanied by hourglass-shaped drums (of the type shown in Plate II, Figure 2). These drums are single-headed and range from two to six feet in length. The open end of the drum is sometimes shaped like the open mouth of a crocodile or bird. Such an important intimacy between New Guinea's music and its environment is often found even in the sounds of such drums, which sometimes are described by natives as imitations of the calls of regional birds.

EXAMPLE 1–2. New Guinea polyphony transcribed from the recording *An Introduction to the Music of New Guinea* (Bergenfield, N.J.: Prestige International Record 25013), side 2, band 2. By permission of Prestige Records, Inc.

New Guinea drums are played primarily by male dancers, so there is often a handle at the waist of the drum which the dancer can grip in his left hand while pounding the skin with his right. The skin is that of a lizard or snake. It is attached with adhesive and tightened with a rattan hoop and heat. Human blood in the adhesive adds mystical power to the drum, and small lumps of gum on the head give it resonance. The hoop is usually removed once the skin is set.

The hourglass drum and the songs it accompanies play a central role in the ceremonial life of New Guinea. For example, in the Hevehe, the long religious drama of Papua, constant musical accompaniment is required for every stage of the cycle, including the making of special houses, masks, and costumes beforehand as well as the actual ceremonial events. When this ceremony still flourished, if often took years to complete one Hevehe, for the entire cycle might stop for six months if a death occurred in the tribe and the resulting taboo on drumming was not lifted by one of the deceased's relatives. The drum was the symbol of the Hevehe dancer's power. It was relinquished by the dancers only at a final ceremony in which they were symbolically (though not actually) killed and their magnificent giant masks destroyed.

Such a concern for ritualistic and spectacular community events seems characteristic of most Melanesian cultures in contrast with other Oceanic groups. In most of Oceania, however, music still pervades many aspects of daily life, not only ceremonials. Thus, in New Guinea there are songs for trading and war as well as for puberty rites and pig killing. Music is also used to establish the relations of individuals to their social matrix. Each family of the Kumaon tribe, for example, has a pair of flutes called *koa*, which represent the tutelary spirits. An essential part of any boy's initiation ceremony is his introduction to the family flutes and the manner in which they should be played. In this way the flutes become concrete symbols of the nebulous but important concepts of lineage and familial continuity.

Such symbolism in music and musical instruments is common to most nonliterate cultures and is found in the music of many literate civilizations as well. (The so-called masculine and feminine cadences of Western art music are an example.) In New Guinea, the masculine–feminine idea is used to explain, among other things, the double rows of tubes found on some panpipes. Such an explanation is not merely fancy; it is a native form of music theory. The native has constructed his theory in analogies because, like the classroom teacher, he has found them to be an effective way of presenting abstract material orally. Of course, such analogies also lock music into meaningful relationships with the things he values in his culture. The important point here is that the lack of music textbooks in a tribal society does not mean that its music is without a

EXAMPLE 1–3. A New Guinean *kawari* canonic chant transcribed by the author from a field tape of Eunice Loeweke. Used by permission.

systematic base. It is, in fact, one task of the ethnomusicologist to look for the logic underlying each culture's music.

By following some of the analytical methods described earlier, it has been possible to discover general melodic tendencies in the music of those areas and tribes of New Guinea that have been recorded and studied. Rather typical of New Guinea is Example 1–2, with its triadic melody, that is, a melody emphasizing tones that can be arranged in thirds (C, E♭, and G in this piece). Except for the "blue" note (A♭) at the end of the opening solo, one also finds in this piece the typical pentatonic scale (shown here as C, E♭, F, G, and B♭). Another common Melanesian melodic style is seen in Example 1–3, with its narrow range and static contour, that is, a melodic contour with little change. A third Melanesian style is like that of Example 1–1B, with its set of narrow-ranged passages descending in a terraced contour, sometimes called a "tiled" melody.[9]

In general, Melanesian music seems less word-oriented than that of Polynesia and Micronesia. This may be because of its heavier emphasis on function and ritual. It also might explain in part why in Melanesia some texts are sung in archaic languages unknown to the performers, or even in meaningless syllables.

[9] See Jaap Kunst, *Music in New Guinea* (The Hague: Nijhoff reprint, 1967). A good example of a Western terraced-contour melody is Verdi's "La donna è mobile."

The characteristics suggested above might make Melanesian music seem rather "dull" to outside listeners. It must be remembered, however, that in most parts of the world (including the West) highly functional music usually has to be highly redundant in order to be effective. A Western chanted psalm or a spell (like "Rain, rain, go away") can be very meaningful to a performer, though neither is more "tuneful" than the Melanesian canonic chant in Example 1–3.

The field collector of Example 1–3 was unable to identify its precise function in her correspondence, though she did mention that *kawari* songs are frequently used in the *sing-sing* meetings which are an important part of tribal and inter-tribal social life. Similar redundant canonic pieces sometimes function in New Guinea in both a medical and a spiritual manner. Their text may be a seemingly meaningless chain of names of local trees, rocks, and geographical locations. Such chants are only sung by the side of a sick person. Their meaning and efficacy become evident once one realizes that medical aid in the New Guinea Highlands is often based on the concept that a person's spirit is capable of leaving the body and a patient cannot be cured until the spirit is brought back. Are these calls to known hiding places for lost souls in New Guinea less curative than many Western psychological methods?

It should be evident by now that melodic style may sometimes be a valid, if only partial, aid in the search for larger views of various cultures. As was implied earlier, the theory and symbolism of the music of a nonliterate culture are also part of the general "world view" (*Weltanschauung*) of that (or any other) culture and thus are best approached from an anthropological as well as a musicological point of view. For example, in order to study the cultural "meaning" of the slit-gongs found all over New Guinea, one must take into consideration the manner in which the large logs are hollowed out and slotted on one side so that the sound can come out in the right "spirit," as well as the particular meaning of the various patterns played upon them. Similarly, one must know the significance of the figures carved on a gong, especially when one end of it is stuck in the ground and the carved head on the other end becomes a totem, the sound of the instrument representing the very voice of a god. Many large horizontal slit-gongs are placed in special houses; the uses of these houses as well as the situations in which the gongs are used may reveal much about the people as well as about their music. Thus, an ethnomusicologist should be a person of many viewpoints in order to appreciate fully the meaning of music in a given culture. The materials of one culture may in turn provide clues about broader musicological theories. For example, the panpipes of New Guinea and other parts of Oceania became grist in the Western musicological mill when the interval relations between the tones produced on them were found to be similar to the intervals of panpipes from such a distant area as South America. The resultant theory of overblown fifths (*Blasquinten*) as expounded by Erich von Hornbostel (1877–1935) became a point of contention in various theoretical controversies concerning the evolution of music.[10]

Though our discussion is necessarily limited primarily to New Guinea, we cannot mention Melanesian panpipes without calling attention to the panpipe ensembles recorded in the Solomon Islands in the 1970s.[11] Not only are the polyphonic texture and variety of sections in each piece compositionally impressive, but the field notes of the recording reveal that the names of the composers and the topics of the pieces are known. This is, in fact, rather common in Melanesia, for compositions or dances are often "owned" by an individual or group, and "copyright clearance" or purchase is necessary for other persons to perform them. Thus, though we have dealt earlier with the high functionality of music in nonliterate cultures, it is equally important to know that the cult of the composer and the building of multisectional forms, well-known in the West, do not necessarily require the trappings of notation and of a literate society. It is true that there is a logical necessity for redundancy in musical illiteracy, for the repetition of some fundamental parts makes possible the building of more complicated strata. When, however, one hears the changes of textures, tempos, and tunes in music of such "primitive" ensembles as the panpipes of the Solomons, it is obvious that individual compositional talent and group rehearsal and diligence are as much a part of the Melanesian islanders' music as they are of European chamber music.

Returning to New Guinea, we find that the artisans who created the panpipes also built another interesting instrument, the bamboo trumpet. Its simplest form is found throughout Melanesia: it consists of a large bamboo tube closed at one end by a node in which a small hole has been made; buzzing one's lips against this hole turns the tube into a trumpet. In its more complex form the bamboo trumpet consists of two vertical tubes connected at the bottom by a horizontal tube, at one end of which is a nodal mouthpiece, and by another horizontal tube connecting the two vertical tubes to form a square-shaped instrument. As in a French horn, the purpose of all these changes in the tube's direction is to produce the sound of a long horn with an instrument that occupies only a small

[10] See Jaap Kunst, *Around von Hornbostel's Theory of the Cycle of Blown Fifths* (Amsterdam: Royal Institute for the Indies, Mededeeling no. 76, Afdeeling Volkekunde no. 27, 1948). Another summary is available in Curt Sachs, *The Wellsprings of Music* (The Hague: Nijhoff, 1962), 102. Hornbostel's own writings are now available in English and German in *Hornbostel Opera Omnia* (The Hague: Nijhoff, 1975).

[11] *Aré Aré,* vols. 1 and 2. Collection Musée de l'Homme. LDM 30104 and 30105.

space. Trumpets in New Guinea are used to frighten the enemy during battles and to signal success when the warriors come home with the corpses of the foe. Trumpets are also used to enhance ceremonies. (The same can be said for the bull-roarer, a common instrument throughout Melanesia.)

We have emphasized a functional view of New Guinean musical instruments, but there are many instruments that are used primarily for self-amusement. Nose flutes, like the one shown in Plate II, Figure 3, serve this purpose. Another common entertainment instrument is the jew's harp or jaws harp. In New Guinea the jew's harp is usually made of a short piece of bamboo in which a thin tongue has been cut. The wood is placed across the player's mouth, and the wooden tongue is made to vibrate by plucking with a finger or jerking with a string. The player then creates a melody by changing the size of his mouth cavity. This type of instrument is found all over the world and is as much at home in its metallic form in the United States and Europe as it is in its bamboo form in Oceania.

Bamboo is used to make many other kinds of instruments in New Guinea, including rattles, beaters, and simple xylophones. It is even used to form a stringed instrument. Strips are cut along a bamboo tube in such a way that they are free from the tube along their lengths but still are attached at both ends. When small wooden bridges are jammed under them, these strips become tight, and plucking them produces a musical tone. Since the strips are cut to different lengths and the bridges are of different sizes, a series of tones is obtained from which melodies can be played. This tube zither looks like the *valiha* of distant Madagascar, although the strings of the latter are now usually of metal and are attached, not cut from the body of the tube (see Plate II, Figure 4). The New Guinea emphasis on bamboo is a useful example of the relation of music to yet another factor, ecology.[12] The more one studies music in a world context, the more one becomes sensitive to and impressed by the delicate balance that continually exists between music and the sociological, psychological, religious, and physical conditions in which a society lives. (Unless, of course, it is inundated by the waves of international synthetics; even then, however, the power of regional tradition has shown remarkable and heartening durability.)

This survey of New Guinean music has revealed a full complement of percussion, wind, and stringed instruments. The presence of polyphonic singing has also been noted, although the predominant style is

[12] See Theodore Grame's "Music and Bamboo," *Ethnomusicology*, VI/1 (1962), reprinted in *Readings in Ethnomusicology* (New York: Johnson Reprint Corp., 1971).

PLATE II. Island Instruments

FIGURE 2. New Guinea drum.

FIGURE 3. Oceanic nose flute.

FIGURE 4. *Valiha* (tube zither from Madagascar).

monophonic. With all its variety, New Guinea exemplifies most of the major styles found in the other islands of Melanesia. To find the musical styles of the more famous Polynesian culture of Oceania we must move farther out into the Pacific.

POLYNESIA

The islands of the Pacific are scattered over such a wide area that one would expect to find a highly varied series of isolated cultures. A combination of amazing navigational skills and migrational incentives, however, has bound the Pacific cultures together in many ways. Our concern will be to point out common characteristics while drawing our examples from special regional forms.

Though a common picture of Oceania today is one of tropical islands filled with lovely girls and easy living, the history of Polynesian societies is generally one of war and oppression. Strict caste systems have predominated, with the aristocracy surrounded by the greatest supernatural power (*mana*) and the most *tabu* (or taboo).

Before the entrance of European diseases, the Polynesians' greatest problem was overpopulation. The consequent needs for territorial expansion brought about extensive warfare. This warfare is reflected in some of the energetic posturing dances still done today throughout Oceania. One of the best-known dance traditions of Polynesia is that of the *haka*, done by the Maori of New Zealand. The music for these dances is sung in a style of declamation that lies between speech and song. This style is called *heightened speech.* The notation of such music is difficult, and some form of graph, like that of Example 1–4, is preferable to the Western five-line staff.[13] The example shows a typical *haka* performance practice in which the pitch rises as the leader calls out the main words before a chorus responds. Vocal sounds and various body percussions such as stamping feet, clapping hands, and slapping thighs help to keep the rhythm. Such performance practice is common in both Polynesia and Micronesia. In general, the music and dance of these areas of Oceania can be considered as extensions of poetry, and thus they contrast in function and style with most of the Melanesian traditions discussed earlier.

Because text is important in Maori music, one finds that the concept of strict rhythm (*whakaeke*) and a proper vocal unison are of equal concern. Such an interest is not merely a matter of aesthetics, because for

[13] Important discussions of the various approaches to the notation of non-Western music are found in a symposium printed in *Ethnomusicology,* VII/3 (1964).

EXAMPLE 1–4. A Maori *haka* dance song transcribed from the recording *Maori Songs of New Zealand* (New York: Folkways Record P 433), side 1, band 6. By permission of Folkways Records and Service Corporation.

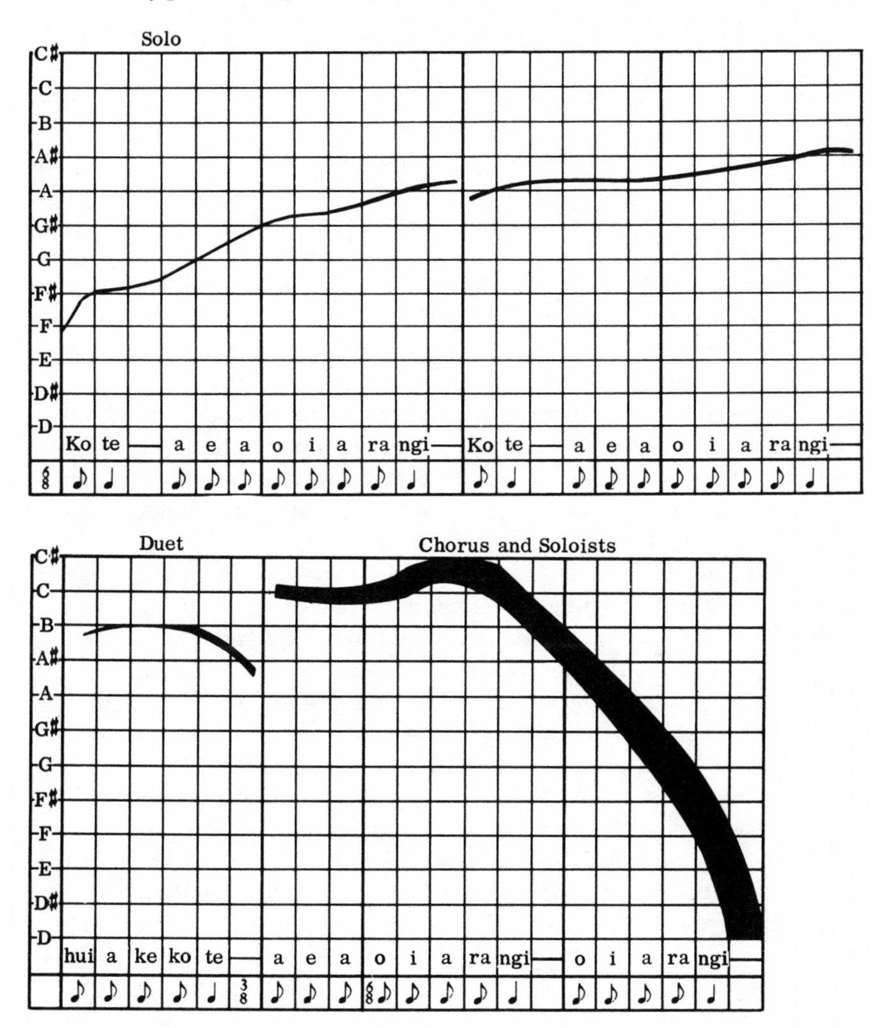

the Maori to break the continuity of a song is to invite death or disaster. This is equally true in the more melodic *waiata* songs and in such reciting chants as the *patere.* The *patere* are of particular importance, for they often deal with the history of the tribe or some personal genealogy. Chants concerning such matters appear throughout Oceania, for the individual's place in the social and political structure of the entire society is largely determined by his family tree. In these preliterate societies, genealogical chants are the best way of keeping track of such complicated information. Thus, insistence on accuracy in the rendition of such chants and seriousness of musical training are important for the social position as well as for the safety of the performer from potential supernatural harm. Under such conditions, musical style tends to remain rather conservative and to resist the influence of other musical cultures. Such is the case in some Polynesian groups.

Maori songs concentrate on a reciting tone called the *oro*. In the genealogical chants and similar forms of tribal historical chants, this tone is surrounded by tones of indeterminate pitch so that no specific scale system emerges. A study of *waiata* songs has shown that seemingly meaningless ornamented solos by the lead singer are actually "cueing" devices which help to distinguish the formal divisions of the piece.[14] But even the more melodic Maori pieces that use specific, accurately sung notes may employ only three or four tones and use an iterative or progressive form. Such limited melodies serve primarily as memory aids in presenting the words; the songs are listened to for the information they contain more than for a musically satisfying effect. Because of the strong word-orientation of such music, many songs are without meter or are heterometric, shifting accent to keep in step with the text.

In analyzing the tonal systems of Maori chants, one often finds tones that do not fit within the tempered twelve tones of the Western scale. These "notes between the notes" are not mistakes. They are reflections of a different cultural concept of standard pitches. When one tries to notate these so-called *microtones* in Western, five-line staff notation, there is obviously a problem. This is sometimes solved by placing plus (+) or minus (−) signs or arrows (↑ or ↓) above the notes that lie outside the Western tempered scale. Unfortunately, this system does not tell the reader how much higher or lower a given pitch may be. This problem was solved by Alexander Ellis (1814–1890) when he devised the *cents system*. He divided the octave into 1200 equal parts. One hundred of these divisions represent the standard Western tempered half step. If, therefore, an interval is 76 cents, its relation to the 100-cent half step or any other size of interval calculated in cents is easily seen.[15] Thus the cents system is an accurate comparative method for measuring intervals which in turn can be used to describe scales. Measurement of an individual pitch, however, is indicated by the number of vibrations per second, for the cents

[14] See Mervyn McLean, "Cueing as a Formal Device in Maori Chant," *Ethnomusicology*, XII/1 (1968).

[15] For specific instructions on how to use the cents system, see Jaap Kunst's book *Ethnomusicology* (The Hague: Nijhoff, 1959), 2–9, or Curt Sachs, *The Wellsprings of Music*, 24–27.

system measures only intervals. Originally both cents and vibration measurements were made by ear with the aid of a device called a calibrated monochord. This consists of a single string stretched over a board on which either cents or vibration figures were marked. The pitch of the string can be changed by moving a bridge along the calibrated board. The ethnomusicologist then tries to match the sound of the monochord with that of the musical tone in question. Today electronic equipment can be used instead, with much greater accuracy.

Not all Oceanic melodies are difficult to notate and describe tonally. There are many lyrical tunes. There are also various forms of indigenous as well as Western-influenced harmonies. They appear in the form of drones, triads, and (occasionally) fourths and fifths. The most common indigenous vocal polyphony of Oceania is a drone which is often sung in the same rhythm as the melody or in a repeating pattern (an ostinato). Much of the polyphonic music in Oceania today, however, reflects the influence of four-part Christian hymns or two-part pieces which had been specially designed for missionary work by using pentatonic tunes and often a call-and-response performance practice. An example of a mixture of traditions is the Tahitian *himene,* whose style of polyphony combines Western-derived counterpoint with an indigenous drone. Though the name is obviously based on the word "hymn," the texts of such music are sometimes secular. When such foreign and native elements are combined, the process is called *acculturation.* This is the basic process shaping Oceanic music today.

A good Oceanic example of acculturation in a musical instrument is the Hawaiian *ukulele.* It is a native version of the Portuguese mandolin or guitar (*bragha*), which was imported to Hawaii in the late 1870's. Today its name is Hawaiian, the chords it plays are Western, and the tunes sung to its accompaniment are a mixture of both. The Hawaiian manner of playing "slack" guitar with different tunings and of stopping the strings with a metal bar or a bottle is yet another aspect of modern Hawaiian music. It may have begun when Latin American herdsmen arrived with the first cattle, but it is very Hawaiian now.

The ukulele also has a Hawaiian ancestor called the *ukeke.* This instrument is a stick of wood to which are attached two strings that are raised from the wood by a bridge at each end. One end is placed on the player's mouth to give the instrument a resonance chamber. It was played primarily for evening serenading, and missionaries forbade its use.

In Hawaii, as in New Guinea, there are many other indigenous instruments, some of which are not adequately described by simplistic Western analogies such as "native guitars" or "primitive clarinets." In the early twentieth century Hornbostel and Curt Sachs (1881–1959) proposed a method of describing and classifying all musical instruments in a scientific manner that would avoid such ethnocentric analogies.[16] The system is based on the materials whose vibrations create what we perceive as sound; in this system there are five classes—*idiophones, aerophones, membranophones, chordophones,* and *electrophones.* We will illustrate this organological terminology by describing the indigenous instruments of Hawaii.

The *ukeke* and the ukulele are classified as chordophones because their sound is produced by the vibration of a string. Actually, there are four kinds of chordophones. The *ukeke,* for example, is a *zither* because its strings are the same length as its soundboard. The ukulele, however, is a plucked *lute* because its strings are parallel to its soundboard and extend beyond it along a neck or fingerboard. (The Western violin is an example of a bowed lute.) The other two types of chordophone are not found in indigenous Polynesian music. They are the *harp,* with its strings at right angles to the soundboard, and the *lyre,* whose strings are suspended from the crossbar of a yoke and are parallel to the soundboard. A Southeast Asian example of a harp is shown in Figure 41 of Plate XV (p. 131); an Ethiopian lyre is shown in Plate V, Figure 14 (p. 57).

Another instrument indigenous to Hawaii is the *puili,* a set of split bamboo beaters played in pairs. This is classified as an idiophone, an instrument whose sound is produced without stretching the basic material of which it is made. The gourd rattle *uliuli,* topped with feathers, is another Hawaiian idiophone; so is the *ili ili,* a double pair of smooth lava pebbles that are clicked like castanets. The double calabash (*ipu*), which is hit on the sides and thumped on the ground, is also idiophonic. The *pahu* skin-head drum, however, is a membranophone, because its tone is generated by a vibrating membrane. Unlike the hourglass-shaped drum of New Guinea and its environs, the *pahu* drum is cylindrical. The sides of the cylinder are often carved into open lattice-work at the bottom so that the lower half of the body is a stand for the drum rather than a resonating part of the instrument. This form of drum and the hourglass type are the two typical forms found in Oceania.

A common form of wind instrument in Oceania is the nose flute (Plate II, Figure 3), which in Hawaii is called the *ohe hano ihu.* It is classified as an aerophone, since its sound is caused by the vibration of a column of air. The conch-shell trumpet of Hawaii is also an aerophone, although the method of setting the air column in vibration differs. These differences are noted in the subclasses of aerophones. If the sound results

[16] See Erich von Hornbostel and Curt Sachs, "Classification of Musical Instruments," translated from the original German by Anthony Baines and Klaus P. Wachsmann in *Galpin Society Journal,* XIV (1961), 3–29. A shorter version is found in Curt Sachs, *The History of Musical Instruments* (New York: W. W. Norton & Company, Inc., 1940), 454–467.

from blowing across a hole, the instrument is a *flute* (end-blown or side-blown, depending on the position of the tube). If the air column is directed to a thin edge someplace below the point of mouth contact, as in a recorder or tonette, the instrument is a *block flute* or fipple flute. *Reed* aerophones use either single or double reeds that can be *free* (not touched directly by the lips) or *controlled* by lip pressure. If buzzing lips create the sound, the instrument is a trumpet or horn. All forms of aerophone appear in Oceania. In Hawaii, however, only the flute and trumpet types are found. The former is played for self-amusement and the latter for signalling and for ceremonial effect.

The main use of Hawaiian idiophones and membranophones is to accompany the *hula,* the characteristic dance of Hawaii. In fact, many hulas are named after the instruments that accompany them, such as the *hula ili ili* or the *hula puili.* Occasionally instruments are used in the main nondance form of Hawaii, the declamatory *oli* chant. As shown in Example 1–5A and B, these two forms reflect the typical chant styles of Oceania. The *oli* transcribed is practically a monotone and completely word-oriented in rhythm. The *hula,* by contrast, uses a three-tone (tritonic) scale, and the words are fitted into an isometric accompaniment on two drums. Note that even in such a restricted music the singer creates great variety by using ten different rhythmic versions of the first two beats of each measure while maintaining continuity with the same rhythm for the last two beats in every measure except m. 16. Such ingenuity is easier to see in notation than to produce in performance. (The art of the *hula* is by no means restricted to the gracefully symbolic and occasionally erotic movements of the dancers.) Once again we see how the native musician displays the human talent for shaping musical materials in an interesting fashion.

EXAMPLE 1–5. *Oli* and *hula* chants transcribed from the recording *Hawaiian Chant, Hula, and Music* (New York: Folkways Record FW 8750), side 1, bands 1 and 2. By permission of Folkways Records and Service Corporation.

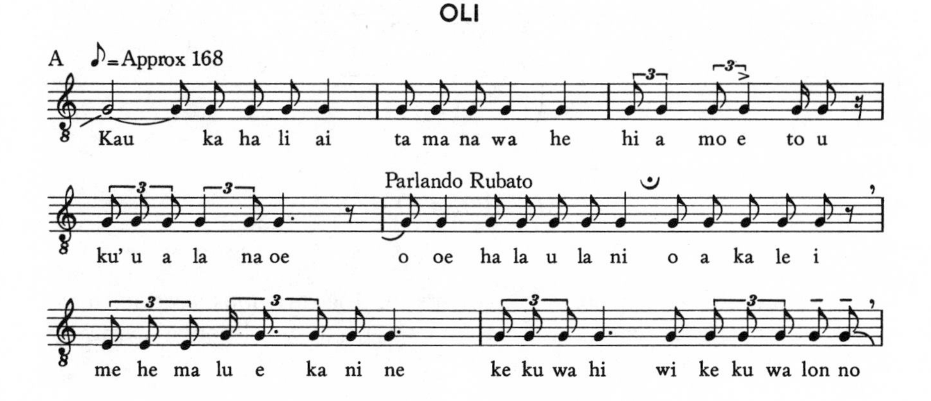

MICRONESIA

Many of our general statements in the previous section have referred to both Polynesia and Micronesia because, although naturally there are differences that must arise between cultures on atolls and islands so distant from each other, our generalities about poetry-orientation and the resultant emphasis on vocal music and dance hold basically true throughout these two areas of Oceania. The first studies of Micronesian music itself resulted from a few early twentieth-century German expeditions in the Caroline Islands plus isolated German, American, and Japanese efforts before and after World War II. These studies reveal a predominantly vocal tradition emphasizing heightened speech or a static melodic style, like that heard in the West when a litany is chanted. Homophony, when it appears, is based on any interval, though parallel fourths seem most common, along with the use of drones. The integration of singing with gesture is perhaps the most impressive aspect of Micronesian music culture: line dances or sitting dances are abundant, and movement is as much a part of a lament as it is of an invocation or a serenade.

The musical instruments of Micronesia are few. The shell trumpet and nose flute (like that in Plate II, Figure 3) are the most common, though standard flutes and jaws harps are found. Occasionally one even finds a single-reed aerophone made of cane or bamboo. A common idiophone in Micronesia is a stick carried by men in certain dances; the performers strike one another's sticks in the course of the choreography. Indigenous stringed instruments are rare, although one can find local imitations of ukuleles and guitars. Membranophones, likewise, are not common, although the hourglass single-headed drum found in New Guinea is also used as far north as the Marshall Islands. In keeping with the ecology of atoll life, the skins of these drums are made of shark's belly or parts of the sting ray, rather than of lizard or snake skin. There are many atolls without any indigenous musical instruments.

On the basis of present information and modern conditions, Micronesia presents the least developed musical culture area of those we have discussed thus far. It must be remembered, however, that the value of this music is best judged by its meaning to a "culture carrier" rather than to a foreigner. For the men and women at a funeral who sing a repetitive lament filled with sliding indistinct pitches, there is great effect in the music, just as there is great release in singing a dance song even if it only uses three notes. The story a song tells or the poetry it supports may be ample reason for its existence, even without the accompanying dance. Music in Micronesian culture today does not loom large in a world survey, but it serves important functions for the people who use it in daily life. One can only wonder what this music might have been like in the days of the great Pacific migrations. Fortunately, centers for Oceanic music studies were established in the 1970s at the University of Hawaii and at the University of Auckland in New Zealand. Through their efforts and those of the new nationalist movements of the late twentieth century, we may find that there is much more to learn, hear, and enjoy in this music that still floats on the tides of the Pacific Ocean.

BIBLIOGRAPHICAL AND DISCOGRAPHICAL NOTES

The bibliographical notes of Chapters 1 and 2 of Bruno Nettl's companion book in this series, *Folk and Traditional Music of the Western Continents,* 2nd ed. (Englewood Cliffs, N.J.: Prentice-Hall, Inc., 1973), cover many of the basic writings about the field of ethnomusicology in general. Of these, Jaap Kunst's *Ethnomusicology* (The Hague: Nijhoff, 1959) and its supplement are repeated here because of their extensive general bibliography of over 5000 items. Current bibliography is found in every issue of the journal *Ethnomusicology.* Bruno Nettl's *Theory and Method in Ethnomusicology* (New York: Free Press of Glencoe, Inc., 1964) speaks further of technical problems of field work and research, while Alan P. Merriam's *The Anthropology of Music* (Evanston: Northwestern University Press, 1964) is the clearest statement of the behavioralist view of music. A useful source for educators is the special "Music in World Cultures" issue of *Music Educators Journal,* LIX/2 (1972). *Readings in Ethnomusicology,* ed. David McAllester (New York: Johnson Reprint Corp., 1971) reprints many items of importance otherwise difficult to locate; relevant to the present chapter are Richard Waterman's excellent "Music in Australian Aboriginal Culture" (originally in *Music Therapy,* V, 1955), Edwin Burrows's study from the Caroline Islands, and Theodore Grame's work listed in footnote 12.

A basic reference is Alice Moyle's "Source Materials: Aboriginal Music of Australia and New Guinea," *Ethnomusicology,* XV/1 (1971). She, along with R. Sheridan and L. B. Glick, also provides an excellent summary of music in the *Encyclopedia of Papua and New Guinea* (Melbourne University Press, 1972). Her important recordings are listed in footnote 2; the Australian Institute of Aboriginal Studies in Canberra, which produced these records, is the major archive for all field tapes, films, and notes in Australia. Other studies are A. P. Elkin and Trevor Jones, *Arnhem Land Music,* Oceania Monograph No. 9 (Sydney: University of Sydney, 1957); Catherine J. Ellis, *Aboriginal Music Making* (Adelaide: Libraries Board of Australia, 1964); and "Aboriginal Music on the Laverton Reservation, Western Australia," by Elizabeth May and Stephen Wild, *Ethnomusicology,* XI/2 (1967). Recordings besides those cited in footnotes 1 and 2 include *Tribal Music of Australia,* Folkways P 439; L. M. West's *Arnhem Land Popular Classics,* Wattle Ethnic Series, no. 3; and *Australia and New Guinea,* Columbia KL 208. Anglo-European music is heard on commercial labels such as *Folk Songs of Australia,* WG 25/S/-5361; and *Freedom on the Wallaby,* Music for Pleasure, MFP A 8131.

The Dieter Christensen and Adrienne Kaeppler article on Oceanic music in the *Encyclopaedia Britannica,* 15th ed. (1974), XIII, 456–461, is a new summary of both music and dance, while drawings of all known musical instruments in Oceania are found in Hans Fischer's *Schallgeräte in Ozeanien* (Baden-Baden: Heitz, 1958). Jaap Kunst's *Music in New Guinea* (The Hague: Nijhoff, reprint 1967) remains basic. F. E. Williams, *The Drama of Orokolo* (Oxford: Clarendon Press, 1940), discusses the Papuan drama cycle in anthropological detail, and references to music in New Guinean ritual contexts are found in Gregory Bateson, *Naven* (Stanford: Stanford University Press, 1958). Melanesian recordings include Columbia KL 208 (cited above); *An Introduction to Music of New Guinea,* Prestige International, INT 25013; and the two volumes of the Collection Musée de l'Homme, *Aré Aré,* Vogue LDM 30104–5. The last-named series includes *Polynesian Traditional Music,* Vogue LDM 30108–9.

Johannes C. Andersen's *Maori Music with Its Polynesian Background,* Memoir no. 10, supplement to the *Journal of the Polynesian Society* (New Plymouth, New Zealand: Avery, 1934), draws together important material from many old sources. More recent and reliable studies are those of Mervyn McLean in *Ethnomusicology,* VIII/1 (1964), IX/3 (1965), and XII/1 (1968). For recordings, hear *Maori Songs of New Zealand,* Folkways FE 4433.

Many of the Bernice P. Bishop Museum Bulletins contain references to music and dance, e.g., no. 34, *Polynesian Religion,* by E. S. Handy, and nos. 162 and 185, *Southern Lau, Fiji* and *The Marianas,* by Laura Thompson. Bulletins 183, *Songs of Uvea,* and 109, *Native Music of the Tuamotus and Futuna,* by E. G. Burrows, and no. 29, *Ancient Hawaiian Music,* by Helen Roberts, are basic sources. *Hawaiian Chant, Hula, and Music,* Folkways FW 8750, is the best recording. *Ethnomusicology* remains the best source for later Oceanic studies, such as those of Adrienne Kaeppler on Tonga dance, XIV/2 (1970) and XVI/2 (1972); Osamu Yamaguchi on Palua, XII/3 (1968); Richard Moyle on Samoan instruments, XVIII/1 (1974); Penelope Sanger and Neil Sorrel on A. F. Gell's New Guinean materials, XIX/1 (1975); and Vida Chenoweth, "Song Structure of a New Guinea Highlands Tribe," X/3 (1966).

TWO
THE PHILIPPINES, BORNEO, AND INDONESIA

The chain of islands that extends from Java through Borneo and the Celebes to the Philippine group contains a variety of cultural-historical influences as well as many indigenous developments. In this survey we shall start at the northeast end of the chain and try to point out some of the ways in which indigenous and foreign styles have interacted to produce a rich variety of musics and musical instruments.

THE PHILIPPINES

If we look first at the remote tribes of the Northern and Central Philippine Islands we find that they share many traits with the peoples of Oceania. For example, Philippine tribes have a large repertoire of orally transmitted histories and mythologies which, like those of many Oceanic peoples, are often sung in litany style with much use of sliding pitches. In addition, many instruments such as jew's harps, end-blown flutes, nose flutes, and tube zithers are shared by the two areas. Some mountain tribes of Luzon, however, use flat bronze gongs, which seems to indicate earlier Chinese contacts. Such gongs in the Philippines are usually played with bare hands like a drum. Groups of performers may play different rhythmic patterns on different-pitched gongs. A tune created in this manner by the interlocking of several different tones or short melodic fragments is known as a *resultant* or *composite melody.*

The dominant foreign cultural forces in the Philippines were Spanish and, in the south, Moslem. The Spanish tradition has spread deep into the interior of the Philippines where, for example, one can find a small, four-stringed, plucked native lute called the *kitara,* a word obviously related to "guitar." Spanish influence becomes ever stronger as one moves toward Philippine urban culture. For example, it is possible to see in a Philippine village a Moro-Moro folk drama about the conflicts between Christian and Moslem knights in ancient Spain. The preservation of this tradition in the Philippines is an example of the principle of *marginal survival,* which holds that the oldest forms of many traditions are not found at the centers of cultures but rather on their more distant fringes. The most common Spanish tradition in the villages and urban districts of the Philippines is the *rondalla* band and its music. The traditional *rondalla* band contains mandolin-type instruments (*bandurría, laud,* and *octavina*), guitars, a double bass (*bajo*) with a fretted fingerboard, and often an accordion. The band's repertoire includes Spanish, Latin American, and vintage American dance forms (waltz, jota, tango, foxtrot) plus arrangements of Philippine folk songs and *kundiman* sentimental ballads. Some of the dances reflect older Spanish styles, whereas others, such as the Tagalog *kumintang* pantomime dances, seem to mix prehispanic and colonial traditions.[1] Even the famous Philippine *tingkling* dance, in which dancers maneuver between clashing poles, shows a mixture of cultural styles: the basic step is said to come from the movements of a native bird, while the arm positions and the musical accompaniment seem to be Spanish.[2]

The dominant style of urban and rural music in the northern and central Philippine Islands is based on the social dances and popular music

[1] A similar kind of compromise can be noted in the urban and rural music of South America, particularly in its western and northern coastal areas.

[2] The relationship of this dance to similar forms in Southeast Asia is of interest. It belongs to the discipline called ethnic dance or ethnochoreology. See "Foundations for the Analysis of the Structure and Form of Folk Dance: A Syllabus," *Yearbook of the International Folk Music Council,* 6 (1974), or the publications of CORD (Committee on Research in Dance).

of nineteenth-century Spain, with some influence also of local *zarzuela* (light operas) and Catholic religious music. However, prehispanic music traditions are still strong in the mountain tribes of the north as well as in the jungles of many of the southern islands. Islam, in addition, is a strong influence in the south, partly because of post-fifteenth-century Indonesian contacts. Musically, the parallels between Indonesia and the Philippines are seen most easily in the many non-Oceanic instruments found among the Moros and other southern peoples. For example, xylophones (*gabbang*), often used to accompany storytellers, Moslem religious songs, or musical flirtation contests, are found in the Sulu Archipelago.

The most obvious Indonesian influence is reflected in the presence of knobbed gongs, particularly as they are used in the Southern Philippine *kulintang* ensembles. These ensembles usually consist of a gong (*babandil* or *tunggalan*) struck with a hard stick, a singled-headed goblet-shaped drum (*dabakan*) or two *gandang* double-headed drums, plus four hanging knobbed gongs (*agung* or *duana*) and a set of eight to eleven knobbed pot gongs (*kulintang*) that are placed on a rack (somewhat like one row of those in the *bonang* shown in Plate IV, Figure 11). The instruments enter one at a time in special rhythmic patterns to create a stratification of sounds somewhat similar to that of Indonesian orchestras. The major difference in a *kulintang* performance is that each piece is based on a so-called rhythmic mode rather than on a melodic theme. As will be seen later in our Indonesian study, however, this emphasis on rhythm and on contour rather than on melody may be a crucial factor in most non-Christian musics found along the chain of cultures from the Southern Philippines to Sumatra.

Another instrumental clue concerning the cultural inheritances of the Southern Philippines is the *gitgit,* a small bowed lute with three strings that is often played by young men as they go courting. It is a diminutive version of the ubiquitous Moslem spike fiddle, known most commonly as the *rebab*. The *rebab,* in its original Near Eastern form, is believed to be not only the distant ancestor of the Philippine *gitgit* (via the Indonesian *rebab*) but also the predecessor of the bowed lutes of Europe, from the medieval *rebec* to the modern violin.[3] A belief in such a widespread relation of instruments is held by adherents of the *theory of diffusion,* which claims that every basic instrument type was invented only once and then spread about the world in variant forms. An opposing *theory of polygenesis* holds that each instrument was invented in several different places at different times; the variants of such separate inventions may or may not have overlapped as each form spread about. So far, neither theory seems

[3] See Albert Seay, *Music in the Medieval World,* 2nd ed. (Englewood Cliffs, N.J.: Prentice-Hall, Inc., 1975), p. 75.

to offer the exclusive answer to the questions of relationships between musical instruments around the world; one can find examples that seem to support each argument. The relation of the *gitgit* to the *rebab,* however, certainly fits best within the concept of diffusion.

Another instrument of the Southern Philippines and Sulu that seems closely connected to Indonesia is an end-blown notched flute around the top of which is tied a rattan band that helps to direct the stream of air. Its construction and playing method are those of the Indonesian *suling.*[4] A more complex relation between cultures is demonstrated by the Philippine *kudyapi* (Plate III, Figure 5). This term is sometimes used generically for native-made plucked lutes, including a diminutive version of the guitar. The *kudyapi* important to this discussion, sometimes called a boat lute because of its shape, is a two-stringed plucked lute with five rather high frets. Some claim that its most distant ancestor may be an ancient Indian chordophone called the *kechapi vina,* but it has many more immediate Southeast Asian relatives, such as the three-stringed crocodile zither (*mi gyaun,* Plate III, Figure 8) of the Mon in Burma, the more abstractly shaped Thailand *chakay* zither (Plate XV, Figure 42), the multistringed Sundanese *kacapi* zither with movable bridges (from western Java; Plate III, Figure 7), and the Borneo *kachapi, kasapi,* or *sapeh* (Plate III, Figure 6), which is a plucked lute with one to three strings that are played in the banjo position rather than horizontally as are the other instruments mentioned. The Philippine *kudyapi* is similar to the Mon and Thailand instruments in its physical characteristics and less like the Sundanese and Borneo instruments; regarding its name, however, the reverse is true. This confusion of names and physical features illustrates the principle of *floating terms,* in which a word is transferred from one concept or instrumental type to a very different form as it moves from culture to culture or even within one culture over a period of time. It is important to note this phenomenon early in our study, because floating terms are so frequent that one cannot presume that the same term will mean the same thing when it is found in a new cultural context.[5]

Despite our discussion of influences and borrowings in Philippine music, one must not think that this is basically a second-hand music tradition. The creative aspects of acculturation have been at work for centuries, and the modern ethnomusicological field worker as well as the

[4] Diffusionists would further connect it with the *nay* (*nai* or *ney*) of the modern Near East as well as the ancient Egyptian *sib*.

[5] Those curious to follow such variants further should refer to Sibyl Marcuse, *Musical Instruments: A Comprehensive Dictionary* (New York: Doubleday & Company, Inc., 1964).

PLATE III. Diffusion Examples from Southeast Asia

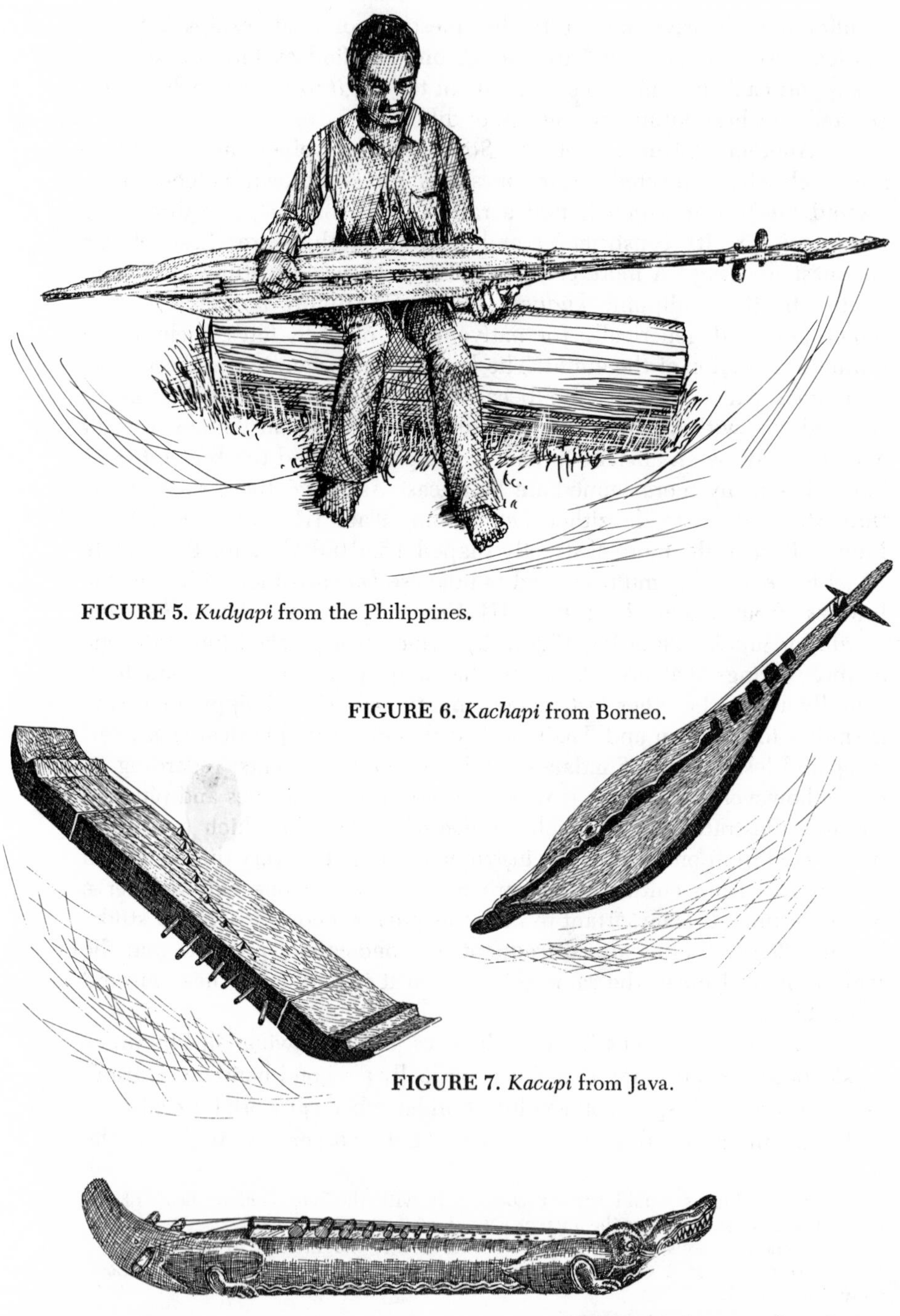

FIGURE 5. *Kudyapi* from the Philippines.

FIGURE 6. *Kachapi* from Borneo.

FIGURE 7. *Kacapi* from Java.

FIGURE 8. *Mi gyaun* from Burma.

nationalistic composer have found and are continuing to find rich stores of native music that reflect the many sides of the musical culture of the Philippines.

BORNEO

As one moves closer to the heartland of Indonesia by way of the islands of Borneo and the Celebes, the frequency of knobbed gongs, gong orchestras, simple xylophones, and end-blown flutes increases. This does not mean that all the music of the islands to the east of Java is Indonesian-derived. The Muruts of North Borneo, for instance, sing in an indigenous drone-based harmony unknown in Central Indonesia. We spoke of similar harmonies in Oceania and New Guinea; they also exist among isolated groups in Taiwan and Southeast Asia, but no connection has been established as yet between these various systems.

Most of Borneo's melody and harmony is not based on Javanese scales but uses a five-tone scale without half steps, the so-called *anhemitonic* pentatonic (see Example 6–3). Though this scale is popular throughout East Asia, its use is so widespread even in other parts of the world that it cannot be said to prove connections between cultures. However, there is one instrument in Borneo that indicates a fairly clear link with the Asian mainland. This is an aerophone consisting of a gourd windchest holding several pipes, each of which contains a free reed. When holes on the pipes are closed, either chords or melodies can be played. Such instruments are believed to be the oldest harmonic instruments in the world. They seem to have originated in Southeast Asia, probably Laos, and spread throughout East Asia. Thus, this tribal instrument of Borneo belongs to a chain of instruments that runs from the folksy *khaen* of Southeast Asia and China (Plate XIV, Figure 40) to the aristocratic *sheng* (Plate XVI, Figure 46) of ancient China and the *sho* of the present-day Japanese court orchestra. Its most recent relatives are nineteenth-century European derivatives called the harmonica and the accordion.

These non-Indonesian examples from Borneo show that even in a seemingly isolated area a complex of influences can be absorbed into the current native style. Change is as much a part of a nonliterate culture as it is of the Western art-music world. Pure native or classical style reflects at best only a single point in a cultural time continuum, albeit a lovely one. It can be stopped on a recording, but it inevitably changes in the living tradition. Thus, in Borneo one can still hear head-hunters chanting heterophonically over an ostinato played on a *sapeh* together with the steady beating of a drum and a knobbed gong, but one can also listen to another tribe singing the English words "bye bye" in indigenous-style harmony based on the pentatonic scale.[6] Both are native for the particular groups involved and for the particular time in which they are performed.

Field workers often feel that Western music has a pernicious influence on non-Western traditions, but if the non-Western culture carriers adapt it to their music, then the new musical resultant *is* the native style. When we turn to the main islands of Indonesia we can still find native traditions that have not yet succumbed to Western influence.

INDONESIA—A HISTORICAL INTRODUCTION

The Indonesians were the last of four large groups of peoples to migrate to the Southeast Asian islands in prehistoric times. We know something of their culture from their many stone and metal artifacts, as well as from commentaries written by the Chinese, who were in contact with Indonesia from at least the third century B.C. Indian influence and Brahman Hinduism entered Java in the first and second centuries A.D. Buddhism appeared in the fifth century and was particularly influential during the powerful eighth-century Sailendra Dynasty. Brahmanism remained in parts of the empire and eventually returned to the central courts, where it merged with Buddhist and indigenous cult traditions. Trade and conflict brought various Indonesian empires in contact with the Chinese, Mongol, and Arab worlds. Islam was present in Indonesia by at least the thirteenth century and was quite prevalent by the fifteenth century. Portuguese, Dutch, English, and other Western influences have increased steadily since the sixteenth century. This long line of cultural contacts has helped to create the rich mixture of musical styles found in Indonesia today, and, as we pointed out, possible relations may be found between the musics of the ancient high civilizations of Java and those of other native cultures along the Southeast Asian chain.

The Gamelan

In Indonesian, *gamelan* is a generic term for a musical ensemble. It may vary in size from a few instruments to over 75. Such variety can be found not only from island to island in the vast Indonesian archipelago but also within each district of one island. Research so far has dealt primarily with some of the different traditions found on Java and Bali, so our discussion will be limited to examples from those two islands. Let us begin with a description of the basic instruments found in a *gamelan* of Central Java.

[6] Compare band 1, side 1, of *Borneo* (Contrepoint MC 20.112) with band 4, side 2, of *Murut Music of North Borneo* (Folkways FE 4459).

Though Westerners often think of *gamelan* music as being instrumental, singing is frequently an important part of Central Javanese compositions. A female soloist (*pesinhen*), a male unison chorus (*gerong*), or a mixed chorus (*gerong bedayan*) may be used, and subtle hand-clap beats can be heard in sections of many modern performances. The delicate, ornamented music of the chorus is said to relate to the melody of the two-stringed *rebab,* a bowed lute (Plate IV, Figure 9), whereas the female soloist part is more analogous to that of the end-blown *suling,* a flute. The *suling* has sometimes been called a ribbon flute because, like the Philippine models, its air is directed toward the blowing edge by a piece of rattan tied around the circumference of the flute. The metal strings of the Indonesian *rebab* are tuned in fifths and fingered without pressing the strings against the pole. The tension of its animal-hair bow is maintained by hand, as is done in the European gamba tradition. In some *gamelan* compositions another stringed instrument is used, the *celempung* (*tjelempung*),[7] a zither called by some a *siter.* It has 26 metal strings tuned in double courses, that is, adjacent pairs of strings are tuned to the same pitch, giving a total of 13 tones.

The most obvious instruments of a *gamelan* are its bronze metallophones. They fall into two basic types, those with slabs or keys and those with knobbed gongs. The *saron* shown in Plate IV, Figure 10, has keys set over a box resonator. It is played with a wooden or sometimes bone mallet (*tabu*). As each new note in a melody is played, the previous one is dampened with the thumb and forefinger of the left hand. In this way the melody emerges clearly.

The *saron* comes in three sizes. The highest and smallest is called the *saron panerus* or *peking,* the middle the *saron barung,* and the lowest is the *saron demung.* In *gamelan* instrument families, there is generally a direct relation between the size of an instrument and the density of its music, the smaller and higher-pitched instruments playing more notes than their larger and lower-pitched relatives.

The wooden-keyed *gambang kayu* xylophone uses a box resonator like the *saron* but is played with padded disks attached to two long thin sticks. Padded disks on short hand-held sticks are also used to play the *gender,* a series of thin bronze keys of fine alloy suspended by strings over individual tube resonators. Plate IV, Figure 12, shows the largest form, the *gender panembung* or *slentem.* It is played like the *saron* with only one stick, but the higher-pitched *gender barung* and its upper-octave companion, the *gender panerus,* are played with two. The combination of key, resonator, and padded beaters produces a mellow, nonpercussive sound. Stopping this resonant tone is a problem in the higher *gender*

[7] The first spelling of this Indonesian term (as of others herein) conforms to a recently adopted official national system; the second is a common earlier romanization.

PLATE IV. Java

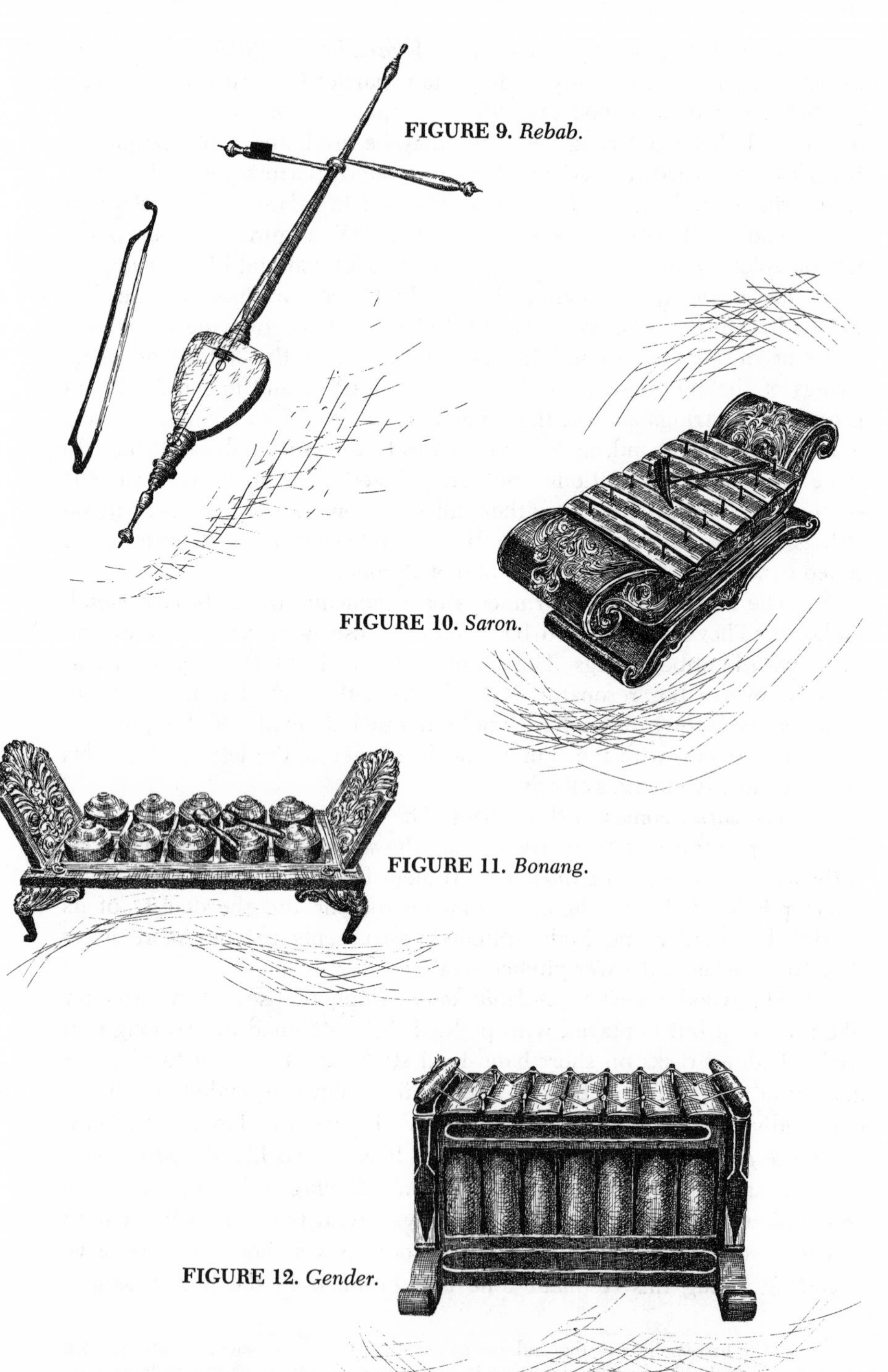

FIGURE 9. *Rebab.*

FIGURE 10. *Saron.*

FIGURE 11. *Bonang.*

FIGURE 12. *Gender.*

because the two hands often play separate elaborating parts. This is solved by a supple wrist action that allows the player to stop the last note played with a finger or the side of his hand while playing the next note.

A prominent member of the knobbed gong family is the *bonang* shown in Plate IV, Figure 11. Its bronze, knobbed gongs are placed on ropes laced in a wooden frame and are played with two padded sticks. Like the *saron* and *gender*, it comes in three sizes. While *bonang* music can be quite elaborate and melodic, the instrument belongs to that class of knobbed gongs whose fundamental function is to mark the time. Thus, the *bonang* holds a vital position in the joining of the mosaic of many layers of sound into one coherent musical event. The time-marking function of knobbed gongs becomes clearer when one observes the actions of four other instruments with the onomatopoeic names of *kethuk, kenong, kempul,* and *gong*. The *kethuk* is usually a small single horizontal knobbed gong set on ropes in a wooden frame and struck with a padded stick to produce a sharp, deadened "kethuk" sound. The *kenong* consists of a set of larger knobbed gongs placed in similar wooden frames. The *kempul* is a set of hanging knobbed gongs, while the *gong agung* or *gong siyem,* which hangs impressively at the back of the orchestra, produces the deepest sound of the four.

In Java there are two basic kinds of *gamelan* playing, the loud style, with an emphasis on the bronze instruments, and the soft style, in which the flute and the stringed instruments may appear.[8] In the soft style, the *rebab* player is the leader, whereas in loud playing the leader uses *kendang* barrel drums with two lashed heads. There are also more intimate chamber music ensembles, such as a trio in Sunda (western Java) that consists of a singer, a *suling* flute player, and a *kacapi* (*kachapi*) zither player (Plate III, Figure 7). In keeping with the floating-term tradition discussed earlier, there are several different kinds of Javanese zithers called *kacapi*. Those of the type shown in Figure 7 have from six to eighteen strings that are tuned with terminal pegs and movable bridges.

Throughout Indonesia there is an endless variety of *gamelan,* including some whose instruments are made of iron or bamboo. Ensembles of the bamboo instrument called the *angklung* have gained in popularity, perhaps under the influence of Western music-education bands. Each *angklung* consists of two or more bamboo tubes tuned in octaves and hung from a frame above a slotted resonator tube in which the ends of the tuned tubes are suspended. When shaken, each *angklung* produces one pitch at as many octave intervals as it has hanging tubes. In order to play a melody it is necessary to have as many players as there are

[8] Compare this with the two styles of orchestra in Southeast Asia discussed in Chapter 5, pp. 123–29.

tones in the scale of the tune (unless some players use two *ankglung* on different pitches). Each player shakes his *angklung* in a different rhythm in order to produce the melody, in a more complicated version of the composite-melody technique sometimes used by Western bell-ringers and by the Philippine gong-beaters mentioned earlier.

In addition to many different kinds of ensembles in Indonesia there are, of course, a variety of musical forms which extend from shamanism to popular music. The *kroncong* popular songs are of historical interest because they were first derived from the traditions of sixteenth-century Portuguese sailors, though today they are a mixture of styles. More powerfully influencing most forms of Indonesian music as well as literature, however, are the tales of the hero Pandji and the local versions of the Hindu *Ramayana* and *Mahabharata*. These stories have been preserved primarily through the oral traditions of the theater and solo songs as well as in orchestral and dance pieces. Of particular interest is the *wayang kulit* shadow puppet theater. The puppet operator (*dalang*) recites entire dialogues and comments to the accompaniment of an instrumental ensemble. Audiences may watch from either side of the shadow screen while the moral truths and conflicts of Indonesian thought are brought to life in epic performances which may last from sunset to dawn. The agrarian, king-centered culture from which such Indonesian art forms developed may prove to show deeply-rooted influences on the very structure of traditional musics as both culture and music are studied more thoroughly. During Indonesia's struggle toward modernization, attempts have been made by traditional artists to relate to a changing society and life style.[9] Music conservatories, notation, shorter performances, and new compositions are reflections of this concern. At this point we have clear information only about the traditional manner in which Indonesian music is put together.

Javanese Music Theory and Practice[10]

The most general Javanese term for composition is *gendhing* (*gending*). While a composition may consist of several sections or movements, the fundamental unit is the *gongan*, consisting of all the events that occur between one stroke of the largest gong and the next. Example 2–1 shows the many layers of polyphonic stratification typical of *gamelan*

[9] Essays concerning Javanese traditional world views can be found in the writings of Clifford Geertz, such as his *The Religion of Java* (New York: The Free Press, 1960). Part of the musical struggle for modernity is discussed in Judith Becker's *Traditional Music in Modern Java* (Honolulu: University of Hawaii Press, 1976).

[10] The following explanation is primarily the result of the research and insights of Professor Judith Becker and her students in the ethnomusicology program of the University of Michigan, though the author takes responsibility for interpretation.

EXAMPLE 2–1. One *gongan* in *ketawang* form and *slendro manyura* mode from "Puspawarna" from the Nonesuch record *Javanese Court Gamelan* (H 72044), side 1, band 1, from the third sound of the gong just before the chorus entry. Used by permission of Nonesuch and Robert E. Brown, field collector.

Kem - bang ken - -
Kem - bang ken -
(basic melody from instruction book)
2
3
(Kethuk)

cur
ka - car - - yan
cur
1
3
(Kenong)

ang - - - gung
ci - - na - - tur.
Ka - car - yan
ang - gung ci - na - tur.
5
6
3
(Kenong)
(Kempul)
(Gong)

music that occur during one *gongan* of the piece "Puspawarna."[11] Beneath the *saron* parts is shown the modern Javanese cipher notation (*kepatihan*). In this notation one can see a series of the smallest melodic units in Javanese theory; these are called *gatra* and are sets of four sonic events, including silences if they occur. Thus in Example 2–1 there are four *gatra:* .3.2, .3.1, .3.5, .6.3.[12]

Since (apart from the *kepatihan*) Example 2–1 is in linear Western notation and is furthermore only a small portion of the whole piece "Puspawarna," it is difficult to visualize the strong cyclic underpinning of the entire musical structure. The insightful Dutch musician-scholar Jaap Kunst (1891–1960) first sought to describe this phenomenon by inventing the term *colotomic* structure, by which he meant a system that marks off music into temporal units according to the entrance of specific instruments in a specific order at specific times. In recent years, studies by both indigenous and Western scholars have suggested a different approach to the structure of Javanese music and to its possible relation with other aspects of Indonesian life. This view considers music as fundamentally a linking-together of temporal cycles which continually subdivide binarily. Example 2–2 is a diagram of the kinds of binary cycles that exist among the time-marking instruments in a Javanese composition set in the temporal form *ketawang* as used in the one *gongan* transcribed in Example 2–1. The *ketawang* cycle is played at double speed in the first *gongan* of this composition, but thereafter, as in most Javanese music, it is repeated at normal speed in each of the *gongan* that follow. In Example 2–2 the entrance of the gong is shown at the top of the circle. The eight sounds of the time-markers are shown with letters outside the circle (T = *kethuk,* P = *kempul,* and N = *kenong*). Each time-marker's divisions are built on those of its immediate successor. Therefore the *kenong* divides the gong cycle in half with its two sounds. The *kempul*

[11] This notation is a composite of several sources: transcriptions from the recording by Francesca Cassara and Richard Wallis and reconstructions for those lines not clearly audible derived from known performance practice and from part books. Additional help was given by Wayne Forrest, the Javanese musician Sumarsam, and the director of the original performance group, Ki Wasitodipuro. A *celempung* zither, the drums, and an additional time marking *kempyang* part have not been included. The actual pitch of tone 6 is nearer Western B♭ than A, and the pitch of note 5 may be closer to F♯ than to G. The placement of barlines is conjectural; they appear here (along with staff notation) for the convenience of Western readers. The actual tonal meaning of the music, outside the limitations and conventions of Western notation, can only be corrected by listening to the actual recording and adjusting one's concept for each pitch. A different version of the same piece in Solonese style is heard in Volume II of *Javanese Court Gamelan* (Nonesuch H 72074)

[12] In order to assist the reader in comparing the transcription with the recording, the notation begins on the gong entrance that occurs on the last note of the last *gatra* of the previous *gongan.*

EXAMPLE 2–2. The *ketawang* temporal cycle.

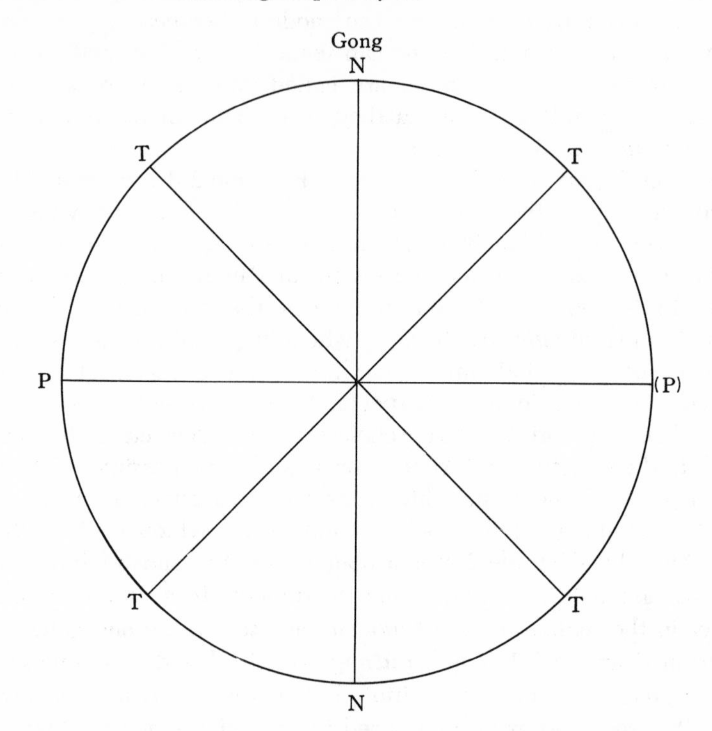

divides the *kenong* part in half with its two sounds which interlock with the *kenong* divisions to divide the cycle into four parts. The *kethuk*'s four sounds slice the total cycle further into eight parts. The first entrance of the *kempul* (P) is shown in parentheses because in some Central Javanese traditions it may be omitted (as it is in Example 2–1). This absence of a time-marker is called a *wela,* an empty place, something that is missing from its assigned position and thus creating a silence, which is, however, still felt as part of a cycle. Listening to the recording from which Example 2–1 is derived will also reveal that entrances of some time-markers such as the *kenong* in m. 3 may be slightly delayed to add extra subtlety to the overall cycle. Final gongs in a composition are often delayed in this manner. The introduction (*buka*) to a piece is often quite free rhythmically, in order not to impose the cyclicity too suddenly on the listener; and the final gong may be followed by an equally free postlude (*pathetan*) for soft instruments like the *gender, suling,* and *rebab.* Thus what appears in print to be a rather rigid system is, in performance practice, often woven in a delicate filigree manner.

A study of the *saron peking* part in Example 2–1 shows that the binary temporal divisions continue as one moves on to the various denser melodic layers of the stratifications. The *gender panerus* part reveals an additional binary division. Such binary expansions or contractions are part of a concept known as *irama.* The *irama* idea has been described as analogous to horizontal lines of dots painted on a balloon. As you blow up the balloon the distance between the dots expands, leaving room for more events to appear between each dot, whereas deflating the balloon brings the dots closer together, leaving little room for more elaborate designs between each dot. In Javanese music, the time-markers' placement remains untouched, but the application of the so-called first, second, or third *irama* to the music expands the distance between notes in other melodic parts like that of the *saron* or, more centrally, the *bonang.* This leaves room for denser lines such as are seen in Example 2–1 in the *gender panerus* part.

It is not possible to explain Javanese rhythmic theory and practice fully in a short survey. Perhaps even these very preliminary examples, however, show the great sense of interdependence that is basic to *gamelan* music. This characteristic is one reason why such a complex multilayered music can be performed and maintained without reliance on detailed linear notation. Another unifying factor in this music is its tone system.

There are two basic scales in Java, the five-tone *slendro* and the seven-tone *pelog.* A study of the fixed tunings of the keys from the *saron* and *gender* of many *gamelan* throughout the island indicates that there is great variety in the actual pitches of, and intervals between, the notes of these scales, though they are very accurately matched within the instruments of one *gamelan.*[13] The *slendro* scale is particularly varied. The difference between the two scales in one *gamelan* is such that a separate set of melodic instruments must be tuned to each in order to have a complete ensemble. Such a pitch difference may be seen in Example 2–3, which shows a typical (note: *not* a standard) *pelog* and *slendro* tuning, with intervals marked in cents,[14] compared with an idealized Western tempered scale of 100 cents to the half step. The word appearing with each pitch is its name in modern Javanese practice; the arabic numbers are those that would appear in present-day Javanese cipher notation. (Both these names and numbers differ from several previous court traditions; since earlier pitch names are found in many studies of Javanese music, the major ones are included in parentheses in their proper positions.)

[13] An attempt to explain this variety is found in Donald Lentz, *The Gamelan Music of Java and Bali* (Lincoln, Nebraska: University of Nebraska Press, 1965).

[14] The specific intervals chosen are derived from measurements for *gamelan* number 5 in Appendices 61 and 62 of Jaap Kunst, *Music in Java* (The Hague: Nijhoff, 1949).

EXAMPLE 2–3. A Javanese tone system.

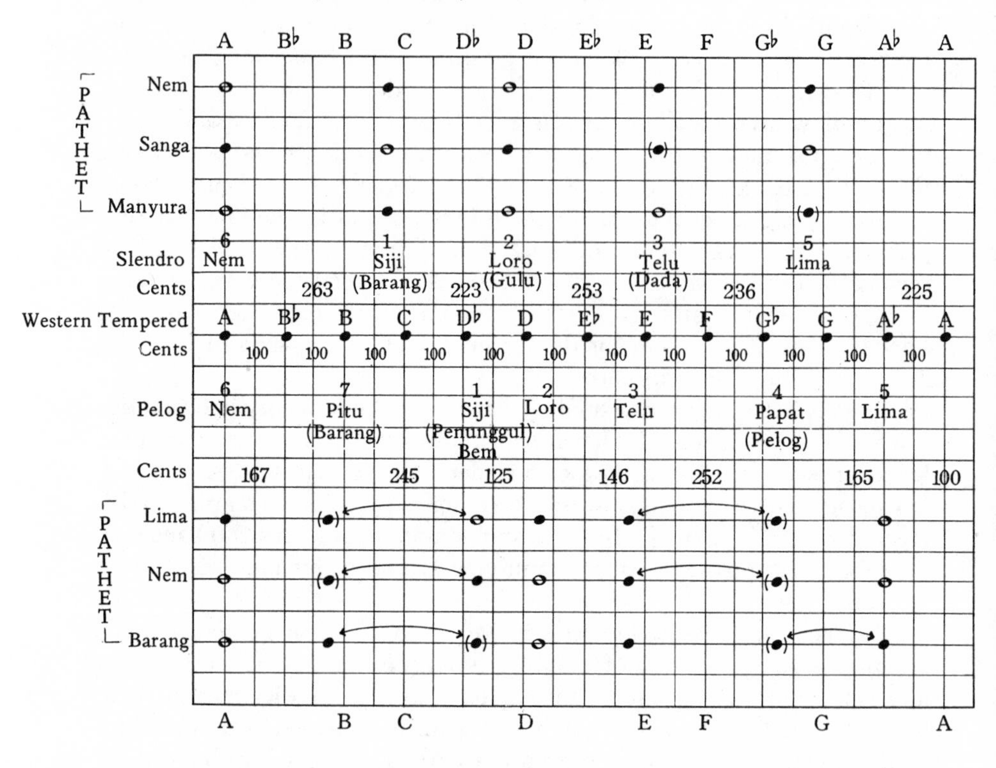

In Central Java each scale has three modes called *pathet* (*patet*). These are shown in the upper and lower portions of Example 2–3. On the basis of material available at the time, earlier researchers felt that specific pitches tended to be used melodically in each *pathet* at moments when the time-marking *kenong, kempul,* or *gong* appeared. Perhaps influenced by the Hornbostel overblown-fifths theory mentioned earlier (p. 15), they found in each *pathet* three so-called gong tones, located fifths apart. Recent research has cast doubts on the indigenous validity of this convenient system. For instance, the large white circles in the *pathet* sections of Example 2–3 indicate those pitches which, on the basis of recent statistics,[15] are used the most frequently in a melody when the gong is struck. The smaller white circle represents the next most frequently used pitch for that position. A pitch in parentheses is one that is avoided both as a gong tone and at other places during a melody in

[15] The data for pitch evaluation are derived from Appendix IV in Judith Becker, *op. cit.*

the *pathet* indicated. In the *slendro pathet nem,* pitches 6 and 2 occur with about equal frequency. As can be seen in their Western note equivalents in Example 2–3, the distance between 6 and 2 is nearly a perfect fourth (A–D), which could be converted into a fifth by placing note 6 an octave higher (D–A). (This logical Western inversion method, unfortunately, is quite outside of the Javanese approach to melody, for the Indonesian musicians think of intervals primarily in terms of the number of slabs between two pitches on a keyed instrument within one octave.)

The predominant pitches of the *sanga* mode in Example 2–3 seem equivalent to a fifth, though it is too big to be a standard Western fifth (712 cents instead of the Western 702). If one searches for fifths between other predominant pitches in other *pathet,* none of the distances in cents between them will match the acoustical 702, nor will they resemble each other (in *pathet lima,* pitches 1 to 5 = 688; in *manyura* 2 to 6 = 714 and 6 to 3 = 739). Thus the Western cycle-of-fifths theory, from both a practical and a scientific point of view, does not seem to be connected directly with Javanese music.

In the *pelog* system, the "avoided" pitches (in parentheses) are used as substitutions (*sorogan*) for their adjacent tones, as shown by the arrows. The use of pitches 4 and 7 or 1 as such alternate tones in the *pelog* modes helps to explain why these three pitches are missing on some keyed instruments (such as a *gender*) in the *pelog* section of a *gamelan.* This absence may cause tonal clashes when a five-tone *gender* and a seven-tone *saron* are playing together in a *pelog*-mode piece; it also relates to an important characteristic of *pathet* recognition, and therefore to the entire Javanese concept of melody, for it would appear that pitches and intervals are often not as important in modes as are the contours of certain melodic patterns (*gatra*) and cadences used. This concept of mode and melody as contour more than as interval structure may be a factor as well in the variety of tunings noted earlier between different *gamelan.*

Another factor in mode recognition is melodic register. Instrumentalists often describe a mode primarily in terms of the general range within which its music falls on their instrument. The *slendro pathet nem* is the mode most easily distinguished this way, for its *rebab* and *gender* parts exploit the lowest ranges of these instruments. Finally, each *pathet,* like other modes in the world, is felt to be best suited to a given mood, function, or time of the day. Together with the few other preliminary facts and theories discussed earlier, the Javanese tone system is impressive evidence of the logical but different system that continually operates in the equally beautiful tradition of Javanese music.

Balinese Music

Among the many different kinds of *gamelan* in Indonesia besides those of Java, the most famous are on the island of Bali. The boisterous brilliance of the Balinese orchestral sound is completely at variance with the generally sedate quality of Javanese music. In Bali, instruments similar to those of the Javanese *gamelan* are found performing analogous functions. However, the Balinese *gender* and *gangsa* (the latter being the equivalent of the Javanese *saron*) are built in pairs or quartets in each octave size. Though all the instruments in a set are in the same scale, half are "female" instruments, which are tuned slightly lower than their "male" companions. When the two groups are played together they create a shimmering throb because of the beats caused by their tuning differences. This lovely sound is characteristic of the Balinese ensemble.

Among the several instruments that elaborate on a nuclear theme (in Balinese, *pokok*) is the *trompong,* a two-octave set of ten knobbed gongs. Unlike the two rows of gongs in the Javanese *bonang,* the *trompong* gongs are set in one row. They are played with the greatest flourish, and the performer's movements come close to dancing. The Balinese colotomic instruments are similar to those of Java, with the addition of small cymbals. The softer *rebab* and flute sounds are less important, and there are two drummers instead of one. In addition, there is often a *reyong,* a set of twelve gongs placed in a row and played by four men. They produce rippling, elaborating resultant melodies by the interlocking of their parts.

The principle of interlocking parts is very important in Balinese music. The two drummers play complementary rhythms that result in one very complex line. The *gender,* and sometimes the *gangsa,* also exploit this technique. Example 2–4 shows two short *gender* excerpts and a *reyong* pattern, and their resultants. Those who know Western music history will recognize this as a more sophisticated version of the old European hocketing technique. The creation and perfection of these resultant melodies is one of the delights of Balinese performers.

In Bali, performers are also in a sense composers because, though one man may create the nuclear theme, he will receive suggestions from the players as he teaches them by rote their various elaborating parts. This group composition method points up the communal aspect of the *gamelan.* Most Balinese *gamelan* are clubs organized within a ward or village. Part of their vitality stems from their democratic base as well as their thorough integration into the social and ritual life of the community.

Another reason for the *gamelan's* survival in the modern world is the fact that its musicians have remained creative. In both Java and Bali, new pieces and new styles of playing are constantly being developed. In

EXAMPLE 2–4. Balinese resultant melodies derived from Colin McPhee, "The Five-Tone Gamelan of Bali," *The Musical Quarterly,* XXXV, no. 2 (April, 1949), examples 19 and 21, pp. 274, 275. Used by permission.

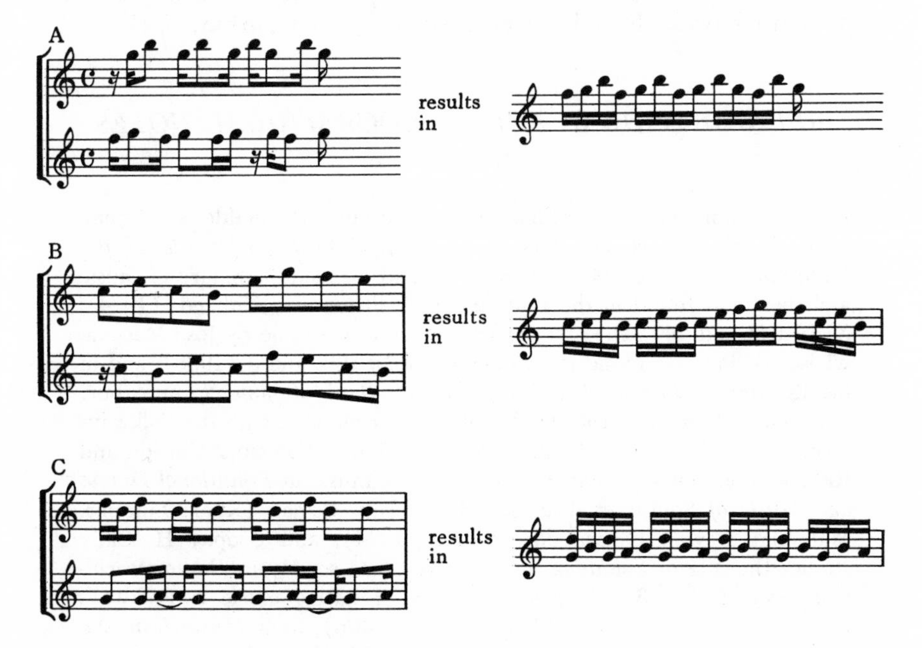

Bali, an individual piece remains only relatively unchanged once it is set. It does not become a fixed, sacrosanct "classic." Some pieces may disappear as new ideas come to the musicians, new dances are created, or the people simply get tired of the piece. Thus the Balinese music and dance world offers a refreshing mixture of traditional and indigenously new art forms.

Conclusion

Despite the many new musical experiments found all over Indonesia, one can still hear traditional sounds such as a quartet of *gender* subtly accompanying an all-night puppet play, a sedate chorus and orchestra performing for a Javanese court dance, or the overwhelming crash of a Balinese *gamelan* playing the entrance music for a witch or a sacred animal in a dance-drama. Such musics are pleasing to the ear, and the theoretical systems that govern their structure are fascinating to the intellect. These admirable features are all the more impressive when one remembers that the high level of artistic ensemble playing needed to perform such music is maintained by rural as well as urban populations.

If we look back over the entire string of cultures surveyed in this chapter, it should be evident that between the village gong ensembles of the Philippines and the court orchestras of Java there is truly a host of wonderful musics available to the listener who will seek them out.

BIBLIOGRAPHICAL AND DISCOGRAPHICAL NOTES

An early summary of Philippine music is Norberto Romualdez's "Filipino Musical Instruments and Airs of Long Ago" in *Encyclopedia of the Philippines* (Manila, 1934), 4, 86–128, and a recent summary of music and theater is found in the *Encyclopaedia Britannica,* 15th ed. (1974), XVII, 241 and 249. The first modern research was done by José Maceda, whose writings are found in *Ethnomusicology* II/2 and 3 (1958), and in his dissertation, *The Music of Magindanao in the Philippines* (Ann Arbor: University Microfilms, 1964). The latter is coordinated with the Folkways recording *Music of the Magindanao* (FE 4536). Professors Maceda and Ricardo Trimillos have written on Philippine music in *Traditional Drama and Music of Southeast Asia,* ed. Mohd. Taib Osman (Kuala Lumpur, Malaysia: Dewan Bahasa dan Pustaka, 1974), and Usopay H. Cady studies the role of *kulintang* music in Maranao society in *Ethnomusicology,* XVII/2 (1973). A good recording of native music is Folkways *Hanunoo Music from the Philippines* (FE 4466), as is *Music from the Tausig of Sulu* (Anthology EST 8000/1). Urban popular music in the Spanish style is heard on Folkways record *Folk Songs of the Philippines* (FW 8791), and professional *rondalla* playing is on the Monitor record *Bayanihan* (332). The Folkways record *Murut Music of North Borneo* (FE 4459) illustrates native harmony and some instruments. Dayak tribal music is heard on the French Contrepoint record *Borneo* (MC 20.112).

Music in Java (The Hague: Nijhoff, 1949), in two volumes, is the classic work of Jaap Kunst. Mantle Hood's *Patet in Javanese Music* (Groningen: Wolters, 1954) is the first detailed study of modal problems; his article "The Enduring Tradition," pp. 438–560 of *Indonesia,* ed. Ruth McVey (New Haven: HRAF Press, 1963), places Indonesian music in its cultural and theatrical matrix, as do sections of Hood's *The Ethnomusicologist* (New York: McGraw-Hill Book Company, 1971). Judith Becker's *Traditional Music in Modern Java* (Honolulu: University of Hawaii Press, 1976) offers new musical and cultural insights. Articles on Java in *Ethnomusicology* include Margaret J. Kartomi, "Music and Trance in Central Java," XVII/2 (1973), and Vincent McDermott and Sumarsan, "Central Javanese Music: The Patet of Laras Slendro and the Gender Barung," XIX/2 (1975). Colin McPhee's *Music in Bali* (New Haven: Yale University Press, 1966) and his charming *A House in Bali* (New

York: The John Day Company, Inc., 1946) are excellent. Walter Spies and Beryl de Zoete show the riches of Balinese theatrical life in *Dance and Drama in Bali* (London: Faber & Faber, 1938), while Jane Belo's *Traditional Balinese Culture* (New York: Columbia University Press, 1970) presents an anthropologist's view. Studies of music from other islands are found in Jaap Kunst, *Music in Flores* (Leiden: E. J. Brill, 1942), and *Music in Nias* (Leiden: E. J. Brill, 1938). Javanese *gamelan* music is best heard on *Javanese Court Gamelan* (Nonesuch H 72044), while excerpts from general Indonesian musics are heard on Folkways *Music of Indonesia* (FE 4537) and Columbia *Indonesia* (KL 210). For Balinese traditions, see Robert Brown's *Music for the Balinese Shadow Play* (Nonesuch H 72037) and *Gamelan Semar Pegulingar* (Nonesuch H 72046), Ruby Ornstein's *Gamelan Music in Bali* (Lyrichord LL 179), and *Dancers of Bali* (Columbia CML 4618, reissued from ML 4618).

THREE

MOSLEM AFRICA, ETHIOPIA, AND THE NEAR EAST

The ancient and modern cultures of both the Near East and Africa contain many rich musical traditions. Our survey will refer to some of the Hebrew, the Christian, and the ancient musics of this vast area, but it will concentrate on the more characteristic tradition of the overall region: Islamic music. In Chapter 2 we have already noted an influence of Islamic music eastward as far as Indonesia and the Philippines, and in Chapters 4 and 5 we shall mention its effects on Central, South, and Southeast Asia. The major topics of this chapter are the music of an area that is called the Near East (or Southwest Asia) as well as the music of North Africa. The chapter will also be concerned with Moslem music from the traditional trade routes along the east coast and the upper half of the west coast of Africa as well as at the southern edges of the Sahara desert. Ethiopia will be treated separately because of its basically non-Islamic tradition. Let us begin at the most southern point of the cultural chain and move gradually towards the better-known Meccas of music in the Near East.

MOSLEM AND BLACK AFRICA

The largest island off the southeast coast of Africa is Madagascar. It is the home of the Malagasy Republic, which is named after a regional culture with a language belonging to the Malayo-Polynesian family and closely related to the speech of South Central Borneo, though it contains borrowings from Arabic, African Bantu, and some French. Thus, the music of this area should reflect a related mixture of styles. Bowed chordophones from the Moslem *rebab* and Western violin family are both to be found in Madagascar, along with French military drums, flutes, trumpets, and clarinets. Such instruments may be combined in many ways to accompany the open-air *hira-gasy* theatricals. These performances consist of music and dance plus long moral songs or proverbial speeches. In some parts of the island, Western drums and flutes have become essential parts of otherwise purely native funeral ceremonies.

Perhaps the most controversial aspect of music on Madagascar is its hypothetical relation to that of Indonesia and Southeast Asia. At least two Malagasy instruments seem reminiscent of traditions found in areas on the opposite side of the Indian Ocean: the *valiha* tube zither (Plate II, Figure 4), with 12 to 18 strings, and the *jejo vaotavo* stick zither, with 4 to 12 strings. The latter looks much like the Southeast Asian model shown in Figure 43 of Plate XV. Both these instruments are used by secular bards. The *valiha* is also found in French-African popular music ensembles, often combined with a guitar and bass. This tube zither is commonly made to sound louder by placing one end of it on an empty gasoline can. Unlike its Asian counterparts, the *valiha* also exists in a boat-shaped zither form. In either form, the *valiha*'s use of diatonic scales and parallel (organal) harmony in thirds is derived from Africa, not Indonesia. Indonesia, however, has sometimes been considered to be the inspiration of the Madagascan xylophones, consisting of sticks of wood placed upon the legs of the seated player.

The Chopi tribesmen of Mozambique, on the coast of Africa west of Madagascar, provide richer materials for potential Indonesian-African comparisons. They play extended dance suites (*ngodo*) with large orchestras made up of many-sized xylophones called *timbila*. These instruments have wooden keys and gourd resonators which, like other resonated African xylophones, have a soundhole thinly covered with a membrane to produce a characteristic African buzzing sound. The poems used in the Chopi suites are topical, not classical as in Java; nevertheless, the *gamelan* concept seems to hover in the background. There have been attempts to show even further relationships with Indonesia through the study of xylophone tunings among the Chopi and in more distant parts of Africa.[1] However, the most common shared traits of these two areas are found in the musical legacies of Islam, for Africa and Indonesia are at two ends of an Islamic cultural stream. This stream is generated centrally in the Near East rather than flowing directly from East to West or vice versa, and it is this Islamic influence on black Africa that offers the most fruitful comparative material.

As implied earlier, Islam extends in Africa over much of the Hamitic and Negritic areas of the East coast, across the Mediterranean littoral, and down through West Africa to the fringes of the Sahara. Since these areas have different pre-Islamic cultures and world views, it is not possible to generalize about the manner in which all respond musically to Islam. In some cases the two traditions seem to have been able to live side by side, whereas in others, particularly those among blacks who moved across the Sahara to North Africa, the Islamic music is colored by indigenous elements. There are some musical changes in black African music, however, which imply Moslem influence (though, at this point, it cannot be proved).[2]

Possible implications of Islamic influence have been found in performances of black singers who ornament their lines with quick, microtonal shakes and mordents and use a tense, nasal voice quality. A Moslem influence may be inferred if, when voices and instruments combine, the accompaniment is not the multiple drums or ostinatos on a melodic instrument as found in Central Africa, but rather a single drum (often of kettle, hourglass, or frame-drum form) or two connected kettledrums or a bowed stringed instrument (like the *rebab*) playing heterophonically. In general, it seems that the polyrhythms of pagan Africa have given way to single rhythmic lines wherever Islam has become dominant. In addition, the several harmonic and disphonic traditions of pagan Africa have become less prominent under Moslem culture, for in general Moslem music tends to be monophonic, although heterophony and drones can also be found. Finally, Moslem influence seems responsible for the appearance in Africa of double-reed instruments.

Interesting if ambiguous mixtures or separations of two musical cultures are found at the terminals of the Sahara caravan routes. The

[1] The best-known and most controversial is A. M. Jones, *Africa and Indonesia: The evidence of the xylophone and other music and cultural factors* (Leiden: E. J. Brill, 1971).

[2] Two discussions of this problem are found in the chapters by Lois Anderson and by Akin Euba in *Music and History in Africa,* ed. Klaus Wachsmann (Evanston: Northwestern University Press, 1971). For a discussion of other Negro African styles, see Nettl, *Folk and Traditional Music of the Western Continents,* and H. H. Nketia, *The Music of Africa* (New York: W. W. Norton & Company, Inc., 1974).

Wolofs of Senegal and Gambia, for example, show such a mixture: they use both cylindrical and pot-shaped single-headed drums in groups to produce African polyrhythms for their secular dances, but when their holy man sings Moslem hymns (*hasida*), a small kettledrum called a *tabala* is used, along with an iron beater; together, these produce simple, single rhythms much more akin to the music of the rest of the Moslem world.

Wolof society has a class of professional entertainers (*gewel* or *griots*) who, in keeping with both Negro and Moslem traditions as well as those of many other cultures, are considered to be lazy, boisterous, and low-class.[3] Nevertheless, they are well paid, for music is an essential, functional part of many phases of African life, just as it is in Oceania. The performances of these musicians reflect a Negro-Moslem mixture, for they sing praise songs—a common pagan African genre—with tense North African voices. They also tell stories to the accompaniment of a plucked five-stringed *halam* lute. The narrative traditions which they use are as old as the camel caravan routes of Moslem and even pre-Moslem Africa. However, whereas the Moslem caravan narrators used bowed, heterophonic accompaniments to their tales, the Wolofs play plucked, drone-like harmonies. Similar mixtures of styles can be found all along the fringes of the Sahara.

ETHIOPIA

So many peoples have traded or fought in the Sudan which lies between North Africa and Ethiopia that its musical culture offers several interpretations. Ethiopia itself, however, has always presented a special cultural image because, despite its basically Islamic environment and occasional Islamic invasion, its fundamental religion has for centuries remained Coptic Christianity. Ethiopia is the home as well of the Falasha Jews, a unique congregation of Ethiopians who adopted yet another ancient religious tradition. In many remote areas, particularly in the South, there also are tribes that exhibit polyphonic styles more typical of neighboring parts of Negro Africa, such as composite flute melodies and canonic singing. Nevertheless, the traditions of Christian Ethiopia remain central to the musical characteristics of the country.

[3] For a discussion of the curiously consistent low position of musicians in world societies, see Alan P. Merriam, *The Anthropology of Music* (Evanston: Northwestern University Press, 1964), Chapter 7.

Ethiopian Coptic chants (*degwa*) as performed by official church singers (*debteras*) exhibit the melodic restraints and repetitions typical of word-oriented music functioning in a ceremony. Like most such religious music, Ethiopian chant at first sounds highly redundant, but a study of the tradition shows a skillful use of ornamentation, with melodic units and tonal emphases that make it possible for one to distinguish specific modes as well as appropriate ritual melodies. The melodies are preserved in a special, rather complicated notation; however, although singers learn to read it well, their basic lessons are given in the rote method, for, as most musicians know, the ear is a more efficient organ than the eye in learning music, particularly if the music is as melismatic as Ethiopian chant.

Few instrumental sounds emanate from the inner sanctum of the round Coptic churches. Outside some rural churches one may find a set of sonorous stone slabs (*dowel*) which are used like church bells, while a drum (*kebaro*) may be heard inside most churches. The jangling sistrum (*tsenatsil*) shown in Plate V, Figure 13, is a Coptic ritual instrument that may also be an example of the marginal survival of an object formerly used in ancient Egyptian, Greek, and Roman traditions.

The large ten-stringed *bagana* lyre is often referred to by Ethiopians as the descendant of David's harp in the Old Testament, but its use is not liturgical. It accompanies classical poetry or songs of religious or philosophical text. The smaller *krar* lyre shown in Figure 14 is an equally interesting instrument and more widely used in Ethiopian secular music, as is the one-stringed *masenqo* bowed lute of more recent Moslem origin. Whatever the "true" origin of any of these instruments, their use in Ethiopia often seems creatively accultural. A possible example of such a mixture of traditions may be heard on side 2, band 2, of *Folk Music of Ethiopia* (Folkways FE 4405). Here a nasal-voiced singer plays a Moslem-like spike fiddle to accompany a Negro-style praise song in honor of his Christian emperor. (By now the reader must realize that the concept of "pure" music is not a very useful one as long as there are frequent cultural contacts in the world and a few good ears attached to imaginative musicians in each culture.)

Although various African groups mentioned in the foregoing section of this chapter show unique variations in their acculturation of musical styles, the general principles stated have given some indications of the directions that Black African music may take under Moslem influences. Our look at an Ethiopian example actually led us beyond Black Africa to an area of Caucasoid dominance—which in turn leads us to North Africa and to the Near East itself.

FIGURE 13. *Tsenatsil.*

FIGURE 14. *Krar.*

THE PAN-ISLAMIC TRADITION

Although we have noted Islamic influence in Africa, the Philippines, and Indonesia (and will note it further in Central, South, and Southeast Asia in later chapters), the mainstream of Western Islamic culture can be found in an expanse of territory extending from southern Spain along the African Coast of the Mediterranean and up through the Near East, where it splits, first in the direction of Iran and second via Turkey into Eastern Europe. At the terminals of this stream the traditions are quite mixed, particularly in Eastern Europe. But within the non-European confines of this core area—that is, from Morocco to Turkey—there is a unity of culture which we shall label the *pan-Islamic tradition,* realizing that historically and geographically the peoples making up this category include such non-Islamic groups as Near Eastern Christians and Jews as well as pre-Islamic Arabs, and that there is an even greater variety of peoples in other Islamic areas to be discussed in later chapters. The pan-Islamic core encompasses a variety of peoples, such as the Turks of Central Asian origins, the Aryan Persians, many kinds of Arab and Semitic peoples, and the Hamitic converts of North Africa. One can expect many differences within such a large grouping of peoples, but the pan-Islamic label is still useful, for the spread of Islam has directly or indirectly brought certain unifying elements to the culture of this vast area.

Our discussion of pan-Islamic music will fall into the general categories of folk, art, popular, and religious music, recognizing that extensive interpenetration of styles and instruments has occurred among them. Under these categories, representative examples will be chosen from one or both of the sub-areas within the basic pan-Islamic world. One is the desert and coast of North Africa, the so-called Maghrib (Maghreb), which includes the modern nations of Morocco, Algeria, Tunisia, and Libya, with Egypt as a cultural buffer zone between this area and the next. The other sub-area is the Near East proper, which includes Iran, Syria, Iraq, Jordan, Saudi Arabia, Lebanon, Oman, Aden, and Yemen. For most of this survey Turkey will be included in this latter area, though its Central Asian background gives it many special traits. Hebraic Palestine (Israel) will be treated separately.

Folk Music

The dominant pre-Islamic peoples of North Africa were the Berbers. With the seventh-century rise of Islam and the eleventh-century migrations of Bedouin Arabs, the Berbers were pushed into the mountains or out onto the desert where they, in turn, displaced Negro groups. Today the Berbers are Moslem, but their present culture often reveals a patchwork of Moslem and indigenous ideas. This can be seen in the life of the Tuaregs, the so-called "Abandoned of God," who control caravan routes in the Sahara northeast of Timbuktu.

Unlike most Berbers, the Tuaregs adopted the Moslem social system while sharing Berber monogamy. Their form of matriarchy is unique (only the men wear veils), as is their writing system (only the women are literate). Their music shows similar contrasts. When women sing, ornaments characteristic of the Moslem music of this area are missing, and the accompaniment is only percussion or handclapping, though a characteristic Arab female yodelling cry is often interjected. The two Tuareg percussion instruments are normally played only by women. One is the single-headed *tendi* kettledrum, played with the hands and tuned by dampening its gazelle-skin head. The other is the so-called water drum—actually an idiophone consisting of a large bowl of water in which a second bowl has been placed upside down. A stick is used to beat out a simple rhythm on the overturned bowl.

Photographs show men playing tambourines, but traditionally women are the instrumentalists. Men, however, do sing, particularly at the sensuous *ahal* entertainment gatherings. They perform highly ornamented love songs to the accompaniment of a one-stringed spike fiddle (*amzhad* or *imzhad*—Plate VI, Figure 15), which is often played by the female object of their song. The heterophonic nature of these songs can be seen in the excerpt shown in Example 3–1.

From this discussion it seems that Tuareg women's music is more oriented toward some non-Moslem style possibly derived from old Berber culture or from the music of their Negro slaves; on the other hand, male music seems Moslem. During the Ramadan holy month the Tuaregs sometimes join with Arabs and Moslem Negros at an oasis for a night of ecstatic dancing. The unique musical mixtures of this trance-filled night offer dramatic illustration of the continuous interchange of ideas in the desert.

Along the coast and in the mountains of North Africa the pan-Islamic style prevails. There are, however, occasional remnants of the Greco-Roman occupation of the land as well as specific Berber and Jewish songs. The expulsion of the Sephardic Jews and later the Moors from Spain in the fifteenth century had its musical effect on North Africa as well. Earlier, during the heydays of Moorish Spain, the various courts in Morocco, Tunisia, and Algeria learned much about Arab classical music from Hispanic artists. The thirteenth-century Bedouin invasion destroyed this Berber culture and its economy, so that today Berber songs and dances are commonly found only in the remote Atlas mountains of Algeria. But even these remnants exhibit traits common to the entire pan-Islamic tradition. For example, one description of Berber mountain dances notes

EXAMPLE 3–1. A heterophonic Tuareg love song transcribed from the recording, *Tuareg Music of the Southern Sahara* (New York: Folkways Record FE 4470), side 1, band 3. By permission of Folkways Records and Service Corporation.

the typical Arab circling line-dance pattern and the use of tambourine accompaniment.[4]

If one goes north of the mountains and out onto the coastal plains, the Islamic influence becomes even clearer. Professional epic poets appear,

[4] See Alexis Chottin, *Tableau de la musique marocaine* (Paris: Geuthner, 1939), Chapter 1.

and they are often accompanied by an end-blown flute commonly called the *gasba* or *qasaba*. The Near Eastern equivalent of this is called the *nay*. Both instruments have five or six fingerholes and tend to be played slanted slightly to the side of the player in a manner reminiscent of both the *sib* of ancient Egypt and the *suling* of modern Indonesia. *Gasba* are made of either cane or metal. Whether such flutes play heterophonic vocal accompaniments or free-rhythmic solos, their florid, breathy melodies are typically pan-Islamic.

A majority of pan-Islamic folk music is purely vocal. It is either performed as a solo or in call-and-response manner with a unison chorus as shown in Example 3–2. If accompaniment is desired, the most common type is a handclap on the main accent of a duple meter (Example 3–2). The most popular instrumental addition is the tambourine. It comes in several distinct forms throughout the pan-Islamic world and is called by a dozen names, the most common of which are *duff*, *taar*, and *bendair*. Its basic form is a circular, single-headed frame drum, either plain or with snares attached beneath the skin. Metal disks may be set in the frame or metal rings attached around the inside of the rim behind the skin. There are also diamond- and square-shaped tambourines. Regardless of its shape or size, the tambourine is a vital element in most lively forms of pan-

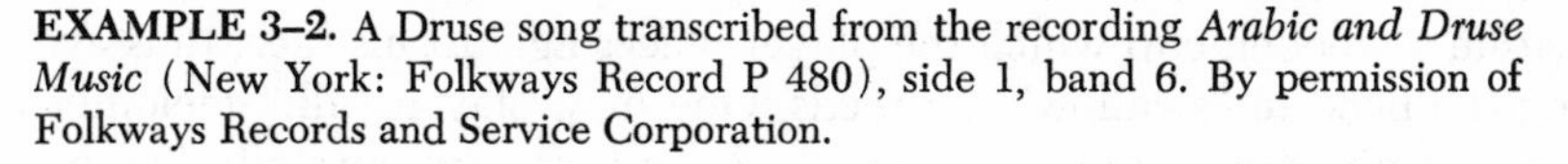

EXAMPLE 3–2. A Druse song transcribed from the recording *Arabic and Druse Music* (New York: Folkways Record P 480), side 1, band 6. By permission of Folkways Records and Service Corporation.

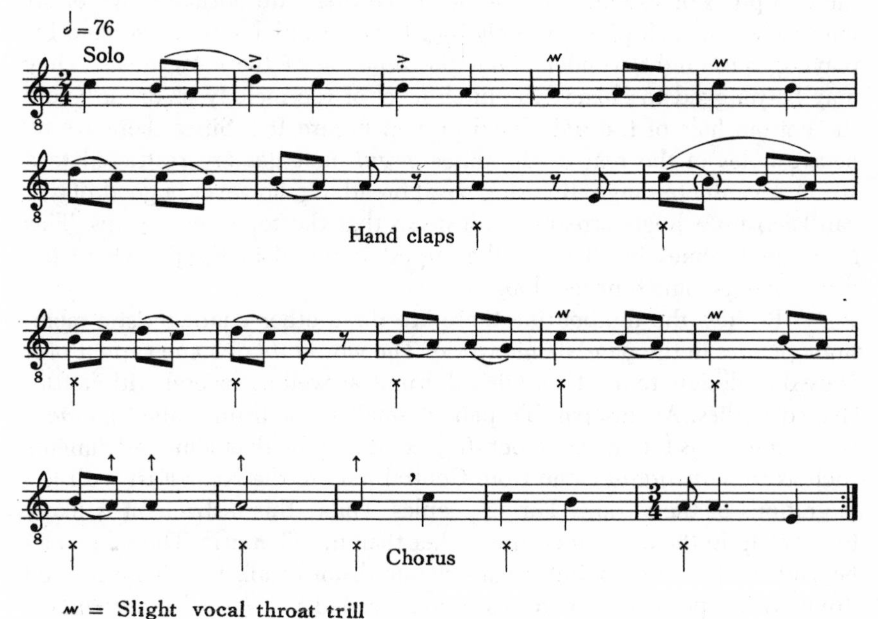

Islamic music—particularly dances, wedding songs, and other music sung primarily by women.

Wedding songs are a significant part of pan-Islamic female music. These are often performed by professional singers hired for the occasion. Weddings also require another typical pan-Islamic instrument, the double-reed aerophone known in the Maghrib as the *zukra, zamr,* or *gaita* (Plate IX, Figure 24). It is more commonly known in the Near East by the Persian term *surnay* or the Turkish *zurna* (*zorna*). This double-reed, conical aerophone normally has seven holes in front and one in the back. The stereotyped Western imitations of Near Eastern music are inspired by its nasal, "outdoor" sound. Most players place the reed inside the mouth so that no lip pressure is possible. When the instrument is played in this way, the bulging cheeks of the player are, in fact, the bag of a human bagpipe. Actual bagpipes with and without drones are found throughout the Maghrib as well as up the Nile River in the Sudan. A more common pan-Islamic aerophone, however, is the double clarinet shown in Figure 16 of Plate VI. Standard names for it are the *argul, yarul, zamr,* or *zamar.* It is sometimes mislabelled as a double flute or double reed. Properly described, it is a double clarinet, for it consists of two cylindrical pipes, each of which has a single beating reed. These are placed inside the mouth and vibrate freely. Sometimes the reeds are within a wooden cup which the player places against his face, thus avoiding the need to "swallow" the reeds. One may play parallel melodies on the two pipes or use one as a drone. Since there are normally five or six fingerholes on each pipe and only four fingers available on each hand for playing, one might wonder about the function of the extra holes. They may be plugged to change the pitch level of the melody or drone (note the bottom hole of the right-hand pipe in Figure 16). Since there are no octave holes in the rear of the pipes, *argul* melodies are restricted to a six- or seven-note range. By using nasal breathing, however, a good player can keep up a lively stream of music so that the tone never stops. This instrument comes in all sizes; the largest is found in Egypt, where the drone pipe is some four feet long.

Besides the tambourine there are three other characteristic membranophones in the pan-Islamic world. The word *tabl* or some variant of it is used to designate most cylindrical drums as well as several with kettle-shaped bodies. An inseparable pair of small kettledrums called *naqqara* is found even as far east as Tibet. Indeed, it may be that some instruments such as these *naqqara* came from Central Asia to the Near East with the migrations of the various Turkic peoples. Today this instrument is likely to show up in the cafe orchestras rather than in folk music. The same may be said for the most popular pan-Islamic drum of all, the single-headed drum with a pottery or metal vase body, called the *darbuka, darabukka,*

PLATE VI. The Near East

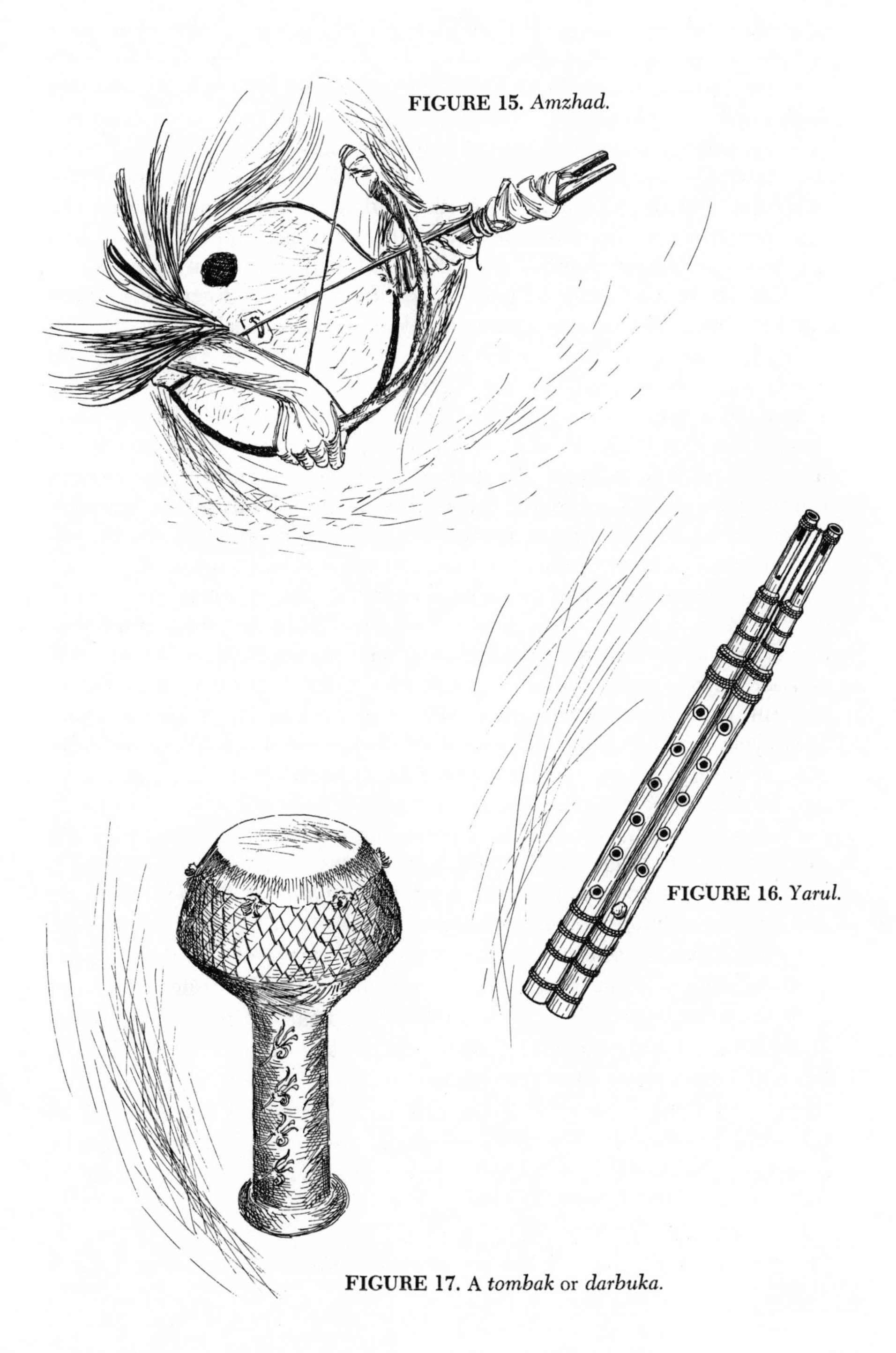

FIGURE 15. *Amzhad.*

FIGURE 16. *Yarul.*

FIGURE 17. A *tombak* or *darbuka.*

or *tombak* (shown in Figure 17 of Plate VI). It can be played in any one of three ways: upright, tucked under the left arm, or held upside down and struck from below. In any position it provides a very lively beat for Arab music of all kinds.

Stringed instruments do not play a significant role in North African folk music except for the bowed spike fiddle (*nabab*) of the street musicians and the plucked lyre of the Sudan and northeast Africa. The Moroccan Berbers, however, do have a three-stringed plucked lute called the *lutar,* and throughout North Africa one can find many homemade versions of the two-stringed *genibri* or *gunbri.* This indigenous plucked lute has a rectangular, skin-covered body and a round neck.

In Turkey and parts of the Near East, several different plucked and bowed lutes can be found in folk ensembles. Figure 19 of Plate VII shows a *tambur,* a popular Near Eastern plucked lute. It has a small, pear-shaped wooden body, a long fretted neck, and from two to ten metal strings in double courses. In Turkey and Turkish-influenced Eastern Europe (including Greece and the Mediterranean islands) there is a wide variety of long-necked lutes, particularly in folk and popular music performances. The most frequent names for such instruments are *saz, buzuq* (*bozuq* or *bouzouki*), and *baglama.* The *kemanchay* (*kemanche*), found in Turkey and Persia, is a bowed lute with three or four strings that found its way into Europe through the many *lira* and other bowed lutes of East Europe and Greece. It is also one of the important ancestors of the European *rebec,* which eventually evolved into the Western violin. This cycle was completed in recent centuries when the Western violin was, in turn, used by Moslem musicians as a substitute for the *rebab,* from which it originated.

So far we have noted as typical pan-Islamic folk forms wedding songs, love songs, epic tales, and line dances (the *dabka* or *debka*). Naturally, there are also camel caravan songs (*huda*). To these we must add various religious songs in praise of the saints or in honor of pilgrims returning from Mecca, as well as the special songs of splinter Moslem sects and the ecstatic chants of the dervish groups. Liturgical music as such is very restricted in orthodox Islam.[5] The calls to prayer (*adhan* or *azan*) by the muezzin from a minaret are usually quite ornate, while the intoning of prayers and sections from the Koran in a mosque is done to specific, restrained chants. Both the calls to prayer and the chants, in fact, are not considered to be music, and therefore are acceptable within the mosque. Another example of such "nonmusic music" in the pan-Islamic

[5] Arguments by Islamic writers for and against music are translated in M. L. Chouchury, "Music in Islam," *The Journal of the Asiatic Society,* Letter XXIII/2 (1957).

PLATE VII. The Near East

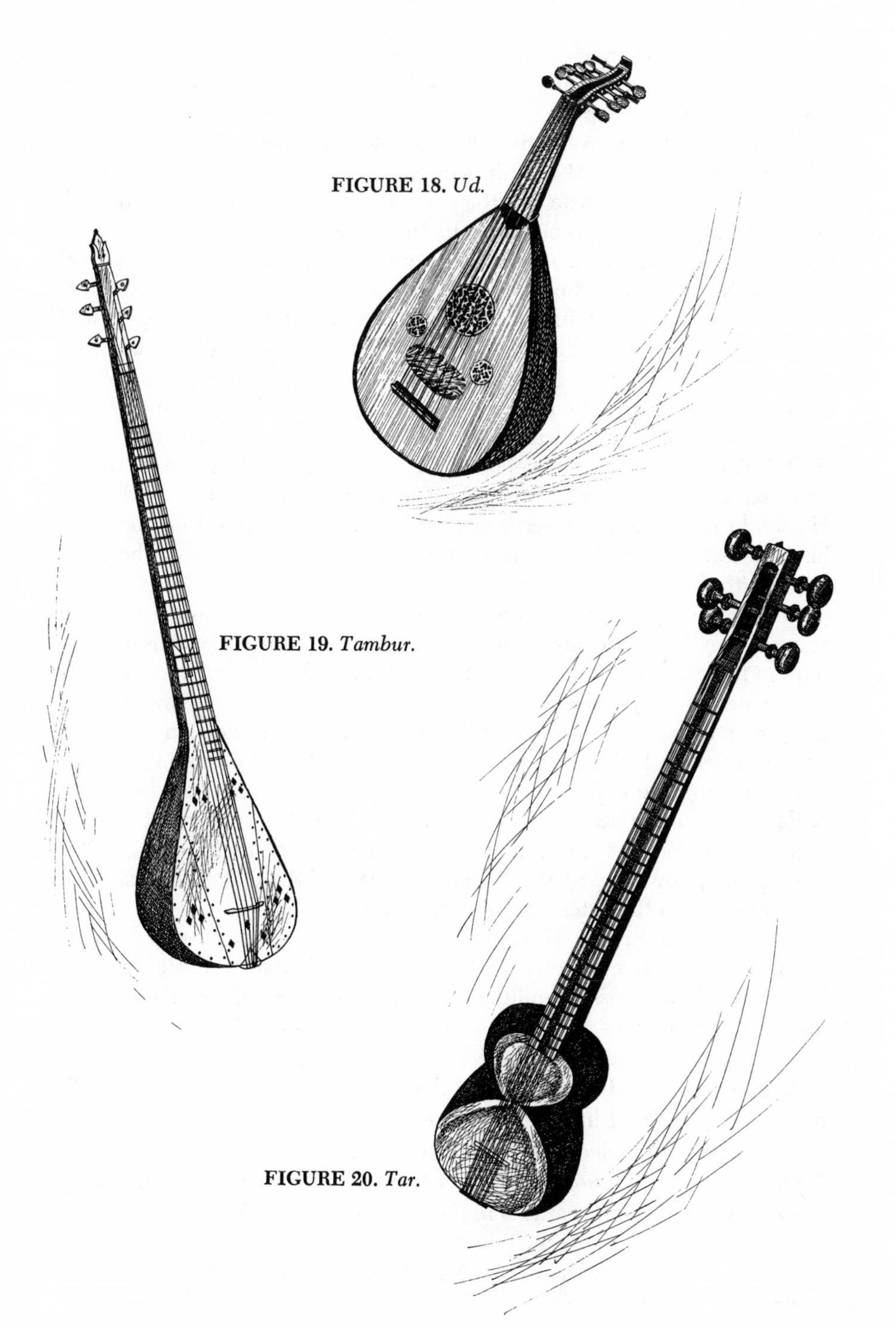

FIGURE 18. *Ud.*

FIGURE 19. *Tambur.*

FIGURE 20. *Tar.*

world is the recitation of certain classical poetry. Both examples are useful reminders of the fact that different cultures have different definitions of the word "music" (cf. p. 4).

Despite the conservative view mentioned above, there is a large number of more mystical Islamic sects which greatly value the functional and spiritual use of music. By the same token, the teachings of the Sufi sect of Islam are often declared to be fundamental to the artistry of both sacred and secular forms of Islamic music. The best-known mystical order is the Mevlevi (Mawlawiyah) sect, whose *sama* part of its services involves men who continue to turn to the accompaniment of prayers and sometimes instrumental music. Though officially discouraged since 1925, the Mevlevi still survive in Turkey and a few other eastern parts of the Moslem world, and their dance style may also have been absorbed into some of the trance-dance traditions of Islamic Southeast Asia. In the Near East today, a similar atmosphere in a secular context is found in the ceremonial exercises of special physical culture clubs such as the *zur khaneh* in Iran. These are accompanied by an epic-singing drummer who, like the leader in a Mevlevi service, marks off the divisions of the ceremony with the sounds of a bell.

Additional Islamic ceremonial music outside the mosque is heard at weddings, funerals, and other family events. Such occasions usually require the service of the wailing *zurna* oboes and various drums. During the Ramadan holy month in North Africa the oboes, and even horns (*neffar* or *nafir*), are used for the call to prayers. In addition, one may hear wandering bards playing one-stringed fiddles and singing *qasida*, songs praising the careers of Mohammed (A.D. 570–632) and the saints. Today these itinerant *qasida* tend to deal with more current events, though they may retain an opening line in praise of their prophet. The term *qasida*, however, is better known as part of the classical music that is heard today in the cafés and in private concerts.

Before discussing classical music, we must mention one Moslem ensemble, especially because of its influence on Western music. It is the famous Turkish Janissary military band, which consists of bass drums (*darwul*), trombones (*boru*), cymbals (*zil*), double kettledrums (*nakara*), and *zurna* oboes. Normally there are nine players on each type of instrument, plus performers who strike the ground with a clanging bell-tree called, in English, a Turkish crescent or Chinese pavilion.[6] Many eighteenth-century pieces *alla turca*, by such composers as Mozart and Beethoven, are imitations of this ensemble; modern variants of it are heard in some Shriners' parades in the United States.

[6] Such a group is pictured on page 119 of Reinhard Pauly's *Music in the Classic Period*, 2nd ed. (Englewood Cliffs, N.J.: Prentice-Hall, Inc., 1973).

Classical Music

Classical and Modern Instruments. Since so many instruments have already been mentioned, it seems logical to continue our organological inventory in a classical context before turning to the complications of the music itself. The human voice, of course, is a major vehicle for Moslem classical music, since much of it is related to poetry. The folk-derived *nay* end-blown flute mentioned earlier is used in classical music, as are tambourines and various forms of the *tombak* drum (Figure 17), known in some areas as a *zarb*. The two small *naqqara* kettledrums can be found in some North African and Turkish classical ensembles.

The chordophone families are particularly well-represented in Islamic music. The most common term for the classical bowed lute is *kamanja*. It may be a two- to four-stringed spike fiddle held upright like the Persian *kamanchay* (Plate VIII, Figure 21) or a western-style violin held either upright or horizontally from the hip. Both positions are used for the *keman*, which is found particularly in North Africa and Turkey; a Moroccan version in the upright position is shown in Plate VIII, Figure 22. Next to it in Figure 23 is the two-stringed Moroccan *rabab*. This small upright bowed lute is unique, for, unlike such instruments as those of Figures 9 and 15, it has a fingerboard that is actually a hollow extension of the body along its short neck to the peg box. The Persian classical *kamanchay* (*kemanche*) of Figure 21 shows clearly why such an instrument is sometimes called a spike fiddle. The spike allows the player to rotate the instrument in order to accommodate the bowing of its two to four metal strings. On some instruments the spike fits into a metal plate so that the player may place the instrument on the calf of his leg. The *kamanchay* has a membrane face of sheepskin and can have a globular or cylindrical body. Note that all the bows being used to play the instruments in Plate VIII (as well as those of most of the other bowed lutes mentioned in this book) require the use of fingers to maintain bow tension.

Long-necked plucked lutes such as the *tambur* (*tanbur*) in Figure 19 float freely among pan-Islamic folk, popular, and art traditions. The word *tar* in the Near East and in Central Asia is used as a final syllable in the names of many such instruments. In Persian classical music an example is the four-stringed *sehtar*. The Iranian *tar* plucked lute shown in Figure 20 is quite different. It has six double courses of metal strings stretched over a membrane-faced figure-eight-shaped body. The gut frets along its neck are movable like those of most pan-Islamic plucked lutes. This is necessary so that the fret positions may be adjusted to the requirements of the various pan-Islamic tone systems (to be discussed presently).

The most famous Moslem plucked lute is the *'ud* (Plate VII, Figure

PLATE VIII. Near Eastern Bowed Lutes

FIGURE 21. *Kamanchay.*

FIGURE 22. *Keman.* **FIGURE 23.** *Rabab.*

18); it has a narrower-bodied, long-necked variant, the *kwitra* (in Turkey the *lauta*). The *'ud* form shown in Figure 18 has five double courses plus a single high string, but there are many variations in the stringing of the instrument. Although the *'ud* often has movable gut frets like the *tar*, it sometimes is played fretless for more flexibility.

Harps and lyres are no longer used in the Near East, though we have noted the presence of lyres in East Africa. A harp called *chang* in Persian is found in historical records and in paintings; however, the present-day *vaji* arched harp of Nurestan and harps among Central Asian archeological artifacts are the only actual instruments of this type found in this area of the world. They are good examples of the principle of marginal survival, as is the *saung kauk* harp of Burma. Zithers, by contrast, are quite widespread. The Persian *santur* (*santir*) dulcimer is of special interest because it is the ancestor of a variety of instruments, from the Western cimbalon and piano to the Chinese *yang ch'in*. Seventy-two metal strings, in quadruple courses, are stretched across a set of bridges set on a shallow trapezoidal body; the strings are struck with two delicate hammers. The florid sounds of Persian music played upon the open strings of a traditional *santur* tend to merge into an exotic mesh of tone color, although there are modern versions of the instrument that have a sound-dampening mechanism like that of a piano and thus are able to separate melodic tones. The stringing method of the *santur* varies: sometimes the pegs (around which the string ends are wound) are on both sides of the body like those of most American hammered dulcimers; sometimes the pegs run along only one side, as may be seen on the *qanun* (*kanun*) shown in Figure 25. This psaltery is found in Turkish and Arab ensembles. Its 72 gut strings are plucked by small picks (seen in Figure 25) that are normally attached to the player's index fingers. Most Arab models have small levers under the strings at the peg side, making it possible to change the pitch slightly for tunings to different scales.

Classical Music Theory. As intimated earlier, there were many centers of musical culture throughout the Islamic world. The oldest was probably Persia, which contained remnants of ancient Babylonian thought as well as some infusions of Greek ideas. This area was conquered by the Arabs in the seventh century and musical traditions were then mixed. As sultanates proliferated along the ever-extending line of Islamic conquests, Moslem musicians and music theorists found patronage in courts as far distant as Samarkand in Central Asia and Salamanca in Spain. The defeat of Islam in Spain in 1492 forced Iberian scholars to flee to North African courts, so that today there is a school of so-called Andalusian classical music in the Maghrib. The rise of the Ottoman Turkish empire from the thirteenth through the sixteenth century led to other centers of activity, such as Alexandria and Baghdad. Although this last great Moslem empire was politically rather static until its demise in the twentieth century, its musicians remained creative and active through at least the eighteenth.

The historical outline given above is reflected in the contemporary scene, for the modern Moslem classical tradition can be divided into four major schools: the Persian, with its center in Iran; the Arab, which flourishes in Egypt; the Andalusian, as it is practiced in North Africa; and the Turkish. Modern practitioners from the various national schools that lie within these four larger traditions continue to expand the theory and practice of their art, but they all retain certain basic concepts that we can label as the ancient pan-Islamic classical music theory.

Studies in musical theories and practice are usually applied to what is called "classical" or "art" music. We implied in Chapter 1 (p. 12) that such terms might be appropriate functionally to any music culture. Used in connection with large urban literate societies, the terms refer to music traditions that were appreciated and supported by the economic or governmental control groups of those societies. In the Near East, however, such aristocratic musics were already well established on both the courtly and tribal levels before the coming of Islam in the seventh century. In the Bedouin tribal camps, the poet-musician (*shair*) occupied a special place in the culture by virtue of his or her shamanistic powers and commentaries on regional society. In pre-Islamic courts like those of Central Asia and Persia, female dancers (*gaynat*) or singers and African musicians were part of a tradition that was happily accepted by subsequent Islamic rulers. They, in turn, increased the import and exchange of all kinds of "exotic" foreign musicians.

Islamic musical scholarship first reached an apogee with the works of such men as Al Kindi (d. *circa* 870) and Al Farabi (d. 950), who combined Greek, Persian, and Arab concepts into brilliant syntheses. Al Farabi's "Grand Book of Music" (*Kitab al musiqi al kabin*) is one of the monuments of music theory; it was read at the medieval University of Paris as well as in Salamanca and Baghdad.

The lives of other famous Islamic music theorists demonstrate the continuing inter-cultural exchange of traditions. Ibn Sina (Avicenna, 980–1037) came from Central Asia to Persia, where he wrote on every intellectual topic of the medieval world, including music theory. A ninth-century musician named Ziryab left Baghdad to work in the Moslem court of Cordoba, Spain; from there his style of performance, teaching, and composing spread to other courts. Later important music scholars were the Persian Safi al-Din al-Mummin (d. 1294), who served the Mongol conquerors of Baghdad, and Abd Qadir Ghaibi al Maraghi (d. 1435), who provided the first extensive examples of Persian music in notation while working for the Turkish Ottoman rulers.

From the surviving literature of many musicians' writings[7] we are able to glean much information about the names of famous musicians and compositions, but most of these works are primarily concerned, like similar medieval European studies, with the science of acoustical music theory. Thus it is appropriate that we begin our discussion of Islamic art music with its theoretical base, although we shall concentrate on the views of modern scholars and musicians rather than on those of their impressive ancient forefathers.

Pan-Islamic classical music is conceived within a system of *maqamat* (plural of *maqam*), which determine the modal as well as the melodic basis upon which musical compositions are formed. Though other terms and spellings may appear (*makam* in Turkey, *dastgah* in Persia, *naghmah* in Egypt, and *taba* in North Africa), the concept itself has remained fundamental to pan-Islamic classical traditions. At first sight there seem to be as many definitions of *maqam* as there are writers about it. A major reason for this confusion may be that some writers view *maqamat* in terms of abstract theory while others see it as a base for performance practice. In this section of our survey we shall take primarily the theoretical approach.

Maqamat theory deals in general with scales and modes. Historically, *maqamat* were often defined as seven-tone scales arrayed within an octave in the ancient Greek style of two four-note units (tetrachords). These scales were divisive; that is, their notes were based on the principle of derivation from various divisions of a vibrating string. Originally, the resulting proportions of these string lengths were permutated mathematically to create several different divisions of the octave and thus different-sized intervals. Using the fretted fingerboard of a lute (the *'ud*, Plate VII, Figure 18) as a diagram, many modes were constructed. These "finger modes" (*asabi*) were arranged in various geometrical figures—such as circles, stars, and polygons—designed to show the relationship of each mode to specific moods, times of the day, seasons, colors, and other extra-musical concepts.

Over the centuries the number of divisions of the Moslem octave changed many times (25, 22, 17, etc.), as did the names and construction of the various scales. Thus, if one views *maqamat* only from the scalar standpoint, little consistency in the use of scale-names seems evident today. This can be seen in Example 3–3, which shows three North African scales, all called *ramal maia* but coming from three adjacent countries. The Algerian example is called *o'shak* (*'ushshaq*) by the eastern Arabs. An Egyptian survey of Moslem music in 1932 showed that the Egyptians

[7] A basic list is given in Henry G. Farmer, *The Sources of Arabian Music* (Leiden: E. J. Brill, 1965).

EXAMPLE 3–3. Three versions of the mode *ramal maia,* from Alexis Chottin, *Tableau de la musique marocaine* (Paris: Geuthner, 1939), p. 181. Used by permission.

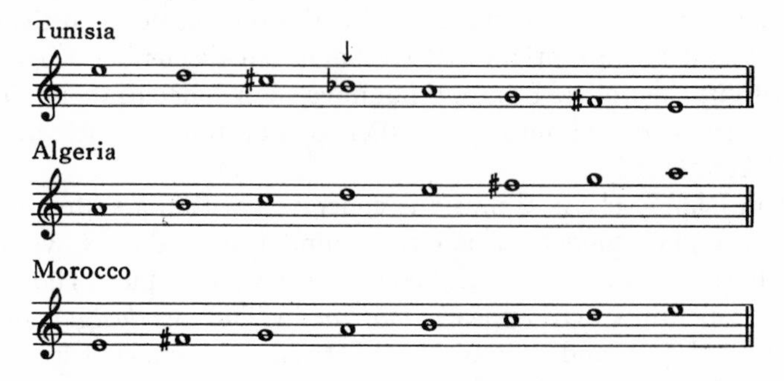

had 52 basic scales; the Syrians had the same number, some in altered form; North Africa had 18, 16 of them the Egyptian scales under different names; Iraq had 37, 15 of them the Egyptian scales under different names; and the Iranians had 7, which they claimed could be permutated into all the others.

In the midst of such variety and musical chauvinism the outsider naturally becomes confused. A partial clarification of the reasonableness of such variety may be made by considering two points. First, we are viewing the *maqam* in the context of a notated abstract scale that in practice hardly exists; actual practical scales are capable of various "translations" out of the aural tradition into such incomplete graphic representations. Second (and this point relates to the first), even the most traditional classical musician will tend to hold to his own interpretation of the modal aspects of a *maqam,* so that various schools of the same tradition may describe a *maqam* in quite different ways. This is also possible in the pan-Islamic tradition, since professional performers, like many other musicians discussed in this book, are more concerned with skills in performance than accuracy in intellectual abstractions. With this important caveat as a prelude we shall discuss briefly one Islamic theoretical system, that of the Iranian (Persian) schools as it is taught today. Where appropriate, information about other systems will be interjected.

Turning first to the concept of tone systems, one finds that Persian music theory presently recognizes 12 modal structures; since the eighteenth century, these have not been called *maqamat* but rather *dastgah-ha* (the plural of *dastgah,* which means scheme, apparatus, or hand position). One interpretation[8] of this system is shown in Example

[8] For others, see the Farhat and Zonis readings cited in the bibliographical notes for this chapter.

3–4. The seven *dastgah-ha* that are considered to be basic are marked with Roman numerals. The remaining five, marked with parenthetical arabic numerals, are felt to be auxiliaries (*avaz*, "songs," or *naghmeh*, "melodies") to a primary *dastgah*, four to *Shur* and one to *Homayun*. Study of Example 3–4 quickly reveals that one cannot easily distinguish a *dastgah* on the basis of pitch alone; for instance, *Mahur* and *Rast panjgah* appear to be the same scale. Each *dastgah*, like an Arab *maqam* or Turkish *makam*, is better recognized in practice by special melodies (*gusheh-ha*, the plural of *gusheh* or *gushé*). These in turn emphasize specific melodic contours, cadence formulas, and conventional final tones (*ist*) or reciting tones (*shahed*). (*Ist* and *shahed* are indicated in Example 3–4 in their most commonly accepted versions.) The auxiliary or satellite modes originally may have been melodies that gained nearly

EXAMPLE 3–4. One abstraction of the Persian *dastgah* system.

equal stature with the primary modes and were referred to in performance by their own name rather than that of their parent *dastgah.* Today their secondary status is noted by the narrower range of their melodies and by the smaller number of compositions based on them in the *radif,* the collection of all the *gusheh-ha* in the Persian art music tradition.

It must be remembered that Moslem musicians do not play scales, they play pieces, and that only in a performance context do the essential characteristics and mood of a *dastgah* emerge. Nevertheless, the tonal abstractions of Example 3–4 give some idea of the rich vocabulary from which such music is constructed. The microtonal arrows in the notation, for example, show that there are obviously more than twelve pitches in the Persian octave. In practice there are an infinite number (though only 7 are used at one time), for individual performers, like many jazz musicians, have their own interpretations of the "correct" pitches of a given scale or piece.

The most common Persian theory continues to view the octave in two tetrachords a whole step apart, each consisting (as in Western scales) of two whole steps and one half step. In the modern Persian system, however, some theorists hold that there are different sizes of seconds: a major second (approximately 200 cents), a minor second (near 100 cents), a neutral second (about 150 cents), and an enlarged second (some 255 cents); the last combined with a minor second can result in a neutral third (355 cents). There is no agreement as to the actual size of these intervals among theorists or among practicing musicians; thus the inaccuracy of our notation in Example 3–4 is appropriate. It is interesting historically to note that the 15, 17, or 24 possible divisions of the Persian octave are often discussed using the old Greek terms *lima* and *comma.* In performance and in scale constructions, however, it is important to know that such tiny divisions, like the Indian *sruti* (see p. 95), are never actually used individually; rather, they are combined into various kinds of larger seconds to form seven-tone scales. Thus there is actually no microtonal "chromaticism" in pan-Islamic music, as is sometimes indicated in writings about such "oriental" music. This descriptive error is usually caused by the "out-of-tune" sound of Near Eastern music (when in fact it is being played very accurately and artfully with the varied intervals mentioned above).

The word *avaz,* besides being used to indicate a satellite scale, is frequently applied to the unmeasured rhythmic style of music that in Iran is most common in classical music. (It is shown in Example 3–6.) In such *avaz* the major rhythmic consideration is that of the classical poetry which so often is part of the performance.[9] Classical pan-Islamic music

[9] Excellent examples are found in Ella Zonis, *Classical Persian Music* (Cambridge: Harvard University Press, 1973), 129–30.

theory, like that of medieval Europe, included a set of rhythmic modes: short rhythmic units constructed from combinations of poetic feet. While these modes may still be discussed academically, they are not used in the living tradition of Persian classical music. Today there are three basic styles of measured pieces. One is the *chahar mezarb,* which has a fast tempo, an ostinato, often a drone effect, and melodic passages that are of rather wide range. The second is the *kereshmah,* which emphasizes variants on the pattern ♩ 𝅗𝅥 ♩ 𝅗𝅥 ♩ ♩ 𝅗𝅥 ♩ 𝄽 . The third is the *zarbi,* a word that simply means "rhythmic"; this style contains many different patterns.

The concept of rhythmic patterns plays a more important role in other parts of the Moslem classical world. The rhythmic mode idea is called *iqa'at* by the East Arabs, *durub* in Egypt, *usul* in Turkey, and *mazim* in the Maghrib. Each country has a varying number of rhythmic patterns in theory or in practice; these range from a few beats in length to as many as 50. Pan-Islamic rhythmic patterns are in general written out in relation to a tambourine or drum mnemonic by which they are learned. Such a mnemonic appears below the Turkish version of the rhythmic pattern *remel* in Example 3–5. Two note positions have been

EXAMPLE 3–5. Two versions of the rhythmic pattern *remel,* after *Encyclopédie de la musique,* ed. A. Lavignac and L. de la Laurencie (Paris: Librairie Delagrave, 1922), pp. 2773 and 3054. Used by permission.

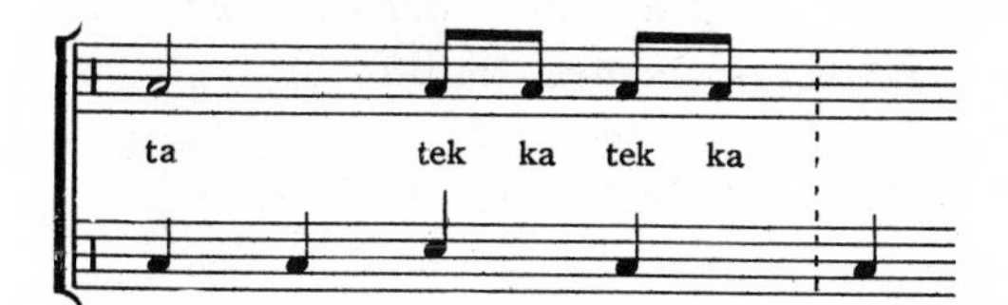

used in the staff notation to help the reader visualize the different sounds on the instrument; they are not intended to suggest absolute pitches. Example 3–5 also includes a modern Arab version of the same-named pattern to show, as in Example 3–3, the variety of interpretations found for the technical terms of pan-Islamic music.

Our few comments on pan-Islamic music theory have implied only indirectly the extensive Moslem studies that exist in the physics of sound and tunings. Further commentary would reveal in Islamic theory a subtle combination of mathematics, aesthetics, and philosophy as well. The real beauty of the system for most people, however, lies in the living art of musical performance.

Classical Music Performance Practice. In order to apply Islamic music theory to performance practice it is important first to recall that the fundamental characteristics of a *maqam* or *dastgah* depend on such things as melodic formulas, contours, and tonal emphases. In the context of an actual composition and performance, it may be more meaningful to concern oneself less with the abstract sonic characteristics of a *maqam* as might be listed in notation (such as Example 3–4) and concentrate more on what has been called the "*maqam* phenomenon."[10] This involves a systematic revelation of the characteristics of a *maqam* by improvisations on a group of melodies that are set on progressively different (usually higher) tonal levels, with the final melody and improvisation returning to the range of the first one. In a Persian *dastgah* the melodic sources for such improvisations are the *gusheh-ha* mentioned earlier. The *dastgah* itself then is a kind of collection of all the melodic *gusheh-ha* that may (but need not) be used in an improvisation set under the title of the *dastgah*. As mentioned earlier, the total collection of all the *gusheh-ha* of Persian music is called a *radif*. Note, however, that such a collection is not like a set of sonatas or symphonies: the latter are constantly reproduced as accurately as possible, whereas the melodies of a *radif* are guides and inspirations, along with poetry, for improvisations no two of which may ever sound the same. They are more comparable to the Moslem calligraphic ideal, which results in many repetitions of the same sacred words on books and buildings in an infinite variety of highly ornamented designs.

Modern Islamic classical music tends to be performed in one of two ways. The first consists of improvisatory solos or duets, as may be seen in the typical Persian *gusheh* of Example 3–6. The second style uses unison instrumental ensembles and choruses that perform accurate reproductions of florid but not freely ornamented traditional melodies.

[10] See further Habib Hassan Touma, "The *Maqam* Phenomenon . . . ," *Ethnomusicology*, XV/1 (1971).

PLATE IX. The Near East

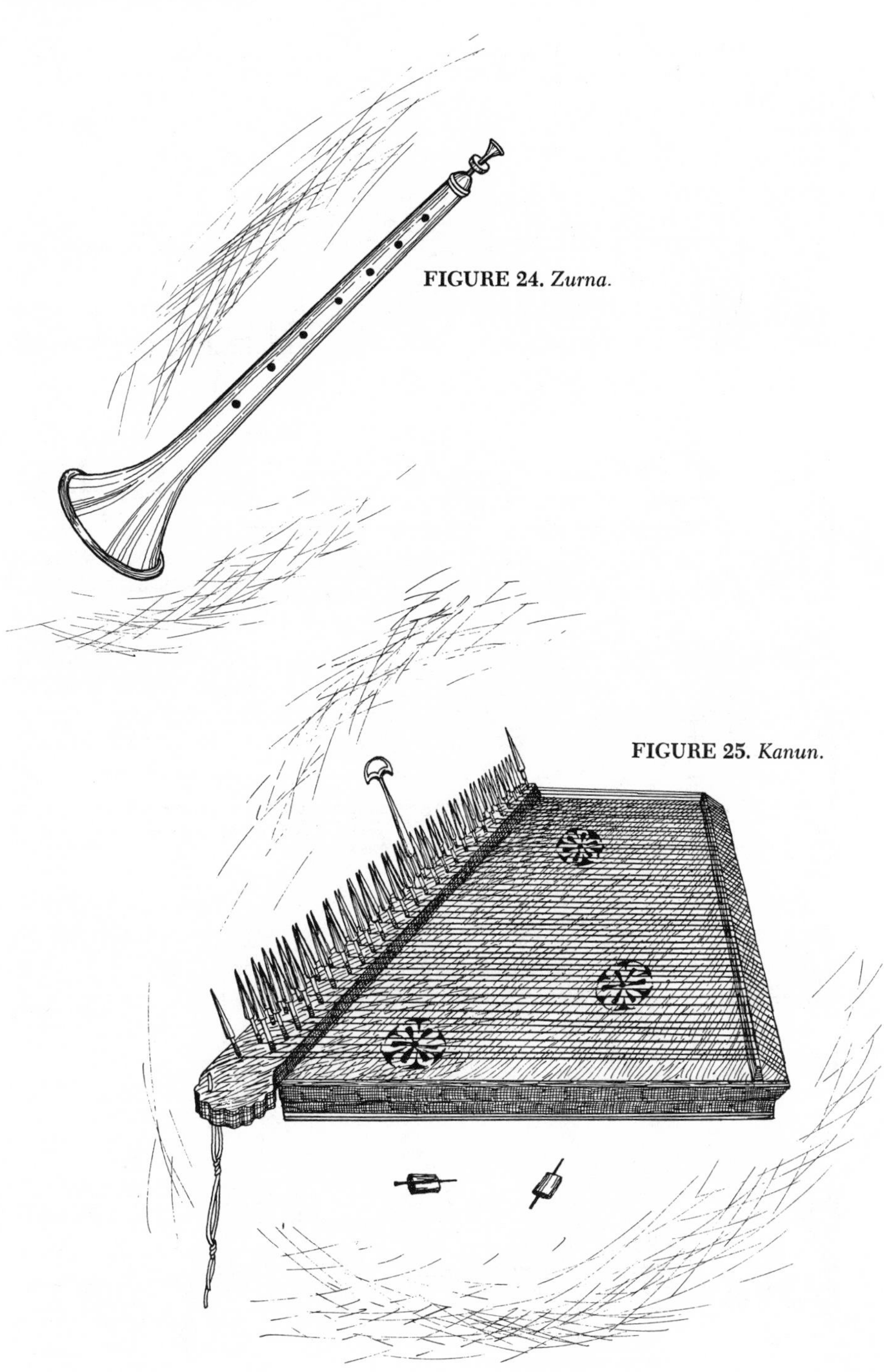

FIGURE 24. *Zurna.*

FIGURE 25. *Kanun.*

EXAMPLE 3–6. A Persian *gusheh* transcribed from the recording *Iran* (Kassel: Bärenreiter-Musicaphon Record BM 30 L 2004), side 1, band 1. Used by permission.

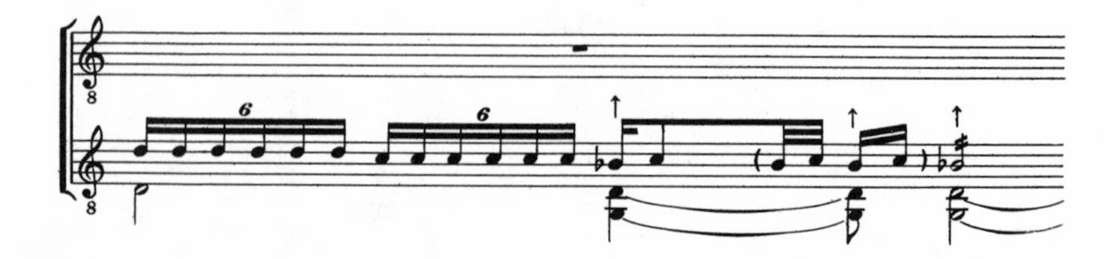

Both styles are heard frequently in Turkey, Egypt, and the Maghrib. Related distinctions in pan-Islamic music are found in how rhythmically free or measured a composition may be and in the degree to which it concentrates on important tonal aspects of the *maqam* in which it was originally set. The particular emphasis of a given piece will depend in part on the form in which it is set.

MUSICAL FORMS. There are as many and as varied forms in pan-Islamic classical music as there are in the Euro-American art-music tradition. In this survey we will speak of only a few of the better-known forms. Vocal forms flourish because of the importance of Arab and Persian poetry in Islamic music, and thus the names of many musical genres are those of poetic forms as well. The classical *qasidah* odes can still be heard sung, along with the shorter strophic *tawshih* songs that grew out of the Moorish-Spanish tradition. Still other songs, the *muwashshah*, are relatively fixed in their rhythm but are felt to be filled with a Sufi spirit of mysticism, a force which, as mentioned earlier, is often said to inspire much of Moslem music. Arab *layali* songs are freer rhythmically; they are often performed by one musician who plays his own accompaniment and improvisations on the *'ud*. The best-known Turkish songs are found in the *beste* and *sarki* forms.

Persian musicians generally speak of a *gusheh* without distinguishing between vocal and instrumental pieces. More specific distinctions between, and extended mixtures of, instrumental and vocal forms are found, however, in the classical suites of other Islamic cultures. The term *nawba* or *nuba* for suite is found in Arab sources as early as the sixteenth century and is still used in that meaning in the so-called Andalusian tradition of North Africa, which came from Moorish Spain in the fifteenth century.[11] In the suites of North Africa and Egypt and the *fasil* suites of Turkey, all the principal sections are supposed to be in the same *maqam*. There may be some eight to ten sections within a suite, and one finds modulations to other modes within a section, but in theory the music should return to the original *maqam* at the end of each digression. Within each movement of a suite there are usually several subsections, called in North Africa the *khana* or *cana*. Both these subsections and the movements themselves may be differentiated by changes of mood or by the particular rhythmic patterns that each employs.

The specific movements played in a given performance of classical music vary. In addition, individual movements may be played separately. For example, both the introductory solo instrumental improvisations (*taqsim* or *taksim*) of Arab or Turkish suites and their vocal equivalents,

[11] For its marginal survival as a ceremonial form of Moslem music, note the Malaysian *nobat* on page 127.

the *gazel,* are frequently heard in solo recitals. Their original function was to set the basic mode, mood, and melodic phrases of the *maqam* of the suite that would normally follow. (This is also the function of the *daramad* that open Persian classical compositions.) However, if the performer is talented enough and there is sufficient rapport between the musician and the audience, the improvisation in this introductory movement may be sufficient for a complete performance. Even the ensemble-and-chorus movements, such as the North African *abyat* and *barwal,* the Turkish *pesrev* (*bashraf*), and the lighter-sounding *samai,* make acceptable concert pieces by themselves because they have within them changes of tempo and mood. When pan-Islamic music is performed in its multi-movement form, however, it displays a subtlety of design and an architectonic structure that reveal the true intents of the Moslem artists. A sense of order is established in these suites through the early presentation of melodic and modal ideas that are then permutated throughout the various movements. At the same time, the set order of rhythmic changes gives to the knowledgeable listener a sense of logical progression in time as well as that feeling of anticipation so important to the active participation of any audience in a musical experience. This does not mean that a Moslem audience must necessarily listen with the kind of specific intellectual concentration that we attempt to instill into Western listeners. Rather, much like Moslem calligraphy, Moslem classical music presents a large tracery of intersecting lines; one may choose to follow the peregrinations of a given melody or simply relax in the beauty of the general design. This attitude is reflected in the circumstances of performance of Moslem classical music, for, although there are some formal concerts in which the arrangement and deportment of the musicians and audience are strictly regulated (as they are in Western concert halls), this music is frequently heard also in cafés. The listener may listen, sip, or converse as he sees fit. Here also, the classical tradition may be mixed with the new and the popular: a *taqsim* may be followed by a love song or by the music of that kind of gyrating female dance for which the Near East is so famous. Classical ideals obviously suffer under such circumstances. Nevertheless, the music of the modern café orchestras of the Near East and the Maghrib is an excellent example of the manner in which musical styles continue to interact throughout the world of music.

Popular Music

There probably has been some kind of topical, easily learned entertainment music in every urbanized culture of the world. Today, telecommunications have created an additional kind of pan-world popular music by making the latest hits of Europe and America instantaneously available throughout the globe. However, the Near East, like the rest of the non-Western world, is not merely a passive receiver of this idiom. In addition to faithful reproductions of Western idioms it has produced its own form of synthesis from a mixture of Western and indigenous elements. Such compromises tend to follow typical lines.

First, Western tempered tuning takes over and those native instruments incapable of performing in that tuning tend to drop out, often to be replaced by some similar Western instruments. The clarinet, for example, is often substituted for the *zurna* oboe. The vocal part becomes less florid and less nasal, and the melodies themselves tend to be phrased in the foursquare manner of Western popular music and to use the reverting rather than the progressive form. If a lead singer is backed by a vocal group, as is common in many Western popular recordings, the group will sing a unison response, an ostinato, or occasionally a drone rather than harmony. Harmony may appear in pan-Islamic popular tunes through the use of a piano or accordion, though sometimes even these instruments will be played in a monophonic manner. One of the most revealing ways to discover the cavalier approach to harmony exhibited in many Arab popular tunes is to follow the bass part. It usually is more concerned with reproducing a standard Near Eastern rhythmic pattern than with establishing a solid harmonic bass progression. Sometimes this native rhythm pattern will be altered, however, to fit into the rhythm of one of the standard South American dance forms such as the beguine, tango, or rumba. We said earlier that music styles do not remain static; pan-Islamic popular music is certainly a case in point.

A Historical Interlude—the Ancient World of the Near East

Although this book deals primarily with the contemporary scene, one cannot ignore the many evidences of music that come from the very cradle of civilization and give us our earliest clues as to the first uses of music by urbanized man.

The oldest records of the ancient civilizations show that music was already a highly organized activity. In Mesopotamia, for example, the presence of guilds of musicians can be traced back as early as the fourth millennium B.C. Among the endless legal documents that dominate the famous cuneiform clay tablet collections one can find contracts for singers from such guilds, employed to intone the psalms in Sumerian temples. Collections of Babylonian liturgies themselves indicate that large numbers of such singers were used, sometimes accompanied by reed pipes, flutes, drums, or tambourines. The excavations of Ur (twenty-fifth century B.C.) have revealed examples of such instruments as double pipes, clappers, and sistrums, along with an eleven-stringed harp that seems to be the progenitor of harps all along the ancient trade routes of the Orient to the far reaches of China and Japan.

Large ensembles of double pipes, percussion instruments, and various styles of harps are seen in the bas-reliefs of later Assyrian and Babylonian ruins. At the same time, written records show us that the ancients knew much about the science of music and acoustics and had evolved a complex theory of the relationship between music and other elements in the universe.

In Egypt, the earliest dynastic records also show a highly evolved art of music. Egyptian art from the twenty-sixth century B.C. shows male musicians playing various harps, reed pipes, and long, end-blown flutes. We noted earlier that the flutes (*sib*) are held to the side as are most *nay* in the Near East today.

Continual change in musical taste was as true in the ancient world as it is today. In the New Kingdom (*circa* 1507 B.C.) foreign female musicians from the Near East became the favorites of the courts, and with them must have come new, "exotic" music. The walls of many tombs and monuments chronicle in much detail the eras of change in Egyptian music history. Yet the musicians who accompany the solemn rites and joyful dances pictured there are mute; no music remains. Like most Near Easterners today, the ancients seem to have taught their music by rote, and the sound apparently died with the performers. There have been, however, attempts to decipher what may be a rudimentary notation involving hand gestures (chironomy) as seen in several wall paintings. In addition, studies of string lengths, frets, and fingerholes in both pictures and artifacts have been used as the basis for inferences about Egyptian scales, and finger positions of harpists in drawings have been used to show the possible existence of harmonies in fourths or fifths.

Most recently, one example of Hurrian cuneiform writing dating from the second millennium B.C. has been transcribed and played on a reproduction of an ancient lyre with the claim that it is the "oldest" known melody—though, like a *maqam*, it may be only a framework for an actual melody.[12]

There has been little agreement in the interpretation of these remnants, or regarding the one supposed example of music notation in cuneiform. This does not mean, however, that the musical legacy of the ancient world is completely lost. The Babylonian connection of music with the universe passed on into the Persian tradition. The Egyptians of Plato's time were still possessors of coveted knowledge in both music practice and theory. Thus, much that we credit to Pythagoras and other

[12] See *The New York Times,* March 6, 1975, I:5 and March 10, 1975, IV 5:4.

great Greek music theorists may have deeper roots in Alexandria and the Nile Valley. In addition, the legacy of ancient Egypt is found in the shapes, tunings, and playing styles of such folk instruments as the *argul* double clarinets in Egypt, the *genibri* of North Africa, the many end-blown flutes of the Near East, the *halam* of the Wolofs, and the sistrums of the Ethiopian Copts and the ancient Greeks and Romans.[13]

One of the most famous Egyptian harp songs was a funeral piece that said, "Let music and song be before you. Leave behind all evil and think only of joy until the day comes when we journey to that land that loves silence."[14] This seems a fitting tribute to the vitality that was, and the silence that now is, the condition of music from the ancient world.

Jewish Music in the Near East

Among the several non-Moslem religious groups in the Near East, the Jews are the most numerous and widespread. Their tradition differs from the Moslem world in two ways. First, whereas the Moslem religion was spread by conversion and conquest, the Jewish tradition remained basically esoteric and nonevangelistic. Wandering Jewish groups spread about the world but remained religiously separated from their host cultures. There was a cross-influence between Jewish and Gentile music cultures, particularly in secular songs, but much of Jewish religious music held to older forms.

The second difference between the Jewish and Moslem musical worlds came with the creation of the state of Israel in 1948. Instead of a continual extension of cultural influence as in Islam, there was in Israel a sudden compression of co-religionists from widely scattered ethnic groups. This concentration of cultures has made Israel (and, for the same reason, cities like New York) a rich hunting ground for ethnomusicologists.

Each Jewish community in Israel today offers special musicological opportunities. The Yemenite Jews, for example, have been extensively studied in the belief that their music represents the oldest Near Eastern Jewish style. The Yemenite religious chant shown in Example 3–7 illustrates their tone-centered, ornamented litany style. The Sephardic Jews, by contrast, are studied for the *romanzas* of Spain that they have preserved since the time of their expulsion (1492). The ghettos of the

[13] For a discussion of the survival of ancient Egyptian instruments, see Hans Hickmann, *Catalogue d'enregistrements de musique folklorique égyptienne* (Strasbourg: Heitz, 1958).

[14] See Miriam Lichtheim, "The Songs of the Harpers," *Journal of Near Eastern Studies,* IV/1 (1945), 178. My thanks go to Professor Carlton Hodge of Indiana University for advice on the paraphrase of the original translation.

EXAMPLE 3–7. A Yemenite Jewish chant transcribed from the recording, *Folk Music of Palestine* (New York: Folkways Record FE 4408), side 2, band 3. By permission of Folkways Records and Service Corporation.

German, Slavic, and Balkan states created the Ashkenazi tradition with its interesting cross-fertilization of European, Russian, and Yiddish musical styles. Jewish communities from the Near East and Ethiopia (the Falasha mentioned earlier), and even congregations from India, have brought their unique musics to Israel. Once settled there, each group of such people tends to use four or five musical styles interchangeably.

First, there is the fairly unified liturgical style. After the destruction of the second temple by the Romans (70 A.D.), the Jewish liturgy turned from sacrificial rites to an emphasis on prayers and invocations.[15] These have been passed on to every congregation. Thus, even groups distant from each other seem to share the melismatic, free-rhythm cantillations of the cantor. Most Jewish cantillations are influenced by the dominant Near Eastern style and may even use modes related to *maqamat*. This is quite evident in the more ecstatic Chasidic and Cabalistic sects.

A second style is found in the singing of religious poems (*piyutim*). These show greater variety with many borrowings from Gentile traditions. The Jews, like the Protestant Christians, have used many secular tunes for such religious purposes. These tunes, in turn, have introduced new melodic styles into the Jewish tradition. For the Near Eastern Jew, Moslem and Armenian-Russian folk songs were a great source. In Europe, each country has made its contributions to such music. The songs without words (*nigun*) of the Chasidic sects are excellent examples of this kind of Jewish music.

A third tradition consists of the secular songs of the Israeli Jew's former homeland. Whether these songs are direct borrowings from a Gentile tradition or specific tunes from a ghetto, they reflect most clearly the land of their origin. Thus, one can hear the difference between a

[15] The Falasha Jews of Ethiopia still maintain the sacrificial rite, but they are a group quite apart from the Hebrew congregation.

German Jew singing a thoroughly Teutonic piece or a Yiddish tune and the old homeland songs of a Rumanian or French Jew.

An Israeli Jew may pick up as a fourth tradition the pan-Islamic style that exists all around him. When he does so he will completely change his vocal style and idiom. Such changes in style are not uniquely Jewish. For example, every American Christian youth uses a voice quality on Saturday night totally different from the one he uses on Sunday morning. This fact, unfortunately, cannot be shown in present-day music notation. Nevertheless, such things as voice quality, facial expression, and gesture should be included in the ideal description of a musical style.[16]

The fifth tradition of the Israelite Jew is the music of the modern state. The bond of Israel is religious and political, not ethnic. Therefore, there has been a concentrated effort on the part of Zionist musicians to "create" a new secular folk music. This music is actually a kind of popular music composed by professional songsmiths and deriving its inspiration from the agricultural, economical, and political aspirations of the state and its citizens. The instruments used to accompany such music reflect the acculturation of styles in Israel. Near Eastern tambourines and goblet drums may be combined with a short block flute (*halil*) and European guitars and accordions, sometimes as an accompaniment for the *hora,* a Near Eastern line dance. The modes of the melodies are often Near Eastern, but they are harmonized with European or Russian chords that discourage the use of indigenous nontempered notes.

The harmonic tendencies of secular music have come into the synagogues, as well, where choirs sing harmony and electric organs play irrelevant chords behind the cantor's melos. As we said before, the study of any music culture presents only moments in a time continuum, not finalities. The unusual polyethnic quality of Israel has created a striking musical mixture.

BIBLIOGRAPHICAL AND DISCOGRAPHICAL NOTES

For general bibliographies and articles dealing with the ancient Near East, see *The New Oxford History of Music,* I (London: Oxford University Press, 1957), and Curt Sachs, *The Rise of Music in the Ancient World, East and West* (New York: W. W. Norton, & Company, Inc., 1943). Hans Hickmann is the major scholar of ancient Egyptian music; his basic work is *45 Siècles de musique dans l'Egypte ancienne* (Paris:

[16] Attempts have been made to include them in style description. See Alan Lomax, *Folk Song Style and Culture* (Washington, D.C.: American Association for the Advancement of Science, Publication No. 88).

Richard-Masse, 1956). Near Eastern religious musics are discussed in *Encyclopédie des musiques sacrées,* I (Paris: Labererie, 1968).

For materials on the first African areas of the survey there are Norma McLeod, "The Status of Musical Specialists in Madagascar," *Ethnomusicology,* VIII/3 (1964), and Curt Sachs, *Les Instruments de musique de Madagascar* (Paris: Institut d'Ethnologie, 1938). Hugh Tracey's *Chopi Musicians* (London: Oxford University Press, 1948) gives considerable cultural and poetical detail on xylophone orchestra music; the sound may be heard in the Folkways album *Africa South of the Sahara* (FE 4503). For Ethiopia, see A. Kebede and K. Suttner, *Ethiopia–The Music of the Coptic Church* (Berlin: International Institute for Comparative Music Studies, 1969) and Michael Powne, *Ethiopian Music* (London: Oxford University Press, 1968) plus the Wolf Lesau records for Folkways, *Music of Ethiopia* (FE 4405) and *Music of the Falasha* (FE 4442). The UNESCO Anthology of African Music includes *Music of the Ethiopian Coptic Church* (BM 30 L 2304) and *Music of the Cushitic Peoples of South-West Ethiopia* (BM 30 L 2305).

A historical view of Jewish music is found in Alfred Sendrey, *Music in Ancient Israel* (New York: Philosophy Library, 1969), and Eric Werner, *The Sacred Bridge* (London: Oxford, 1958). A. Z. Idelsohn's *Jewish Music* (New York: Holt, Rinehart and Winston, Inc., 1929) is a standard general reference. Edith Gerson-Kiwi shows her talent in both Arab and Jewish studies in *The Persian Doctrine of Dastgar Composition* (Tel Aviv: Israel Music Institute, 1963) and "Women's Songs from the Yemen," in *The Commonwealth of Music,* ed. Gustave Reese and Rose Brandel (New York: The Free Press, 1965). Joel Walbe, *Der Gesang Israels und seine Quellen* (Hamburg: Christians, 1975) contains excellent studies.

Islamic folk musics are found in Folkways *Wolof Music of Senegal and Gambia* (FE 4462), *Music of South Arabia* (FE 4421), *Arabic and Druse Music* (FE 4480), *Kurdish Folk Songs and Dances* (FE 4469), and *Kurdish Folk Music from Western Iran* (FE 4102), as well as *Coptic Music* (FR 8960) and *Islamic Liturgy* (FR 8943). The Folkways *Tuareg Music of the Southern Sahara* (FE 4470) is documented by Geoffrey Holiday, who also wrote "The Tuaregs of the Ahaggar" in *African Music* I/3 (1956). Wolfgang Laade produced three volumes of Tunisian folk, religious, and art music on Folkways *Tunisia* (FE 8861, 8862, 8863). Popular music is heard on Folkways *Arabic Songs of Lebanon and Egypt* (FW 6925); that company's *Songs and Dances of Turkey* (FW 8801) contains a mixture of styles, as does its *Folk and Traditional Music of Turkey* (FE 4404). The two Westminster records *In Israel Today* (W 9805, 9806) show some of the variety of music in Israel. Dozens of modern Israeli music records are available, particularly on Elektra and Vanguard labels.

Egypt has produced a set of folk and classical examples in *La musique populaire d'Égypte* (United Arab Republic Ministry of Culture, EST 52–53), as have the Japanese in *Niru no uta* ("Song of the Nile," Victor JL 66–71). UNESCO Musicaphon has one volume of classical music, *Tunisia* (BM 30 L 2008); two in the Persian style, *Iran* (BM 30 L 2004–05); and two of the Mevlevi, *Turkish Music* (BM 30 L 2019–2020).

Ella Zonis has produced both a record, *Classical Music of Iran* (FW 8831–32), and an excellent book, *Classical Persian Music: An Introduction* (Cambridge: Harvard University Press, 1973). Two valuable theses are Homoz Farhat, *The Dastgah Concept in Persian Music* (Ann Arbor: University Microfilms, 1966), and Karl Signell, *The Turkish Makam System in Contemporary Theory and Practice* (Ann Arbor: University Microfilms, 1973). Valuable articles in *Ethnomusicology* include Johanna Spector, "Classical ud Music in Egypt . . .", XIV/2 (1970); Gen'ichi Tsuge, "Rhythmic Aspects of the Avaz . . ." in the same issue; Habib Hassan Touma, "The Maqam Phenomenon. . .", XV/1 (1971); Lois Ibsen al Faruqi, "Muwashshah . . .", XIX/1 (1975); and Bruno Nettl, "Persian Popular Music in 1969," XVI/2 (1972).

Several older studies still remain basic, such as Rauf Yekya Bey, "La musique turque," and Jules Rouanet, "La musique arabe," in *Encyclopédie de le musique . . .* , A. Lavignac, ed. (Paris: Librairie Delagrave, 1922), Part 1, V.

Baron Rodolphe D'Erlanger presents fine transcriptions of Hispanic-Arab, Berber, Jewish, and Negro music in *Mélodies tunisiennes* in the *Bibliothèque Musicale du Musée Guimet,* First Series, III (Paris: Geuthner, 1937). He also produced a six-volume collection of Arab theorists, *La Musique arabe* (Paris: Geuthner, 1930–49). One of Alexis Chottin's several excellent writings on North Africa is *Tableau de la musique marocaine* (Paris: Geuthner, 1939). The articles in *Grove's Dictionary of Music,* 5th ed. (1954), by Henry George Farmer on Berber, Moorish, Maghribi, Persian, Syrian, and Turkestani music are useful summaries. Farmer's orientation is usually historical, as in his *A History of Arabian Music* (London: Luzac, 1929). More about the living tradition is found in F. Salvador-Daniel, *Arab Music and Musical Instruments* (New York: Charles Scribner's Sons, 1915).

FOUR
CENTRAL AND SOUTHERN ASIA

Central Asia is an immense landlocked area extending from the Caspian Sea eastward to China and Mongolia, with Siberia to its north and Afghanistan and Iran to its south. Its terrain varies from mountains to grassland steppes and arid deserts. Southern Asia consists of the subcontinent south of the Himalayan mountains and Afghanistan. For centuries the musics of Central Asia and Afghanistan have interchanged their indigenous styles with those of the Near East and South Asia. Thus, for us they are excellent geographic and cultural areas through which to move on our musical journey from the Near East to Southern Asia.

MUSIC OF THE SOVIET CENTRAL ASIAN REPUBLICS

Although the Southern Republics of the Soviet Union (Georgia, Armenia, and Azerbaijan) on the west shores of the Caspian Sea are filled with numerous traditions from their many neighbors, our discussion will be limited to the Central Asian Republics of Kazakhstan and Turkmenistan on the eastern shore, and Uzbekistan, Tadjikstan, and Kirghizstan still farther to the east. For most Westerners this area is a *terra incognita,* but historically it has been a land of many civilizations and many visitors. Some of its travelers have been merely observers or merchants—like Marco Polo—but a majority of those who crossed the borders of Central Asia had more militaristic or evangelistic intentions. A list of these visitors includes the feared names of the leaders of every horde that poured out of Inner Asia to plunder Europe and the Near East, such as Jenghiz Khan, Kublai Khan, and Tamerlane; it also includes the eastward-moving standard-bearers of Islam as well as the westward-directed advance guards of ancient Chinese armies. In a word, this area, plus Afghanistan to the south, contained the major routes of commerce and conquest for centuries. The results were a series of colorful and generally short-lived cultures as varied as the outside influences that pressed in upon them.

Today, the major influences to be found in Soviet Asia are the Persian and the Arab. This is easily seen in the presence of such musical instruments as the end-blown flute (*nai*), the conical oboe (*zurna*), and various double clarinets. The tambourine (commonly called the *doira* here) and a small pair of kettledrums (*nagora*) are also present. All the chordophones of Persia can be found, particularly in the art music ensembles of Tadjikstan, Uzbekistan, and Azerbaijan. Such ensembles play suites in the best pan-Islamic tradition. In Tadjikstan and Uzbekistan these suites are known as *makom,* while the Azerbaijan suites are sometimes called *dastgya.* These two terms obviously relate to the Near Eastern words *maqam* and *dastgah,* though their meanings are changed. Many other terms, such as mode names and the titles of movements within the suites, relate to the pan-Islamic tradition discussed in the previous chapter, but their uses often reflect specific Central Asian national styles.

We have noted that several centers of Moslem music theory were located in Central Asia. Al Farabi himself is said to have been born in Turkmenistan, and the eleventh-century theorist Ibn Sina (known in the West as Avicenna) was educated in Bokhara. These men were but two of many scholars who contributed to the general progress of Moslem music theory. Of more importance to the Central Asian art-music tradition was the work of Kaukaba (*d.* 1526). He made a definitive analysis of the *Shashmakom,* the basic collection of *makom* suites upon which all modern Tadjik and Uzbek classical performances are based. Another important innovator was Njaz Mitzabashi Kamil (*d.* 1889), who created a tablature called *khorezm* notation, in which the entire *tambur* part of the *Shashmakom* was written.

If one moves from the art music of Central Asia to the folk and

EXAMPLE 4–1. A *komuz* song from Kirghizstan transcribed from the recording, *Folk Music of the U.S.S.R.* (New York: Folkways Record FE 4535), side 4, band 3. By permission of Folkways Records and Service Corporation.

popular idioms, many variations upon Near Eastern instruments can be found. Variants on small-bodied, long-necked plucked lutes such as the *tambur* (Plate VII, Figure 19) and *setar* are found in the two-stringed *dutar,* the three-stringed *komuz,* and the two-stringed *dombra.* The last comes in a great variety of shapes, some of which are influenced by still further variants of the same chordophone (for example, the *balalaika*). Despite the interrelations of the instrumental types, the musics played upon these various forms are not necessarily the same. Example 4–1 is the beginning of a Kirghiz song with *komuz* accompaniment. Organum-like harmonic accompaniments in parallel fifths or fourths and heterometric structures like those in this example are common throughout Central Asia and seem to be indigenous elements in this highly acculturated music. There is also a fondness in Central Asia for double clarinets (somewhat like those in Figure 16 in Plate VI) or for two oboes, one of which plays only a drone, a tradition equally common in Turkey.

Another important feature of Central Asian music is the presence of long epic narratives. From the traditionally unaccompanied songs of storytellers, many of the famous folk epics of this area have been recovered. Kazakh and Kirghiz musicians often play textless narratives in which the entire story is pictured instrumentally. Competitive songs are also found, in which the contestants vie with each other through improvised verses in a manner quite like that found throughout the Romance-language countries of Europe.

Modern Soviet Asian music has been subjected to considerable collectivization under the general communist policy of "reconstruction," in which folk art must, by Marxist definition, reflect the social and political conditions of the people. This policy produces several curious results. First, field collectors are instructed to collect only such music as falls within these ideological goals and to admonish singers who persist in performing overly religious, sarcastic, or sensual musics. Secondly, the analysis of such music as is collected is made to conform to certain specific state doctrines such as the predominance of the 12-note chromatic scale system in peoples' music. In Central Asia the latter policy is the cause of much scholarly hedging, since many "wrong notes" show up in the Islamic ornamented styles. Finally, the goal of collecting is not solely the archival preservation of traditional materials (though much valuable work is done in this area); rather, the music collected is primarily raw material for the use of Western-style composers who must produce new "realistic" music based on national idioms.[1] The music is also frequently arranged for state-supported "folk" orchestras and choruses, which then become the major media through which the music is made available to the people in performances and on records.

Many individual folk singers are honored by the state, particularly if they create new socialist-oriented songs. However, the emphasis is on ensemble and choral music; this reflects the basically collectivist nature of the Soviet attitude toward music. Since the original idiom is often soloistic, this musical collectivization is bound to affect such characteristics as ornamentation and tuning. The specific arrangements of reconstructed music reflect a strong orientation toward such ideals of the central conservatory in Moscow as Western harmony and tempered scales. Thus, reconstructed Central Asian music often sounds suspiciously like nineteenth-century Russian romanticism. In the 1970's, however, transcriptions and actual recordings of regional styles began to appear, and state support of performance and research in national idioms has shown encouraging signs of constructive rather than reconstructive action.

[1] The specific doctrines of Marxist music can be read in Rena Moisenco, *Realist Music* (London: Meridian, 1949).

AFGHANISTAN

The twentieth-century country of Afghanistan shares borders with China, India, Pakistan, Iran, and Asiatic Russia. In ancient times these borders, like those of the Central Asian republics just discussed, were crossed many times by the routes of commerce or conquest. One artistic result of this constant flow of cultures can be seen in the amazing statuary found in the ruins of Afghanistan's ancient cities. The physical features of these statues are those of every type within the Indo-Caucasian family plus a liberal sprinkling of the Mongoloid types. Thus Afghanistan is an important link in the chain of cultures binding Europe and Asia together.

Musically, this linkage can be heard by listening to pieces from various regions of Afghanistan. The western and northern musics of the country are dominated by Near Eastern or Central Asian styles, whereas eastern Afghan music is heavily Indian-oriented. The former tend to use a slightly nasal, quickly ornamented vocal line, while the latter prefers a softer, lower tone quality and artful portamento slides. Though the Soviet border has been closed for some time, the traditional wanderings of the many ethnic groups of Central Asia have created fairly large pockets of "minorities," many of whom maintain their earlier musical traditions. A study of northern Afghan musical life[2] has shown that the major sources of most musical events are the local and regional markets. Their tea houses are filled every market day (usually twice a week) or religious holiday with men who enjoy gossip and the entertainment of at least a lute-player (*damburachi*) and singers who often perform in Uzbek or Tajik styles. The modern administrative or industrial cities rely more on the national radio from the capital, Kabul, with its mixture of idioms in a popular style similar to that discussed in the last chapter. There are, of course, a few regional or big-city musicians who maintain traces of the classical traditions of earlier Central Asian courts or who have taken up the Persian tradition. In addition, the Nurestan peoples in the isolated mountain regions of the northeast use an arched harp (*vaji*) which may be a marginal survival of an instrument often found in the archaeological remains of ancient Near Eastern cultures.

The major nomadic (*kuchi*) culture of southern and western Afghanistan is the Pashtun or Pathan. Its fundamental musical style is vocal and normally consists of folk poetry (*lundai*) set to various standard tunes. If songs are accompanied, the long-necked *tambur* or *dambura* lute is used commonly, though other Central or Near Eastern instruments, such

[2] Mark Slobin, "Music and the Structure of Town Life in Northern Afghanistan," *Ethnomusicology*, XIV/3 (1970).

as the two-stringed bowed *ghitchak* (*ritchak*) lute, also appear. The *ghitchak* is related to the Near Eastern *rabab* although, like its Central Asian counterpart, its body is often made of a rectangular gasoline can. The term *rabab* also appears in Central Asia and Afghanistan, but there it usually refers to a plucked lute, thus demonstrating the concept of floating terms discussed in our second chapter (see p. 31). Tambourines, flutes, and jew's harps are found as well, once more reflecting a potential mixture of indigenous and Moslem traditions. In contrast, the two-headed *dhol*, a barrel drum common in eastern Afghanistan, points just as clearly in an Indian direction. If we wandered further out into the Central Asian steppes or studied tribal peoples in Afghanistan who had come from that region, we would encounter traditions related to those of Mongolia or even Siberia, but our present musical trail leads more logically to South Asia.

SOUTH ASIA–A HISTORICAL INTRODUCTION

The Indian Peninsula from the Himalayan Mountains and Karakorum to the island of Sri Lanka (Ceylon) includes a wide variety of peoples, languages, religions, and political divisions. The history of this wide area began with the Dravidian civilization (2500–1900 B.C.), which was in turn supplanted by an Aryan invasion. The caste system and the Hindu religion were already ancient traditions when Gautama Buddha (563–483 B.C.) appeared. Though the Buddhist religion eventually found its greatest strength outside India, the island of Sri Lanka remained a Buddhist stronghold. On the mainland, Hinduism was the dominant force until the Moslem invasion of the thirteenth century. The resultant Moghul courts of North India produced brilliant new Islamic-Hindu art forms, while South India became the center of Hindu tradition. The British occupation of the nineteenth and twentieth centuries introduced many Western ways, but the basic cultural patterns of India remained those of the Moslem-Hindu world. The political separation of Pakistan from India in the mid-twentieth century and the creation later of Bangladesh are reflections of this split cultural heritage.

The musical divisions of South Asia are many, but the best–known classical traditions are two: *Hindustani music*, the music of Pakistan and North India, where Moslem influence is often strong, and *Karnatak* (*Karnatic*) *music* of the south, which claims to be more indigenous. The Karnatak system prevails in Madras, Mysore, Anghra, and Kerala. Hyderabad may be said to be the dividing line between the Hindustani and Karnatak traditions. Though these two traditions use different instruments and vary in their nomenclature, their basic concepts are the same and have been cultivated in South Asia for centuries.

Ancient Indian Music

The study of Indian art music begins with the *Vedic* hymns, sacred Aryan texts to which other materials have been added over the centuries. The Rig Veda is the earliest form still surviving. Some of its verses were rearranged later into the so-called Yajur Veda. The Sama Veda contains selected verses from the same source as used in liturgies. The Atharva Veda is a set of different texts derived from folk religious magic and incantations. The Rig Veda and Sama Veda in India are somewhat analogous to the Catholic and Orthodox Christian chant tradition of the West for, although both sets are actually performed and known only by special groups, their early texts and theoretical implications are considered to be the foundations of many later styles. The Vedic tradition belonged to the higher caste cultures and, because of its religious nature, was the subject of rigorous essays concerning its correct performance. Metaphysically, the physical vibrations of musical sound (*nada*) were inextricably connected with the spiritual world, so that the validity of a ritual and the stability of the universe itself might be adversely affected by a faulty intonation of sacred texts. The rules of Rig Veda chanting emphasize syllabic singing with attention paid to word accent, as shown in Example 4–2. Other schools of Rig Veda singing, as well as most of the Sama Veda tradition are, by contrast, quite wide-ranged, melismatic, and generally unconcerned with word accent.[3]

EXAMPLE 4–2. A Rig Veda hymn transcribed from the recording *India* (Kassel: Bärenreiter-Musicaphon Record BM 30 L 2006), side 1, band 2. Used by permission.

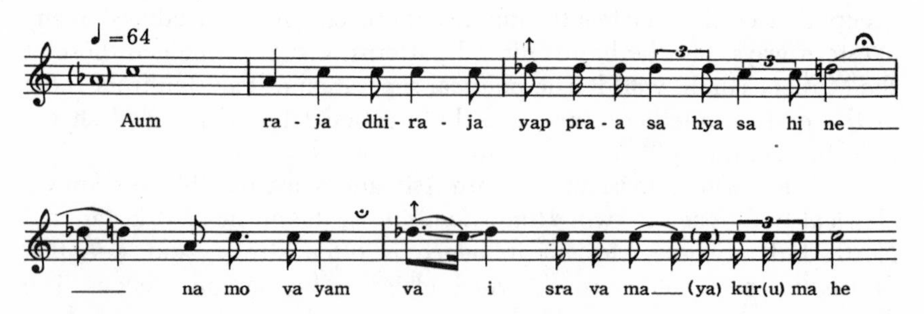

[3] For notated examples of several different Vedic forms, see Nazir Jairazbhoy's "Legacy of India: Indian Music" in *Cultural History of India* (Oxford: Clarendon Press, 1974).

Though the entire Vedic tradition is little practiced today, its nomenclature and some of its musical world views were carried on through religious and secular epics performed for lower-caste Indians. The *Natya-Sastra,* attributed to the sage Bharata (*circa* 5th century A.D.), is said to have been a kind of manual for productions of theatrical forms of this tradition, which were sometimes also called Veda. The original book is most commonly dated in the fifth century A.D., although some place it as early as the second century B.C., while others feel that it is a compilation of the works of many men done between the fifth and seventh centuries A.D. Whatever its date, it is the traditional link between ancient India and the classical eighteenth- and nineteenth-century musics as they survive today, for music and dance are discussed in it along with various dramatic elements. Other important theoretical sources for Indian music are the tenth-century *Brhaddesi* by Matanga, which is the first text to use the term *raga,* and the thirteenth-century *Sangita-Ratnakara* by Sarangadeva, written during the time of pressures from Near Eastern ideas brought in by the Moghul rulers. From the sixteenth through the twentieth century Indian theorists continued to attempt further syntheses and standardizations. In this manner the ancient terms remained, but their meanings began to vary greatly; in some cases the words refer to what they might have meant in ancient music, whereas in others the terms are applied to the musical practices of the time when the book in which they appear was written.[4] In any case, it is obvious that the basic concepts and terminologies derived from the Vedic hymns, as well as the many studies of later centuries, are necessary sources for an intellectual understanding of Indian classical music. They may even apply indirectly to the much larger world of Indian folk and popular styles. Let us turn first to classical Indian theory.

Indian Music Theory

Because word meanings in Indian music have changed so greatly over the centuries, we can deal here only with the more commonly accepted interpretations of musical terms and must leave their subtler and older meanings to the writings of specialists. The very simple outline of basic Indian theory shown in Example 4–3 begins with *nada,* the concept of musical sound vibrations with their implied extramusical implications (as mentioned earlier). In ancient India, the smallest interval perceptible to the ear was called a *sruti.* Theoretically there were three different sizes

[4] For an outline of many such sources, see Nazir Jairazbhoy, *The Rags of North Indian Music* (Middletown: Wesleyan University Press, 1971), 16–26, or Walter Kaufmann, *The Ragas of North India* (Bloomington: Indiana University Press, 1968), 37–58.

EXAMPLE 4–3. The Indian theoretical system in outline.

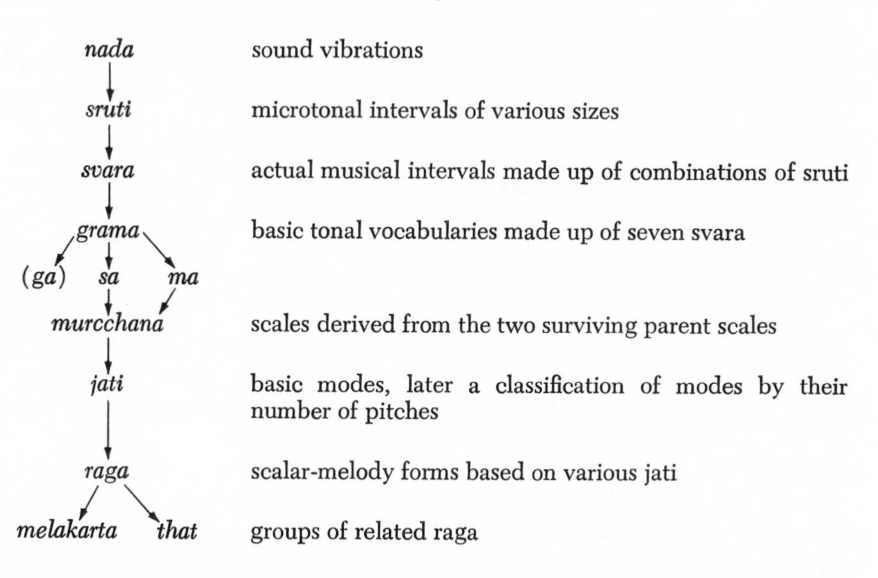

of *sruti*[5] and a total tonal vocabulary of 22 such nonequidistant units within an octave. Like Near Eastern theorists (see page 74), Indian music theorists did not consider the movement just from one *sruti* to an adjacent one as an interval. Rather, two to four *sruti* were combined to form a *svara,* an actual musical interval or step. In musical practice today the complete tonal vocabulary seems to include only twelve tones, though each has a fairly wide range of tolerance as to actual pitch.[6]

Both ancient and modern practice generally create seven *svara* to arrive at an octave (a *saptaka*). The seven *svara* have special names,[7] but only the first syllable of each name is generally used when writing about these tones. Thus, the sounds *sa, ri, ga, ma, pa, dha, ni*—like the Western *do, re, mi*—have become basic terms for discussing or singing Indian music.

In ancient theory, seven *svara* played in order became a *grama,* a scale. Three such scales (the *sadjagrama, madhymagrama,* and *gand-*

[5] Fox Strangways claims them to be approximately 22, 70, and 90 cents in his *The Music of Hindostan* (London: Oxford University Press, 1914), 115–17.

[6] The variability of actual intonations in the contemporary performance of North Indian *raga* is discussed in Jairazbhoy, *op. cit.,* 164–69. Its relation to ancient *sruti* traditions is questionable. In any discussion of music theory it is important to remember that many excellent performing musicians have no overt knowledge or interest in the topic.

[7] In North India they are *sadj, risabh, gandha, madyam, pancam, dhaivat,* and *nisad.*

haragrama) are said to be the basic "parent" scales of Indian music, but by the time of the *Natya-Sastra* only the first two are mentioned. (Hence we have parenthesized the third in Example 4–3.) The two surviving scales are normally called by their abbreviated names, *sa-grama* and *ma-grama,* and often are listed with their tone names and *sruti* distances as shown in Example 4–4. Very rough analogies with Western notes are

EXAMPLE 4–4. The theoretical *sa-* and *ma-grama.*

Sa-grama

pitch name	sa		ri		ga		ma		pa		dha		ni		sa
number of *sruti*		3		2		4		4		3		2		4	
Western analogy	D		E		F		G		A+		B		C		D

Ma-grama

pitch name	sa		ri		ga		ma		pa		dha		ni		sa
number of *sruti*		3		2		4		3		4		2		4	
Western analogy	D		E		F		G		A		B+		C		D

shown by letters in the example, for comparison's sake, but the actual pitch of any Indian music, like much Western vocal music, is set by the performer. (Until its association with Western music, Indian music did not concern itself with perfect pitch as opposed to perfect intervals.) The tiny differences in the intervals between the pitches *ma* and *pa,* and between *pa* and *dha,* in the two scales seems very subtle indeed, especially when one remembers that modern practice bears little relation to ancient theory. The *grama* are historically important, however, because they were the theoretical parents of five *murcchana* scales, two of which use a raised third (*antara ga;* a pitch equivalent in Example 4–4 would approximate an F♯) and three of which use both the raised third plus a raised seventh (*kakali ni;* a Western analogy would be C♯ in Example 4–4). By the time of the *Natya-Sastra* the term *jati* appears as well, to imply modes within the two parent scales, the original seven *murcchana* being called "pure" *suddha jati,* and an additional eleven being "modified" *vikrta jati,* some with five or six tones rather than seven (pentatonic *audava,* or hexatonic *shadava,* rather than heptatonic *sampurna*).

All the terms used so far appear in the *Natya-Sastra,* but the meaning and actual use of such words has changed greatly since then. For example, the word *sruti* today is usually used in the South to mean a basic ground tone of a drone (called *sur* in the North), though Hindustani musicians sometimes call a microtonal ornamentation in performance a *sruti.* Similarly, the term *svara* (often *svar* in the North) may mean either a tone or an interval, just as a Western musician uses, for example, the word "third" to mean both the third note of a scale and an interval of three tones. One early use of the term *jati* was as a means of classifying modes according to the number of notes they contain; to this has been added special melodic characteristics of compositions in a *jati,* as well as extramusical connotations and mood (*rasa*). It is thus through *jati* that we arrive at the better-known concept called *raga.*

The term *raga* (the term is *rag* in the North or *ragam* in the Tamil language) can be defined as a scalar-melody form; that is, it is both the basic scale and the basic melodic structure. The term is derived from a Sanskrit root, *ranj,* which means to color with emotion; thus the name implies many features beyond those of actual pitches. While such extramusical aspects are important to many practitioners of *raga* music,[8] we will discuss only a few of the most essential elements found in any *rag* or *raga* from either North or South India.[9]

The actual scale of a *raga* should be shown in both its ascending and descending forms, for they may differ. In addition, the notes may not always proceed in only one direction: many *raga* change direction, repeating or adding new tones in a quasi-melodic fashion. Also, specific notes within a *raga* sometimes have special ornamentations (commonly called *gamaka*). The so-called ground tone upon which the scale of the *raga* begins is called the *sa.* It is the most common note among those comprising the drone that accompanies all contemporary performances of classical music. (It is not known when this practice began.) In Hindustani theory there are two "important" tones (*amsa*) that dominate each *raga:* the *vadi* and the *samvadi.* The *vadi* today is often considered to be the most important pitch melodically in a *raga,* while the *samvadi* may be second in importance. The *vadi* is often *not* the ground tone of the *raga.* The *samvadi* is usually a fourth or fifth above the *vadi,* although, like the reciting tones of other musical traditions (such as Christian chant), there are various distributions of fundamental tones. Similar reciting tones (*jiva svara*) appear in Karnatak music, but they are given less theoretical significance. Theoretically, thousands of *raga* may exist. In Indian books there are occasional lists of up to 1000 *raga* actually named or described. In either Hindustani or Karnatic practice today, however, some 50 *raga* tend to appear most frequently, though individual performers may know a great many more.

[8] In his *Northern Indian Music* (London: C. Johnson, 1949–54) Alain Danielou lists fifteen essential items.

[9] In Indian musical terms such as *rag* and *raga,* the presence of a final "a" means that a Sanskrit spelling is being followed, rather than the Hindi version. This is generally true of South Indian music terms (*svara* rather than *svar, druta* rather than *drut,* etc.) and is used in this survey. North Indian terms often use English plurals (*jati–jatis, bol–bols*) but these are not used in this book.

Given the large number of possibilities, it is only logical that Indian theorists should organize *raga* into related groups. Perhaps the most controversial arrangements are those which attempt to determine the times of the day at which specific *raga* are most suitable.[10] Though not popular today, there was at one time another tradition which arranged tonal materials in terms of *raga* and their *ragini* (wives), each often associated with scenes from romantic or mythological literature or the emotional setting of such scenes. The best-known result of this method was not music, but rather the *ragamala* miniatures which have been found in some schools of Rajput-style North Indian painting since the sixteenth century. Traditionally, thirty-six scenes are depicted, each titled only by the name of its proper *raga* or *ragini*. Of more significance musically are the divisions of *raga* into *that* or *mela* (*melakarta*). In the South Indian *Caturdandi-Prakasika* of 1620, Venkatamakhi suggested the grouping of Indian tone systems into 72 *melakarta*. These were scales based on connecting six possible tetrachords (four-note groups) within a fourth (for example, C D E F) with another set of six within the next higher fourth (like G A B C). This created thirty-six possible scales ($6 \times 6 = 36$), but the total was doubled by adding another six lower tetrachords, these within an augmented fourth (like C D E F♯).[11] Though this larger vocabulary was not actually in use at the time, it did serve as an inspiration for the "invention" of new *raga* in following decades. In the 1930's Bhaktkhande organized a framework (*that*) of 32 seven-tone scales to which the many *rag* of the North Indian tradition could be related.[12] Ten of these *that* were considered basic.

We turn now to the Indian theory of musical time. The core of this system is the concept of a cyclic measure of time called *tala*. It can be called a cycle because its basic characteristics continue to appear (like markings around the face of a clock) in repeated sequences as long as there is a steady beat. The actual tempo (*laya*) of Indian music may vary from fast (*druta*) to medium (*madhya*) or slow (*vilambita*). Major factors that contribute to the use and understanding of *tala* remain constant, however. First, there is the Hindustani *matra* and Karnatak *akshara*, or basic beat. Like the Western quarter-note pulse, this beat is capable of

[10] See O. C. Gangoly, *Ragas and Raginis* (Bombay, 1958), 90–92, or Kaufmann, *op. cit.*, 14–20.

[11] The clearest explanation of this method, with charts of the *melakarta*, is in Harold Powers, *The Background of the South Indian Raga System* (Ann Arbor: University Microfilms, 1963), I, 17–23.

[12] For a detailed study of the *that* system, see Jairazbhoy, *op. cit.*, or the writings of Bhatkhande listed in Jairazbhoy's bibliography. The *raga* classification system's development is somewhat analogous to that of Gregorian chant, which moved from a multitude of materials to a system of eight medieval modes.

small divisions in the context of melodies or details of rhythmic patterns. In the *tala* the *matra* and *akshara* are like the *tact* of a Western meter (p. 7) or the clicks of a metronome. They come to life when they are placed in a *tala* cycle (*vibhaga* or *avarta*), which may total from 3 to 128 beats in length, though 7- to 16-beat cycles are more common. Each *tala* is subdivided into groups of beats. Though these subdivisions are important to both classical traditions, the Karnatak musicians are more prone towards theoretical details and terminology. In the South Indian *tala* the rhythmic groups are known as *anga* and can be categorized as belonging to one of three types: *anudruta,* which consists always of only one beat; *druta,* made up of two beats; and *laghu,* which may have one of five different lengths (of 3, 4, 5, 7, or 9 beats) known as *jati.* Example 4–5 shows *tala* from both of the classical traditions; the two *tala* share the same length (ten beats) but illustrate some of the differences between the Northern and Southern systems. The Hindustani *jhaptal* is divided in four parts (2 + 3 + 2 + 3), whereas the Karnatak *jhampa* has three *anga* in the categories *laghu, anudruta,* and *druta* (7 + 1 + 2). Both traditions consider the first beat of the entire *tala* (the *sam*) very important, though their approaches to the internal structure of the *tala* may be different. North Indian musicians use the term *tala* to refer to other secondary accents on the first beats of subdivisions. When such first beats are "felt" strongly but seldom actually stressed they are called a *khali* beat. This is seen on the sixth beat of *jhaptal* in Example 4–5 which also contains the other terms just described. Sometimes one can actually see units of the subdivisions enacted visually during a performance, for some musicians as well as listeners will keep track of a *tala* by clapping their hands on the *sam* and *tali* beats while waving the right hand sideways on the "silent" *khali.*

The *jhaptal tala* in Example 4–5 includes inside the circle the onomatopoeic mnemonics (*bol*) by which a player learns a specific drum pattern (*theka*) characteristic of the *tala.* This tradition is particularly strong in Hindustani music, and a drummer will remain rather close to the *theka* pattern throughout a composition in order that the melodic performers can move with confidence into extended rhythmic flights. Because both the melodic and rhythmic performers in Karnatak music pay closer attention to the *tala* and its *anga* as such, basic rhythm patterns need not be followed as closely.

Students of European medieval music will recognize the *tala* as a more complex version of the concept of *talea.*[13] However, the combination of rhythmic units of different sizes, common to Indian music, illustrates

[13] See Albert Seay, *Music in the Medieval World,* 2nd ed. (Englewood Cliffs, N.J.: Prentice-Hall, Inc., 1975), 133–34.

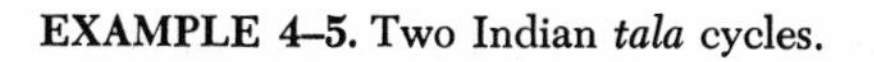

EXAMPLE 4–5. Two Indian *tala* cycles.

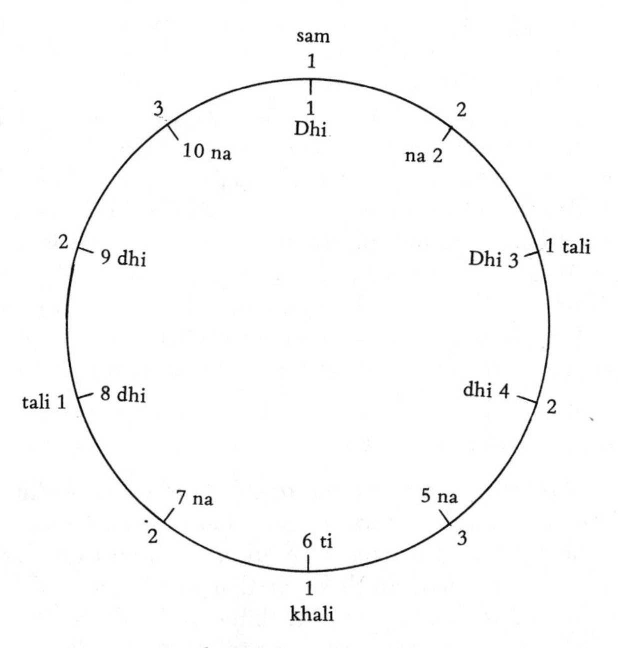

a. The Hindustani *jhaptal tala.*

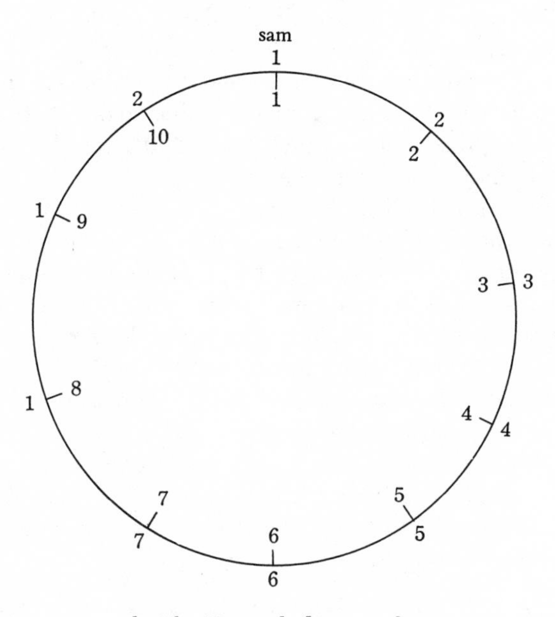

b. The Karnatak *jhampa tala.*

the *additive* approach to rhythm in contrast to the *divisive* method normally found in the even subdivisions of a measure in Western music.[14] It would seem that the Western fascination with harmonic structures and the South Asian enchantment with melodic and rhythmic systems propelled these two grand traditions in very different directions. The Western musician needs to sing solfège and recognize chord progressions by ear in order to feel and understand his past tradition, while the Indian musician needs to practice his *sa, ri, ga, ma* and be able to beat and wave the divisions of basic *tala* in order to be a true part of *his* musical world. Whereas the Western professional becomes aware of subtle variations in harmonic structures, the Indian becomes equally sensitive to the rhythms that tend to have become characteristic of each *tala*. Some of this sensitivity will be revealed when we discuss actual performance practice.

Indian Music Practice

An Indian musician must thoroughly absorb some threescore or more *raga* and many *tala* before he can obtain any professional status. This is done first by singing each *raga* and *tala* in an extended series of pedagogical exercises similar to those familiar to Western music students. The Indian's rhythmic training is rather different, however, for in addition to beating and waving the stresses of the *tala,* he must also, as we noted earlier, chant the mnemonics (*bol;* in Karnatak, *sollukattu*) which are syllabic vocalizations of the strokes to be played on the drum. The object of Western exercises is primarily instrumental technique plus familiarity with traditional tonal systems; these goals are also sought in Indian pedagogy, but there is also a larger goal, which is so deeply to indoctrinate the student in the possibilities of each *raga* or *tala* that he can get to the heart of much Indian music—improvisation.

The art of Indian music has been called guided improvisation, by which is meant that at all times the musician must be guided simultaneously by the *raga* and the *tala*. In truth, all improvisation that is not merely personal musical rumination must be guided by some rules. Great freedom of improvisation is possible only when there are many rules for guidance. Jazz, for example, with its comparatively simple rules of order, eventually was felt to be too restricted in its improvisational scope, leading progressive jazz musicians to seek new rules, including some Indian concepts, in order to expand their improvisational range. The Indian musician, by contrast, has before him a dazzling array of rhythmic and melodic possibilities, thanks to the thoroughness of the rules which serve as guides to his improvisations.

[14] See Curt Sachs, *Rhythm and Tempo* (New York: W. W. Norton & Company, Inc., 1953), 24–25.

The Indian performer is also a creator. Like his Western counterpart, he must practice diligently the pedagogical materials of music. Such practice makes it possible for the Western musician to play a given piece time after time without the slightest noticeable variation. There are some compositions in Indian music which require that same precise, non-improvisatory performance; however, the general aim of Indian practice is for the performer to reach the stage where he can play each *raga* in a new way every time without losing its characteristics, which are his guides.

This important distinction in purpose results in a different kind of artist-audience relation. The knowledgeable Western audience listens for a faithful reproduction of the composer's intention and reacts to a combination of the composer's skill, the performer's artistry, and the personal "meaningfulness" of the composition. The Indian audience reacts not to the challenge of reproduction but to the performer's ability to create his own music within given bounds. In both cases, the listener must have some foreknowledge in order to appreciate the art of the performance. In the West, this consists of knowledge of the piece, the idiom, or the form. The same kinds of knowledge are useful to the Indian but, in the case of form, the intent is different. Western classical forms of the eighteenth and nineteenth centuries were constructed to introduce the listener to the basic tonalities and themes so that their development and return could be followed. Indian classical forms are designed to acquaint the listener with the *raga* (and, sometimes, a basic theme) while still leaving room for the performer to reveal the beauty of the *raga* in terms of his own imagination. Because form follows function, one can expect Indian forms to differ from those of the West.

Most Indian forms begin with a rhapsodic, free-rhythmic introduction called the *alapana* or *alap*. Its function is to reveal gradually the notes of the *raga* plus its special melodic characteristics. Even before these notes appear, however, one hears a drone on the "ground tone" (*sa*) of the *raga* plus its fifth. In *raga* not having a perfect fifth in their scale, the drone uses the fourth or an ostinato figure like *ni, ṡa, ṡa, sa* (in a heptatonic scale, 7, 8, 8, 1). An ostinato-like drone is also found in many performances of other *raga*, particularly if played on a *tambura* drone chordophone. Such patterns differ from the traditional Western ostinato in their general lack of a distinctive rhythmic pattern related to the rhythm or tempo of the composition. Whatever the style of the drone, it is essential in most Indian music today, for it serves as a constant reminder of the music's starting point throughout the performer's peregrinations in the introduction and all the sections that follow.

Since there are at least as many different forms in Indian music as there are in the Western tradition, it is impossible to generalize about what will happen after the close of an *alap*. The most common indicator that the *alap* is over and that the piece proper has begun, however, is the entrance of the *tala,* usually in the form of a drum part. An informed listener can, in addition, distinguish which type of piece is being played and its Karnatak or Hindustani origin or performance style.

The Karnatak tradition concentrates on forms based on songs, so that one might say that it has no uniquely instrumental compositions. Quite often the performance involves the actual singing of the song along with "dialogues" between the singer and an instrumentalist, both using the melody of the song. Virtually all of the texts are religious. The best known form is the *kriti* (or *kirtana*), a devotional song which, after the *alap,* consists of three sections, the *pallavi, anupallavi,* and *caranam* (*charanam*). Each section contains or is derived from a setting of religious poetry along with improvisations on the setting's melody, such as the one in the excerpt given in Example 4–6. Though certain artists are able to

EXAMPLE 4–6. Karnatak flute variations transcribed from the record, *Anthologie de la musique classique de l'Inde* (Paris: Ducretet-Thomson Album 320 C 096-8), side 6, band 4. The performer is the famous Madras musician Tanjore Viswanathan. Used by permission of Pathé Marconi.

A. Rama-pria raga

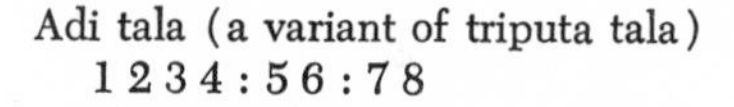

introduce new ornamental pitches during performances, the basic *raga* is not changed throughout a traditional piece.[15] Different notes or ranges, however, are often emphasized in different sections of a piece so that one feels a sense of tonal progression within the overall one-*raga* composition.

The *dhrupad* of North India is comparable to the strict religious songs of the South; the freer *khyal* is the North's more popular vocal-instrumental form. The *khyal* text itself is shorter than that of the *dhrupad,* and some of it may be left out or sung with ornamentations which make the words incomprehensible in parts of the two sections of the form, the

[15] In North India today one may sometimes hear a so-called *ragamala,* in which a piece does modulate from one *raga* to another and back.

B. "Sandehamunu" by Tyagaraja

sthayi and the *antara.* Perhaps the ultimate in purely vocal music forms are the *tarana* of the North and *tillana* of the South, in which there is no text at all but rather sets of meaningless syllables. There also are sections of other pieces in which the Indian sol-fa syllables (*sa, ri, ga,* etc.) or drum mnemonics are sung for a considerable time; this is particularly common in dance accompaniments. There are, in addition, lighter vocal genres such as the South Indian *javali,* as well as purely instrumental light forms, the most popular of which is the North Indian *gat.*

The mention above of a few Indian music forms is as lifeless as the word "sonata" unless one imagines each in terms of a live musical event. This can be done in a book like this one only through discographies and descriptive evocations. In the latter spirit let us remember that during the formal progress of a piece the performer may not only be playing upon the notes, ornaments, and melodic characteristics of a *raga* and maintaining the rhythmic framework of a given *tala,* but may also be using a well-known melody composed by someone else. This is suggested by Example 4–6, which contains the preliminary lines of the *pallavi* section (after the *alap,* which is not shown but can be heard on the recording) of a performance by a Karnatak flutist based on the song "Sandehamunu" by the composer Tyagaraja (1767–1847). The *raga* and *tala* of the composition are shown in Example 4–6A; the B section of the example starts with one version of the first line of the melody. (The original tune was transmitted orally and is therefore open to various interpretations.)

The first few lines of the actual flute performance are arranged in what is called a *comparative score,* a system in which related lines of music are shown immediately below their counterparts in the original line. This method is used in many transcriptions that involve highly varied pieces in either folk or art music. In this case, one can see that the flutist first repeats a florid version of the basic melody. This is followed by the repeat of a so-called *sangati* (fixed variation) which is normally used at the beginning of every performance of this piece before launching into different material or the much more improvisatory variations which will emerge as the performance progresses. The opening beats of the *mridanga* drum part have been included to illustrate how that instrument enters. Like the opening bars of a symphony, this transcription barely touches the heart of the music but it does suggest some of the artistry of the Indian art music tradition.

When more than one player is involved in Indian art music, the performance becomes something of a contest. If a drummer is present, he may try to trip up the other musicians with complicated permutations of the *tala* rhythm. The other players, of course, can play with the *tala* as well. Notice in Example 4–6 how even the composer has set the basic accents and phrasing of his melody in a very subtle relation to the *tala.*

A common North Indian rhythmic device is a *tchai,* in which a pattern, often beginning on the upbeat of an unaccented beat, will be so constructed that three repetitions of it will always end on the first beat (*sam*) of the *tala.* Such a pattern can be extended to such a length that it will be "out of phase" for three complete cycles of a *tala* only to land miraculously on the first beat of the fourth cycle. On such occasions one can hear sighs or see head-shakes of satisfaction among the audience. They have experienced in music the kind of thrill one gets from watching a tightrope walker execute a difficult balancing act and end with a graceful leap upright on the wire. For the traditional Indian, however, the experience has been more than a ravishing of the senses. The ethical aspects of Indian music have already been implied. We should note further that most famous composers, such as Tyagaraja (composer of the original on which Example 4–6 is based), are considered saints. This attitude is reflected as well in the concept of the teacher as a *guru.* Ideally, the teacher's intent is to guide the disciple spiritually through music. As a result, professional musicians may continue to burn incense before the picture of their *guru* in remembrance of their perpetual debt to him musically and spiritually. The latter aspect of this dual debt is beyond the scope of this short essay, though it is worthy of further deliberation on the part of the reader so inclined. From a strictly musical standpoint, our discussion should have made it evident that the basis of almost all sacred and secular Indian art music lies in the drone-based, *raga-tala*–oriented improvisations found in vocal and instrumental concert and theatrical forms. We need now to discuss the means used to reach many of these artistic ends, the basic instruments of India.

Basic Indian Instruments

From all that has been said about Indian theory and practice, one can expect three basic requirements in the construction of instruments suitable for such music. First, there must be a flexibility in pitch production and tuning in order to accommodate the many *raga* and the sliding techniques typical of their melodic ornamentations. This need is reflected in the absence in India of the fixed-pitched metallophones and xylophones found throughout Southeast Asia and Indonesia (though the Western harmonium has become a common part of some North Indian ensembles). A second consideration is the necessity of a constant drone. Because of this, drone strings are common to most Indian chordophones and some instruments are capable of playing only drone pitches. Finally, the importance of rhythm in Indian music necessitates drums as well as rhythmic devices attached to basically melodic instruments. With these three principles in mind we shall now discuss briefly the major components of India's instrumental treasure-house.

The basic drums in Indian art music are the South Indian *mridanga* and the North Indian *tabla* (a pair of smaller drums, one for each hand, called *tabla* and *baya* respectively). The *mridanga* (Plate X, Figure 26) is a two-headed barrel drum related to the *dhol* mentioned in our Central Asian discussion and found also in Indian folk forms. It is laid across the lap so that both drumheads may be subjected to the subtle flights of the performer's fingers and palms. The pieces of doweling seen under some of the straps are used to help tighten the heads. The right head has a semi-permanent black paste tuning-patch made of boiled rice and manganese filings. The doughy patch on the left head is made of cream of wheat (*suji*) and is applied freshly for each performance in order to lower the pitch and enhance the bass quality of that head. Similar but permanent patches are found on the single heads of the kettle-shaped *baya* (Figure 28) and the *tabla* (Figure 27). The traditional account of the origins of the *baya* and *tabla* has it that they were created by cutting a *mridanga* in half; their present shapes and materials would seem to contradict this, though they both have tuning patches and are played together by one performer. Both shapes can be found in larger sizes. There also exists a half circle of tuned drums (*tabla tarang*) that can be used melodically like a similar set of bowls called *jalatarang,* which one tunes by filling them with different amounts of water and plays by striking their edges with two thin wooden sticks.

The melodic instrument in Example 4–6 is the unadorned side-blown cane flute (*venu* or *bansri*). In the Indian double-reed family there are many variants of the *shahnai* derived from Near Eastern instruments mentioned in the previous chapter (see Plate IX, Figure 24).[16] South India's most distinctive oboe is the *nadasvaram* (*nagasvara, nagasura*). Its thick, large double reed is attached to a body some 87 cm. long in which there may be more than seven fingerholes, the "extra" holes being plugged with wax to regulate the basic pitch of the instrument. It is often accompanied by another conical double-reed, with fewer holes, which plays only the drone.

The most famous instrumental creations of South Asia are chordophones. Since instrument-making in India is still basically a hand craft, there are many local variations on any given instrument, but the instruments found in Plates XI and XII show some basic types. On Indian chordophones, three kinds of strings may be found: melodic strings, drone strings, and sympathetic vibrators. This can be seen clearly in the evolution of the *vina.*

[16] See Nazir Jairazbhoy, "A Preliminary Survey of the Oboe in India," *Ethnomusicology,* XIV/3 (1970).

PLATE X. Indian Drums

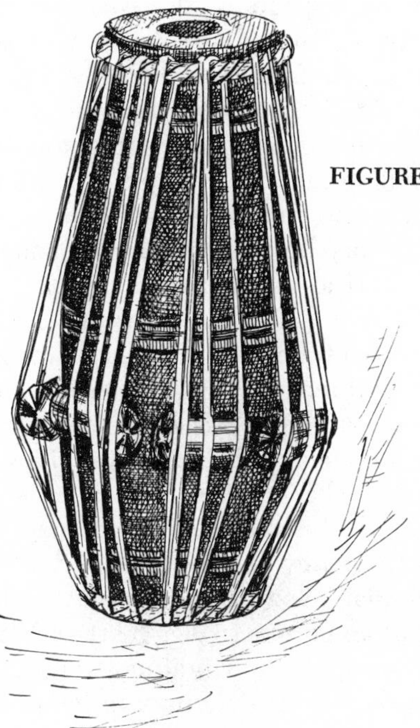

FIGURE 26. *Mridanga.*

FIGURE 27. *Tabla.*

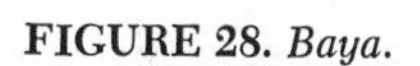

FIGURE 28. *Baya.*

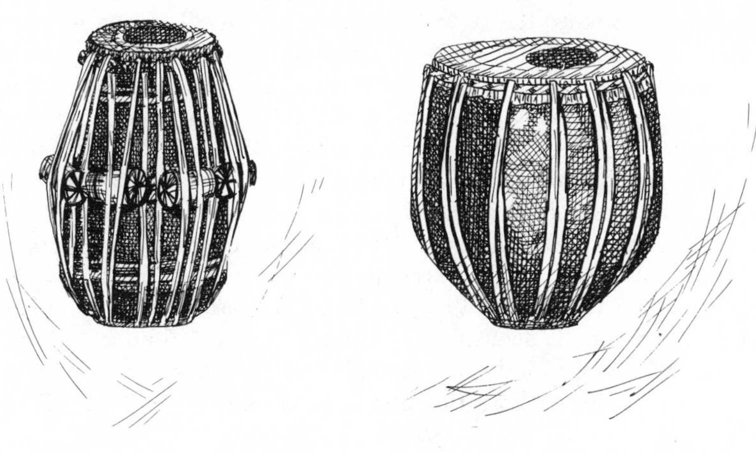

In ancient times the term *vina* referred to a type of arched harp much like those of the ancient Near East. As can be seen in Plate XI, however, the surviving variants of the *vina* are either zithers or lutes. Figure 29 shows the North Indian *bin,* a tube zither with two large calabash resonators, high frets, four melody strings, and three drone strings, two on one side and one on the other. The high frets make it possible to play the important ornamentations of individual notes by pressing down or pulling the strings to the side. Figure 30 is a *bin sitar,* a little-known variant found in Poona; we include it because it helps to illustrate the evolutionary potentials of instrumental design, though it is not necessarily a historical link between the *bin* and later instruments. The two gourd resonators are present, but they are attached to a trough zither body rather than a tube. The number of strings used varies, but the example shown has all three types: five melodic, two drone (on the side), and eight sympathetic vibrators. The frets are quite different from those of the *bin,* for they are metal rods held to the sides of the trough by gut. Such an arrangement makes it easier to adjust the pitches to those of a specific *raga.* This method is probably an adaptation of the movable fret systems noted earlier on many plucked lutes of the Near East.

The South Indian *vina* in Figure 31 maintains the tradition of melody strings (four) and drone strings (three), Karnatak classicists finding the tone of extra sympathetic vibrating strings distasteful. It should be noted that the drone strings of the *vina* can be used to keep track of the *tala* by stroking them in a proper rhythmic pattern. The *vina* frets are metal rods, although they are set in walls of blackened beeswax rather than tied with gut as are those of the *bin sitar* (Figure 30). The important difference between the Karnatak *vina* and the *bin* and *bin sitar* is that on the *vina* one of the calabash resonators has coalesced with the fingerboard, turning a zither-type instrument into a lute. Also, the upper gourd has become basically decorative rather than sonically functional, although it is used to help balance the instrument when playing. The carved head at the top of the instrument is somewhat functional, as it encloses a storage compartment with which a can of coconut oil is kept; this is used to lubricate the performer's fingertips to facilitate their gliding over the metal strings and frets. On this instrument the melodic ornamentations are most often made by pulling the string to one side.

The Hindustani *sitar* (Figure 32) is the Indian chordophone best known in the West. It is a lute developed by Moslem musicians through a combination of Indian principles and those of the Near Eastern *tambur* family (see Plate VII, Figure 19). The *sitar* often has an upper gourd that, like that of the *vina,* is acoustically nonfunctional. In addition to four, or sometimes only two, melodic strings and three drones, the *sitar* may have as many as 13 strings whose function is to vibrate sympathetically with

PLATE XI. Indian Plucked Chordophones

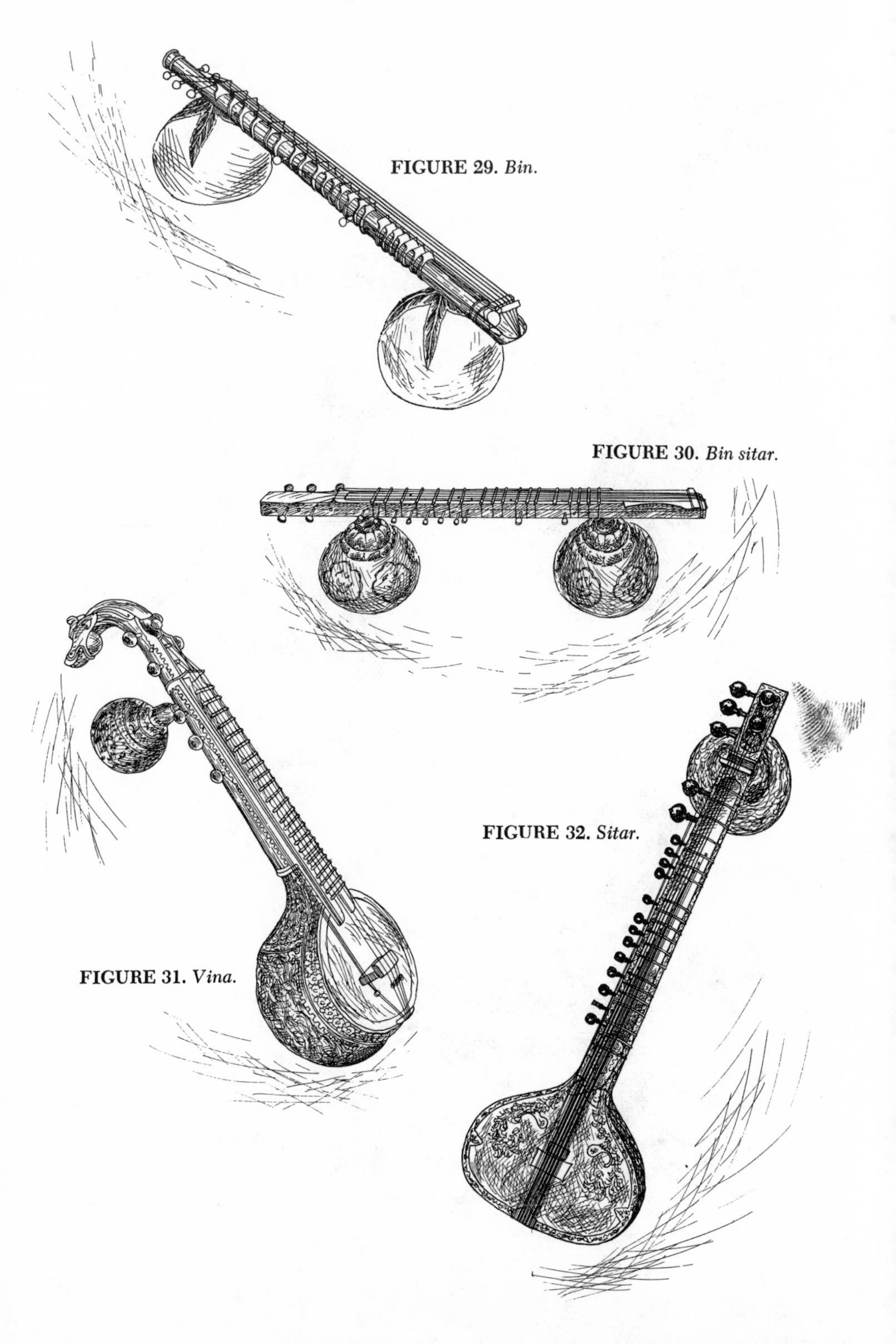

FIGURE 29. *Bin.*

FIGURE 30. *Bin sitar.*

FIGURE 31. *Vina.*

FIGURE 32. *Sitar.*

PLATE XII. Indian Bowed and Plucked Lutes

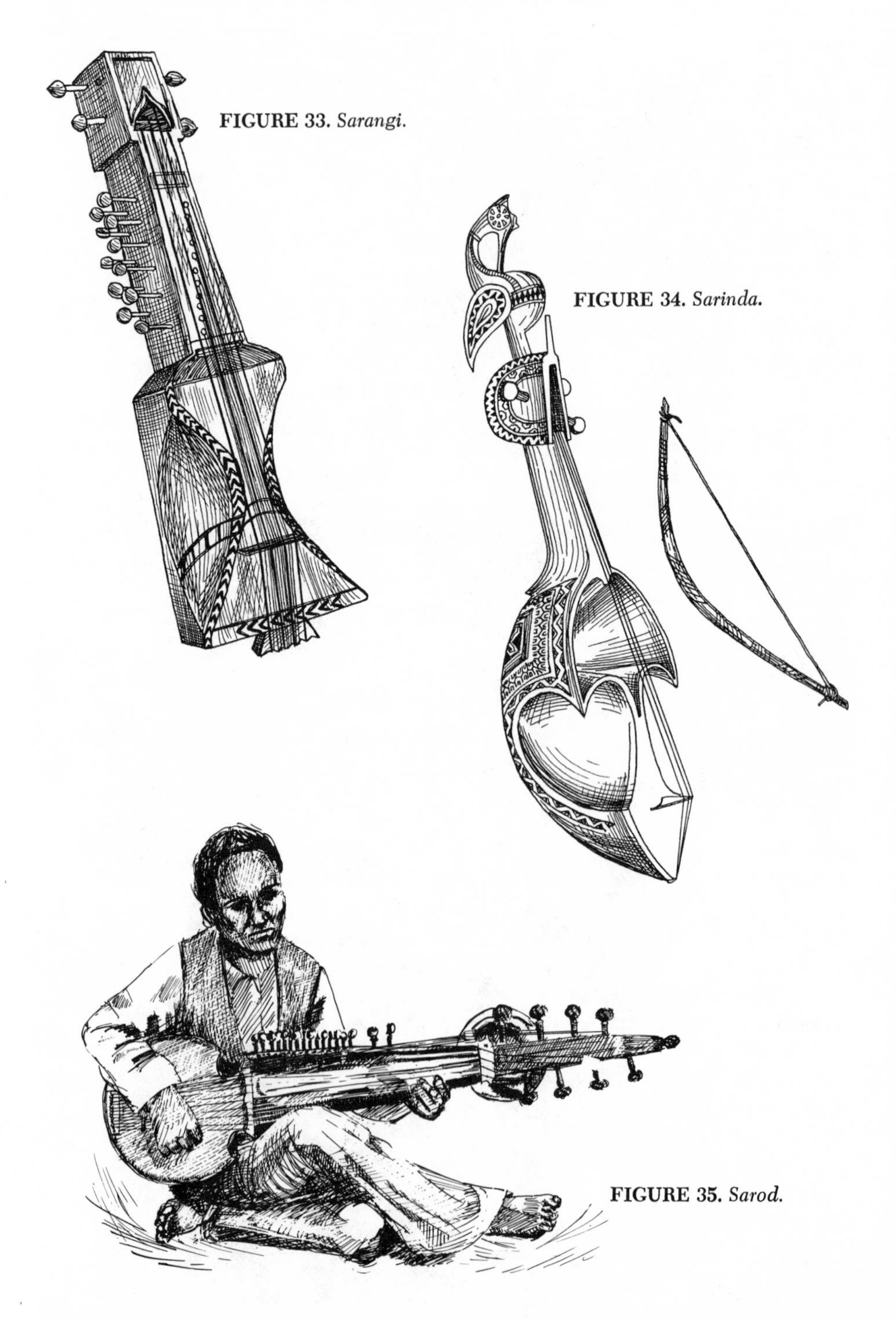

FIGURE 33. *Sarangi.*

FIGURE 34. *Sarinda.*

FIGURE 35. *Sarod.*

notes played on the melody strings. These sympathetic strings give the *sitar* that special hollow sound familiar to devotees of Hindustani music. Room is made beneath the frets for all these strings by having a concave trough along the fingerboard and convex frets tied with gut onto the walls of the trough. These convex frets also make it easier to pull the strings sideways when playing ornaments.

Another well-known but shorter Hindustani lute is the *sarod* (Plate XII, Figure 35). Normally, its six melodic and two drone strings are plucked. Several sympathetic strings pass inside the deep body of the *sarod,* which has a parchment soundboard and a metal fingerboard. Perhaps a better-known plucked, long-necked Indian lute is one that plays no melody at all; this is the *tambura,* whose four (occasionally five or six) metal strings are always played unstopped, in order to produce the vital drone accompaniment for vocal and instrumental performances. The *tambura* is often complemented or replaced by a small one-note hand-pumped reed organ (*sur-petti* or "*sruti* box").

The scattered presence of various Near Eastern bowed lutes in South Asia is a reflection of India's extended historical contact with the Near Eastern tradition. Karnatak music reflects the Western experience as well, with its frequent use of the violin, which, however, is braced between the chest and foot rather than held under the chin, and is tuned to the drone tones of tonic and fifth. Its fretless fingerboard is suitable for performing Indian pitches and ornaments properly. Another common bowed lute in India is the *dilruba,* which is a kind of "bowed sitar." Figure 33 shows a *sarangi,* an Indian bowed lute that combines melodic and sympathetic strings, whereas the *sarinda* in Figure 34 has only three melodic strings. Large indentations on the sides of both of these instruments accommodate the movements of the bow as it changes from string to string. Note that only the lower half of the face of the *sarinda* is covered by a membrane; the *sarangi* produces a richer tone, with its face fully covered by a membrane. It is used in the accompaniment of vocal or dance concerts. The *sarinda* is most often found in the hands of street musicians.

The main Indian box zither is the *svaramandala,* which is historically related and physically similar to the *qanun* (Plate IX, Figure 25). It also shares with some *qanun* the lack of any damping device, and thus it is commonly used to create a wash of sound as a supplement to the drone texture behind the melodic instruments that deal with the tones and embellishments so important in the Indian *raga* system. The ubiquitous missionary harmonium, with its rigid vocabulary of the Western twelve-tone scale and its harmonic orientation, is inappropriate for South Asian music, but it enjoys an unfortunate popularity in several northern idioms.

Some Indian Folk, Popular, and Theatrical Music Traditions

Perhaps the Indian folk instrument best known in the West is the *pungi,* a double clarinet with free reeds encased in a gourd. Despite all the Western cartoon pictures of oboe-playing fakirs, it is the *pungi* that is the snake charmer's instrument. But the true world of Indian folk music, and much of its art music as well, is found in singing. The fascination of Indian art music has overshadowed folk music as an area of serious study. Even a superficial look at Indian folk music, however, reveals a richness worthy of the lifetime of any field collector. In the central part of India (Nagpur), in the northeastern Naga hills, and on many offshore islands there are collections of tribal peoples whose musics are more reminiscent of Arnhem Land, Borneo, and the jungles of Southeast Asia than they are of Hindu and Moslem India. Antiphonal and responsorial songs, harmonies in fourths and fifths, and even occasional singing in seconds can be found in such regions. At the same time, the lovely boatmen's songs of Bangladesh and the melodies of Kashmir display casually ornamented lines based on *raga* prototypes and sung with soft-toned vocal qualities like those of Indian art music. A treasure of folk songs can be found in each of the hundreds of dialects spoken throughout India. However, the systematic collection of this music has only recently begun; it is to be hoped that eventually more of it will become available in the West. At present, searches for examples of Indian songs most frequently end up with a collection of popular tunes derived from the enormous number of Indian films produced by the huge native film industry. Such music is a natural part of transistorized urbanization and is equally worthy of study, since it is, after all, the primary idiom heard by most Indians. It is not "serious" music, but it often is very creatively Indian. The simpler characteristics of popular music discussed in the previous chapter (see page 81) naturally apply to film-derived music as well, but let us never underestimate the sociological value of this medium and its messages.

Theatrical music of many kinds exists in South Asia: accompaniments on double-reeds, drums, and cymbals for religious exercises at the many kinds of temples and shrines; the music for a classical dance or dance-drama form; curved trumpets and massed drum ensembles accompanying a parade of elephants; and accompaniments for a night club routine in Bombay. We shall discuss only the first two types.

Indian theater and dance have traditionally been connected with religious activities. This is easily seen in the Kathakali dance-drama of Malabar, which originally presented its tales from the *Ramayana* and *Mahabharata* in the open-air courts of temples. The accompaniment of these pantomimes and dances consists of drums, cymbals, and narrating singers. Drums form the major part of the accompaniment for the Kandyan dances of Sri Lanka, which relates to the special Buddhist festivals of that island.

The orchestras for the accompaniment of the better-known classical dances of South India are more elaborate. These dances, based on the precepts of Bharata's *Natya-Sastra* mentioned earlier, also have religious undertones, for they were originally performed by temple girls (*devadasi*), though today their performers are usually middle- and upper-class women. A standard accompaniment for such dancing is a dance-master (who also sings), another singer, a *mridanga* drum, a *vina* and/or a violin, plus a drone instrument and perhaps a flute or clarinet. The dance-master (*nattuvanar*) plays the *talam,* a pair of small hand cymbals that are essential in guiding the rhythmic movements of the dancer. Rhythmic mnemonics and Indian solmizations, in addition to poetic texts, are used by the singers.

The major form of North Indian classical dancing, Kathak, is an indigenous dance style based on the *Natya-Sastra* but influenced by the secular court dances of Persia as introduced by the Moghul rulers in India from the fourteenth century. The accompanying orchestra also shows a mixture, with instruments such as the bowed *sarangi* and the plucked *sarod, sitar,* and *tambura* being combined with the *tabla* and *pakhawaj* drums. A singer is always present.

Though the Kathak and Bharata Natyam dancing are the heart of the Indian classical dance tradition, there are many regional and folk traditions that maintain independent styles.[17] Their accompaniments vary from bagpipes in Northern Pakistan to small bowed lutes with coconut-shell bodies in Manipur. The most common instrument to accompany such dances is a double-headed drum of the *dhol* or *dholak* type, though many other types can be found. One particularly interesting form is a small hour-glass-shaped drum called the *damaru,* which is played by twisting it so that the knotted ends of a cord tied around its waist will strike the skins alternately. This drum is closely connected with the cult of Siva in India; variants of it are found throughout Tibet and East Asia in connection with Buddhist activities (cf. page 140).

Nationalist sentiment in South Asia has led to state subsidies for many of the dance and theater forms mentioned above. The real strength of these forms, however, lies in the fact that, despite great efforts at modernization and Westernization, there is still an audience in the Asian subcontinent that follows them, as traditional arts, with interest and pride.

[17] For details see Balwant Gargi, *Folk Theater of India* (Seattle: University of Washington Press, 1966).

A Theoretical Postscript

As we study the various musics of the world we normally find the traditional idioms on the defensive against Western intrusions. India seems to be an exception. Western art music is hardly taught, and the music of the schools is still almost exclusively Indian. Why? A possible answer may be in the early existence of a thoroughgoing theoretical system with which the native musician could explain himself when confronted by the analytical Western mind. For most non-Western musicians, the only answer to the question "Why do you play your music in this manner?" is a shrug and a statement like "I play it thus because that's the way it's supposed to go." The same kind of answer can come from many professional Indian or Western musicians. Among them, however, there also exist persons who can analyze their music and show, note by note, where it comes from and "why." Perhaps what is needed in other music traditions of the world are in-depth studies that will make equally explicit the rules of order underlying each system—rules which the traditional performers may know only subliminally. Such constructions could be dangerous misinterpretations of the traditional world; however, if correct, they could give the traditional artist a vocabulary with which to explain his music to the outside world. In India, at least, there seems to be evidence that a well-organized music theory and a flourishing performance tradition can absorb the shock of foreign confrontations and react to or imitate them without destroying the special beauty of the indigenous heritage.

BIBLIOGRAPHICAL AND DISCOGRAPHICAL NOTES

Victor Belaiev's fine Russian work of 1962 has been translated by Greta and Mark Slobin under the title *Central Asian Music* (Middletown: Wesleyan University Press, 1975), and Barbara Krader has reviewed Soviet folk music research since World War II in *Ethnomusicology,* VII/3 (1963). Mark Slobin has written *Music in the Culture of Northern Afghanistan* (Tucson: University of Arizona Press, 1974), *Kirgiz Instrumental Music* (New York: Society for Asian Music, 1969), and the Central Asian music section of *Encyclopaedia Britannica,* 15th ed. (III, 1124–27), as well as articles in *Ethnomusicology* and *Asian Music Journal.* He has also produced a set of three excellent records, *Afghanistan* (Anthology Record AST 4001, 4004, and 4007); other examples are found on the Folkways records *Music of the Russian Middle East* (FE 6916) and *Folk Music of the U.S.S.R.* (FE 4535). For details on the growth of Soviet materials and their sources overseas, see Pekka Gronow, "Ethnic Music and Soviet Record Industry" [*sic*], *Ethnomusicology,* XIX/1 (1975).

Nazir Jairazbhoy's entry "Music" under "South Asian Peoples, Arts of" in *Encyclopaedia Britannica,* 15th ed. (XVII, 150–58), and his "Legacy of India: Indian Music" in *Cultural History of India* (Oxford: Clarendon Press, 1974) are good starting points. Indian studies in English of the two major traditions are V. N. Bhatkhande, *A Short Historical Survey of the Music of Upper India* (Bombay, 1934), and P. Sambamoorthy, *South Indian Music,* 6 vols. (Madras: Indian Music Pub. House, 1958–69). A. H. Fox Strangways' *The Music of Hindostan* (London: Oxford University Press, 1914) is sensitive if dated. Basic Hindustani *raga* studies include Jairazbhoy's *The Rags of North Indian Music* (Middletown: Wesleyan University Press, 1971), Alain Danielou's *Northern Indian Music* (London: C. Johnson, 1949), Walter Kaufmann's *The Ragas of North India* (Bloomington: Indiana University Press, 1968), and O. C. Gangoly's *Raga and Raginis* (Bombay, 1958). Harold Powers' Princeton dissertation, *The Background of the South Indian Raga System* (Ann Arbor: University Microfilms, 1963), explains the Karnatak system, and his article "Indian Music and the English Language," *Ethnomusicology,* IX/1 (1965) effectively reviews all the basic English writings on Indian music to that date. Elise B. Barnett compiled "Special Bibliography: Art Music of India" in *Ethnomusicology,* XIV/2 (1970), and *A Discography of the Art Music of India,* Special Series No. 3, Society for Ethnomusicology (1975).

Among the many records of Indian music available in the West we can mention but a few. The Ducretet-Thomson *Anthologie de la musique classique de l'Inde* (320 C 096–8) is a good general collection. Specific genres and instruments are to be heard in the UNESCO series *India* (Musicaphon BM 30 L 2006, 2007, 2017), and a star-filled *The Anthology of Indian Music* (World Pacific WDS 26200; with a lecture by Ravi Shankar). Shankar and other artists have released several records under the World Pacific label (for example, WP 1403, 1416, 18, 21, 22, 26, and 1430–38), and Nonesuch has produced many recordings of both Northern and Southern performers. Yehudi Menuhin's explanation of Karnatak music is part of *Classical Indian Music* (London CM 9282). Folkways has several offerings, of which *Music from South Kerala* (FE 4365) is of special interest because of its harmonic examples and excerpts from Kathakali plays. *Religious Music* (FE 4431) and *Raga* (FE 3530) contain some notation. *Ritual Music of Manipur* (FE 4479) contains theater music from that region. Odeon has a series of regional Indian recordings of interest, and commercial music is found on Capitol's *Modern Motion Picture Music of India* (T 10090).

FIVE
SOUTHEAST ASIA

The area known as Southeast Asia encompasses the twentieth-century countries of Burma, mainland Malaysia, Singapore, Thailand, Cambodia, Laos, and Vietnam. Over the centuries the names and cultural conditions of these various areas have changed often. The magnificent ruins of Angkor Wat, for example, are a monument to only one of several brilliant kingdoms that flourished in Southeast Asia between approximately the seventh and fifteenth centuries. The jungles and mountains that surrounded these high civilizations ensured separate tribal ways, many of which have survived to the present day. Even if the growth of colonialism and nationalism, particularly in the nineteenth and twentieth centuries, has made inroads into indigenous cultures, there is still much in Southeast Asia that speaks of its ancient and its tribal traditions.

The music of Southeast Asia today reflects a mixture of indigenous genius with various combinations of influence from four main external traditions: Indonesia, China, India, and, in more recent times, the West.

Hybrid musics have bred further hybrids, so that today it is very difficult to separate the many interminglings and cross-influences. Southeast Asian music shows variation not only among all its nations but also between geographical regions within each country. Rather than attempting to discuss subtle cross-currents like Sino-Thai and Malayo-Indonesian influences, or regional differences like the Khmer and Champa styles, let us begin by discussing Southeast Asian tonal systems in general, then go on to consider the various media and kinds of music based on those systems, in the following order: (1) percussion-dominated ensembles, (2) string-dominated ensembles, (3) wind music, (4) instrumental solo and chamber music, particularly for strings, (5) sacred and secular vocal music, (6) folk and tribal music, and (7) theatrical, rural, and popular music. Although these categories are not mutually exclusive, they will serve to illustrate certain cultural continuities as well as some of the variety in Southeast Asian music. For example, all the major genres rely on oral learning rather than notation, and most musics are related to or inspired by some form of theater. Each country, however, has different forms of theatricals and uses different terms for the styles of music and the instruments that relate to the general Southeast Asian tradition. We have tried to pick typical examples in each of the categories given above and to mention some regional variations, without pretending to include every nation's terminology or variations.

SOUTHEAST ASIAN TONAL SYSTEMS

The most famous tone system of Southeast Asia is the so-called equidistant seven-tone (heptatonic) scale. In theory these seven tones are 171.4 cents apart, but the manner in which instruments are tuned often alters the actual distance. Example 5–1 shows this equidistant tendency, which in staff notation is indicated by a higher-than-Western seventh (1026 cents, theoretically). In performance these notes give a "neutral" effect (as does the whole-tone hexatonic scale in the West, although its pitches are very different). Some Southeast Asian groups that have had contact with the West tend to adjust these tones to tempered pitches. The origin of the equidistant scale is open to considerable conjecture; at least one theorist has proposed that it is the lost *ma-grama* of ancient India.[1] Perhaps rural ensembles may provide information on the more ancient tonal systems since, like the Indonesian *gamelan,* they contain keyed in-

[1] See Alain Danielou, *La Musique du Cambodge et du Laos* (Pondichery: Institut Français d'Indologie, 1957), pp. 2–3.

EXAMPLE 5–1. A Burmese orchestral melody transcribed from the recording, *Burmese Folk and Traditional Music* (New York: Folkways Record P 436), side 1, band 5. By permission of Folkways Records and Service Corporation.

struments and gongs of rather fixed pitches. One of the most intriguing tone-system arguments of the twentieth century revolves around the tuning of a set of supposedly ancient stone keys found in Vietnam in 1949. Many things can be "proven" according to one's interpretation of the age, tuning, and function of these stones.[2]

Example 5–2 presents yet another of the many scales found in Southeast Asia. This example has an equidistant tendency in the upper three notes, but the resolutions to C of the "neutral" D♭ (i.e., a pitch about halfway between a Western D♭ and a D natural) and the "gap" between B♭ and G create a totally different effect from that found in Example 5–1. This is particularly evident if one listens to the recording from which the example was transcribed. To the American ear, Example 5–2 sounds surprisingly like the blues; the similarity arises because the American Negro has also exploited neutral tones in his traditional music. Example 5–2, however, is a thoroughly indigenous piece.

There are seven-tone scales in Southeast Asia that concentrate on a pentatonic "core." The two notes most often de-emphasized in such scales are the fourth and the seventh. There are also purely pentatonic pieces (see Example 5–4). A majority of these are of the well-known, no-half-step (anhemitonic) variety. Even this seemingly simple scale is subject to tonal refinement, for in Southeast Asia it has modal forms, and certain melodies that seem to use a six- or seven-note scale may actually be shift-

[2] A convenient summary of research on these stones is found in Curt Sachs, *The Wellsprings of Music* (The Hague: Nijhoff, 1962), 106–8.

EXAMPLE 5–2. A Cambodian wind ensemble piece transcribed from the recording *Cambodia* (Kassel: Musicaphon Record BM 30 L 2002), side 1, band 7. Used by permission.

ing between one five-note mode and another.[3] These melodic "modulations" are extremely important to the flow of music in such basically nonharmonic traditions as those of Southeast Asia. Here the forward-moving

[3] Such a technique has been labeled *metabole* by Trân-Văn-Khê in his *La Musique vietnamienne traditionnelle* (Paris: Presses Universitaires de France, 1962), 225.

dynamism of the music is solely dependent on melodic and rhythmic tensions. This flow is further aided in Southeast Asia by the emphasis in each scale on certain "pillar tones"[4] that are melodically consonant; that is, they seem to be at rest and require no further melodic resolution. Other notes in the scale are melodically dissonant or tense and seek resolution into one of the pillar tones. The notes F and C and A might be considered pillar tones in Example 5–1, while B♭ and F form the pillars for Example 5–2, the remaining tones being melodically tense and in need of further resolution.

Some Southeast Asian tonal traditions have been thought to reflect outside influences. The anhemitonic pentatonic is too widespread and common to imply any such thing, but major-minor pieces usually show hymn, march, or popular-music inspirations. Islamic influence is more difficult to pinpoint tonally but does seem to appear in some Malaysian musics (such as Example 5–3).

Attempts have been made to link Southeast Asian tonal systems with those of India by comparing contemporary Indian *ragas* with specific Southeast Asian scales, particularly those used in Hindu-oriented theatrical or religious pieces. The existence of certain beliefs concerning the mood of each scale also implies such a relation. In addition, some Southeast Asian musics use special ornaments on specific notes in each scale, much like those of India. However, some Southeast Asian melodic ornaments involve notes outside the given theoretical scale; this inconvenient fact is mentioned to emphasize that a major problem in musical cultural comparisons is not unlike one found within a single culture: the contrast between theory and practice. On the basis of selected performance practice alone one could compare Indian and Western music if their written theoretical systems did not exist to confound the thesis. When one of the cultures chosen is Southeast Asia, however, the comparison is easier (and potentially more sophistic) because indigenous theoretical writings are rare. Such books that do exist tend to be reflections of Chinese or Indian theory interpreted in terms of local practice. As our knowledge of regional sources in indigenous languages improves, it may be that we shall discover Southeast Asian theories as thoroughgoing as those of India, the Near East, East Asia, and the West. Progress in this direction was implied in our discussion of Indonesia (p. 43), but at present we must rely, for mainland Southeast Asian music, on performance practice, sure in the knowledge that the native performer and listener (like similar participants in Western musical events) are sub-

[4] The term was first applied to Southeast Asian music by Jaap Kunst in *Music in Java* (The Hague: Nijhoff, 1949), I, 92 and 94. It is derived from the *Gerusttone* concept of earlier German theorists.

liminally aware through cultural conditioning of an aggregate of tonal and aesthetic principles that help form their responses to the beauty and logic of the music. A foreign listener does not enjoy this advantage; but a conscious awareness of a few principles, such as those mentioned above concerning Southeast Asian tone systems, may help in learning what to listen for in such music.

INSTRUMENTAL ENSEMBLES

Percussion-dominated Ensembles

The best-known percussive ensemble in Southeast Asia is the Thai *pi phat* band. *Pi phat* ensembles vary from 6 to 14 players. A standard instrumentation includes paired idiophones which, like the sets of three *saron* and *gender* in the Javanese *gamelan*, have different ranges. The 21 wooden keys of the *ranat ek* xylophone (Plate XIII, Figure 36) carry the main melodic load, assisted in a lower register by its 17-keyed companion, the *ranat thum*. Their metal-keyed counterparts are the 21-keyed *ranat ek lek* (or sometimes *ranat thong*) and the 17-keyed *ranat thum lek* metallophones.

Circles of knobbed gongs are essential to most of the Southeast Asian percussion ensembles, such as the *pi phat*. In Thailand there are two forms, the lower-pitched 16-gong *khong wong yai* (Plate XIII, Figure 37) and the higher-pitched 17- or 18-gong *khong wong lek*, of which the two lowest-pitched gongs are nonfunctional. Two kinds of cymbals are also found in a *pi phat*. The smaller ones (*ching*) resemble the small dance-orchestra cymbals of India, while the larger (*chap*) are like the knobbed cymbals found in the Buddhist rituals of Tibet and China. Along with a hanging knobbed gong (*khong mong*) they provide a colotomic structure. Two kinds of drums also assist in this function. One is a large, laced-head barrel drum called the *tapone*, both heads of which are played with the hands. The other is a pair of tacked-head barrel drums played with sticks, called the *glong that*. Tuning paste is applied to the heads of both types of drums.

The only instrument that keeps the *pi phat* from being completely percussive is the *pi nai* oboe (in Cambodian, *sralay*) (Plate XIV, Figure 38). This instrument is novel in several ways. Its bulging shape is totally different from that of the standard *sornay-zurna* type found elsewhere in the world or in other ensembles of Southeast Asia (compare Figure 38 with Figure 24). It can be tuned by extending its thick teakwood body with a rim of wax at the lower end. The most novel feature of the *pi nai*, is its reed, which is not the standard double, but rather quadruple

PLATE XIII. Southeast Asian Idiophones

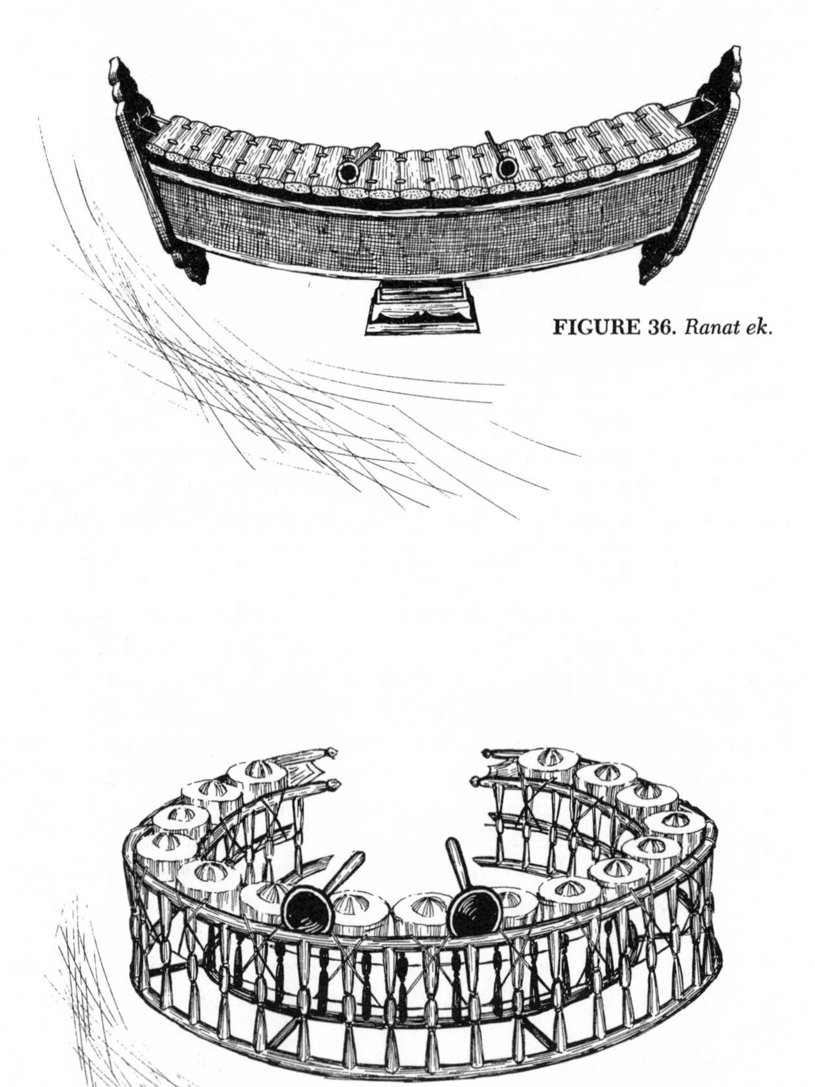

FIGURE 36. *Ranat ek.*

FIGURE 37. *Khong wong yai.*

PLATE XIV. Southeast Asian Aerophones

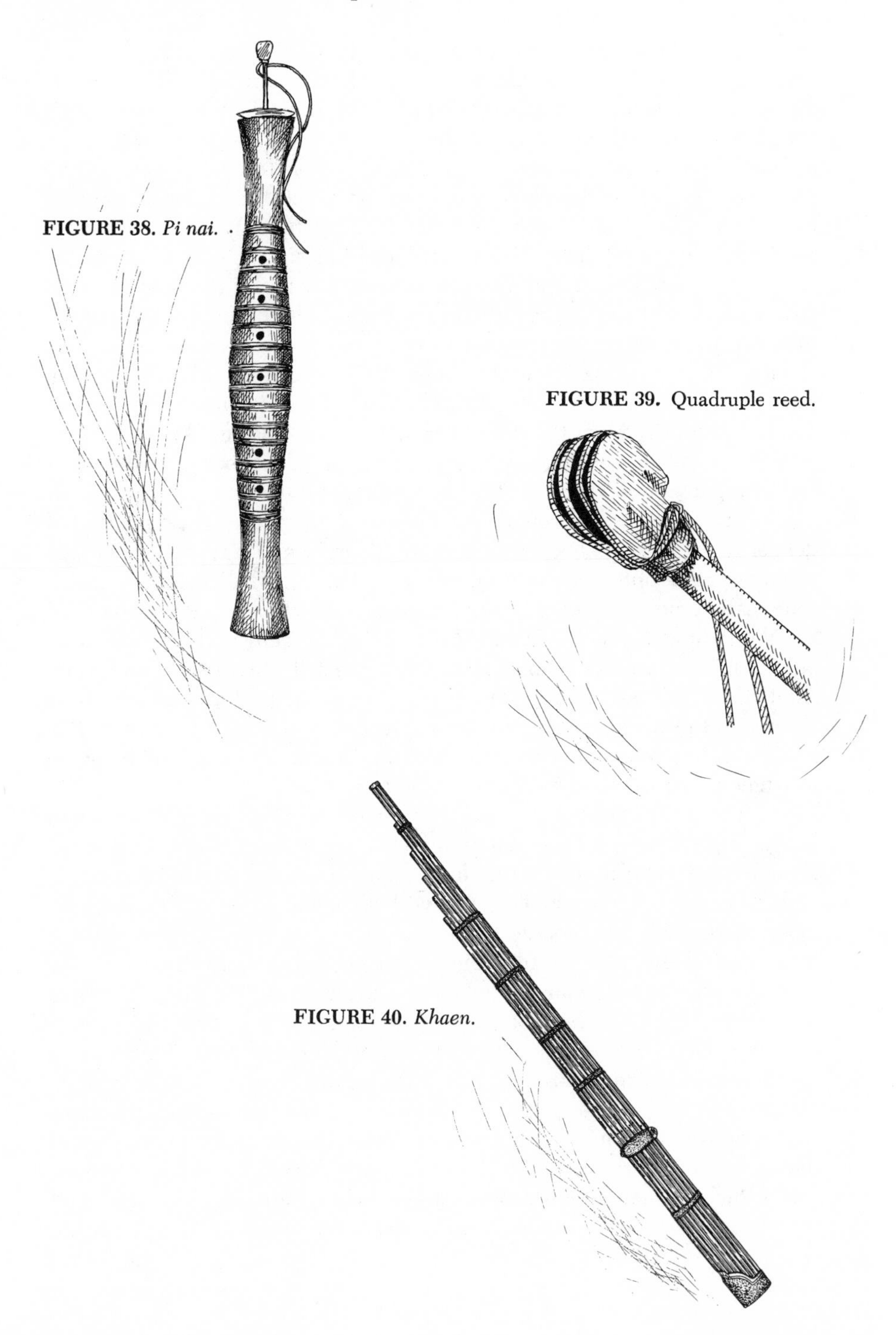

FIGURE 38. *Pi nai.*

FIGURE 39. Quadruple reed.

FIGURE 40. *Khaen.*

(Figure 39). Four short rounded reeds made of dried palm leaf are bound to a metal tube inserted in the top of the instrument. These reeds are set in a position vertical to the lips rather than in the western horizontal position, and the set is "swallowed"; that is, it is placed within the mouth cavity rather than on the lips. The reason for the novel vertical placement is so that the player's tongue can touch the edges of some of the vibrating reeds and stop the outer two layers, thus allowing him to produce different pitches with only six finger holes.

The Cambodian and Laotian *pi phat* ensembles are similar in instrumentation to the group just described. All three were mostly heard in the royal palaces, where they accompanied official ceremonies and classical dramatic presentations. Some private academies of ensemble playing now exist, as do various rural orchestras. This music, however, is derived primarily from the days of courtly power and, unlike Indonesian *gamelan* music, has little support among the populace except as it is used to accompany public theatricals or new national functions.

The Burmese percussion orchestra (*saing waing ah-pwe*) has deeper roots, perhaps because it is more itinerant and travels from village to village in support of the public theater (*pwe*). This orchestra, sometimes called merely a *saing* or *saing waing*, derived its name from its most novel instrument, a set of 21 tuned drums (*saing waing*). These are hung on an ornate circular screen which, while partially hiding the performer from view, adds a decorative visual pleasure to the performance. Such an interest in the visual appeal of instruments is characteristic of most Southeast Asian instrumental traditions, and the nonfunctional parts of many instruments are overlaid with traceries and colorings.

The rest of the Burmese ensemble consists of a circle of 21 knobbed gongs (*kyi waing*); a large hanging barrel drum (*segi*); large and small cymbals (*ya gwin* and *si*); two long bamboo clappers (*wa let kyong*); and a double-reed aerophone (*hne*) with a conical bore and a very large, loose, metal bell. The melody for *hne* given in Example 5–1 is an excerpt from a *saing* ensemble performance. As in the other orchestras of Southeast Asia mentioned so far, the melodic instruments in the *saing* ensemble may create together a kind of stratified polyphony. This, and our description in general of various percussion ensembles and their functions in Southeast Asia, brings to mind the Indonesian *gamelan*. Also, the prevalence of melodic idiophones and knobbed gongs, as well as the close connections of the music with dance or drama, are certainly reminiscent of the *gamelan* tradition. Unlike the Indonesian *saron* or *gender*, however, few of the continental Southeast Asian melodic idiophones are capable of sustaining long tones, and their melodic style thus tends to be more incisive.

There are many Burmese percussion ensembles in which the major or indeed the only melodic instrument is from the quadruple double-reed family described above. Players of such instruments normally use nasal breath in order to maintain a pitch or melody indefinitely, as in the style of Example 5–2. The Burmese *hne* excerpt in Example 5–1 illustrates possible idiophonic influence with its short-breathed lines and sudden changes in melodic direction. Its use of heterometer is atypical of Southeast Asia. Example 5–3 shows a very different florid style from Kedah, in

EXAMPLE 5–3. Malaysian Islamic procession music transcribed from a videotape of the author's 1968 field trip.

Malaysia, played on a *serunai* quadruple-reed aerophone in a *gendang keling,* an ensemble used for Moslem ceremonial events and processions. Despite the use of the quadruple–reed and one portable knobbed gong, the combination of a simple rhythm pattern played with sticks on the two heads of a laced barrel drum (*gendang*) with a melismatic tune in an "exotic" tonality played on a reed aerophone gives this ensemble a Turkish flavor. A clearer Islamic influence in Malaysia is found in the *nobat* ensemble connected to the courts of regional sultans. Its two barrel drums are called merely *gendang nobat,* but the use of the term *nobat* (cf. p. 79) and of a small *nenggara* kettledrum, a *nafiri* trumpet, and the *serunai* reveal its relation to similar groups in Moslem India and the Near East. We shall see the *serunai* in a very different ensemble in our later discussion of theater music.

String-dominated Ensembles

The main function of *mahori* orchestras is to accompany songs and plays. Like the *pi phat,* they find their main patronage in the capitals, although individual bowed instruments are widespread rurally. Though a *mahori* includes many other instruments, such as xylophones, circle gongs, cymbals, drums, and end-blown flutes, the overall sound is softer than that of *pi phat* groups. The common terms for bowed chordophones are *saw* in Laos and Thailand and *tro* in Cambodia and among the Mons of Burma. There are three basic kinds of bowed lutes in such groups; let us describe primarily their Thai forms. The first type is a three-stringed spike fiddle called the *saw sam sai.* Both its shape and its separate bow relate it to the *rebab* (see Plate IV, Figure 9) and, in fact, the *rebab* itself is used in certain theatrical musics of Malaysia. The second type is the *saw duang* (in Vietnam, the *cai nhi*). Its two strings lie one above the other, vertical to the body, like those of the Chinese *hu ch'in* (Plate XVII, Figure 47), rather than horizontal to the body, like the strings of a Western violin. The bow passes between the strings like that of the *hu ch'in,* rather than over them in the style of the *rebab* or the violin. The body of the *saw duang* is cylindrical and open (like Figure 47). The third type of bowed string instrument, the *saw u,* is like the *saw duang* except that the body is usually made of half a coconut shell. Other Chinese-style bowed chordophones with four strings and coconut-shell or cylindrical-shaped bodies also exist in Southeast Asia.

The basic styles of bowed lutes described above are graphic reflections of the confrontation of East and West in Southeast Asia; when the string pegs are inserted from the rear, the influence is clearly that of China, whereas lateral pegs mean a Moslem or Western origin. The term "Western" has been added because the origin of violin-like instruments in Asia is not always clear. A four-stringed violin held horizontally under the chin or at waist level is generally Western-derived when found in South or Southeast Asia. However, the ensembles of the Mon people of Burma use three-stringed fiddles which are held in a vertical position like the Near Eastern or Indonesian *rebab,* but because of their Western violin-shaped bodies, they look like North African *keman*—except for the special Southeast Asian designs on their scrolls. Organological diffusionism strikes again (along with the imagination of creative indigenous instrument makers)!

Though historically the ancient Mons seem to have used only percussion instruments, their present ensemble includes, besides two of the fascinating violins just mentioned, two small drums, an end-blown flute, and the *chakay* or *mi gyuan* crocodile zither (Plate III, Figure 8), a zoomorphic variant of the ubiquitous Southeast Asian plucked chordophone called in Thai the *chakay* (Plate XV, Figure 42). The latter is already familiar to us from similar instruments noted in Plate III from the Philippines (*kachapi*), Borneo (*kudyapi*), and Java (*kacapi*). India also may play a role in the labyrinthian search for the distribution of such an instrument. The manner in which the three gut strings of the Thailand *chakay* pass over high frets is reminiscent of the *vina,* though the *chakay* sound is less resonant, its playing style is less florid, and it is plucked by a pointed ivory dowel rather than by *vina*-like finger picks.

Another plucked chordophone found in *mahori* bands is the *grajappi* lute. This instrument has four strings in double courses and a long fretted neck whose thin, curved line forms a lovely visual image. The Cambodians make great use of this instrument under the name *chapey-thom.* The *dan nguyet* is a Vietnamese variant. Other Vietnamese lutes reflect Chinese origins, such as the four-stringed *dan ty ba,* which looks like the *p'ip'a* (Plate XVI, Figure 45), and the three-stringed *dan day,* which is a long necked version of the *yueh ch'in* (Plate XVII, Figure 49). Organological borders are never fixed, and the use of Western guitars and banjos has increased since the mid-twentieth century. One drum of particular interest is the single-headed pot-shaped *thom* or *thap,* which resembles the Near Eastern *tombak* (Plate VI, Figure 17).

Wind Ensembles and Instruments

The most famous wind ensemble of Southeast Asia consists of a group of *khaen* (*can* or *khen*). As seen in Plate XIV, Figure 40, the *khaen* is itself a kind of ensemble, since it can play chords and melody at the same time. It consists of from 6 to 16 long bamboo pipes (from 100 to 200 centimeters) joined in the center or bottom by a single wind chamber. Each pipe contains a single free reed that vibrates when a hole on the side of the pipe is closed. The harmonic, melodic, and drone aspects of *khaen* music can be seen in Example 5–4. Nasal breathing allows the performer to keep the air chamber filled and thus maintain the sound. When *khaen* are played in ensembles, the separate parts are primarily for reinforcement rather than for the addition of new polyphonic lines. The *khaen* is be-

EXAMPLE 5–4. A Thai *khaen* piece transcribed from the recording *Music of Thailand* (New York: Folkways Record FE 4463), side 1, band 1. By permission of Folkways Records and Service Corporation.

lieved to have originated in Laos, but as we saw in Borneo (p. 33) it is widespread throughout South Asia. In addition to being the predecessor of the Chinese *sheng* (Plate XVI, Figure 46), it may also be a distant precursor of the Western organ. In any event, it is one of the more complicated and widespread folk instruments of Southeast Asia. In its folk form, the pipes may stick out of one side (as in the *sheng*) rather than penetrate the gourd.

A variety of both horizontal and end-blown flutes exists in Southeast Asia. The latter include open-end and closed-end notched flutes as well as block flutes. In Thailand they all tend to fall under the term *khlui.* The Thai block flute is perhaps the best known ensemble aerophone, since it appears frequently in *mahori* orchestras. The opening of the block is at the back of the instrument rather than at the front (as on the Western recorder). In addition to six fingerholes, it has one hole that is covered with a thin membrane to create a soft buzzing sound.

Another important aerophone found in ensembles as well as in solo music is the *pi saw*, also called sometimes a *khlui.* A relative of the *khaen*, it consists of a single free metal reed inserted near the closed end on the side of a long bamboo pipe in which six or seven fingerholes have been drilled. The instrument is held sideways (somewhat like a horizontal flute) with the reed portion covered by the mouth. This instrument has a soft, clarinet-like tone and produces a pleasant buzzing resonance. It is commonly used for evening serenades in villages. It can be heard in the Laotian ensemble transcribed in Example 5–2. Mention has been made of the quadruple-reed aerophones, which seem to be another distinctive Southeast Asian organological contribution.

STRING MUSIC–SOLO, ACCOMPANIMENTAL, AND CHAMBER

One of the most lovely instrumental solo traditions of Southeast Asia is that of the *saung kauk* harp of Burma (Plate XV, Figure 41). It is used in classical music to accompany the simple *cho* songs as well as several more esoteric kinds of vocal music, such as the *yodaya.* The *yodaya* are based on a Thai style of song and use a different tuning, rhythmic mode, and melodic style from those of the *cho* songs. The tuning of the harp is changed by twisting the braids that attach its 14 (formerly 13) strings to the pole. The rhythmic changes in Burmese songs and harp music can best be heard by following the sounds of a pair of small hand

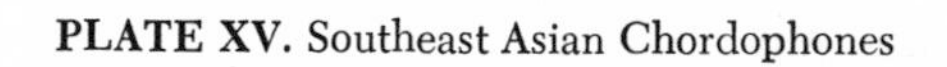

PLATE XV. Southeast Asian Chordophones

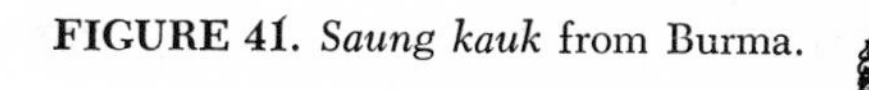

FIGURE 41. *Saung kauk* from Burma.

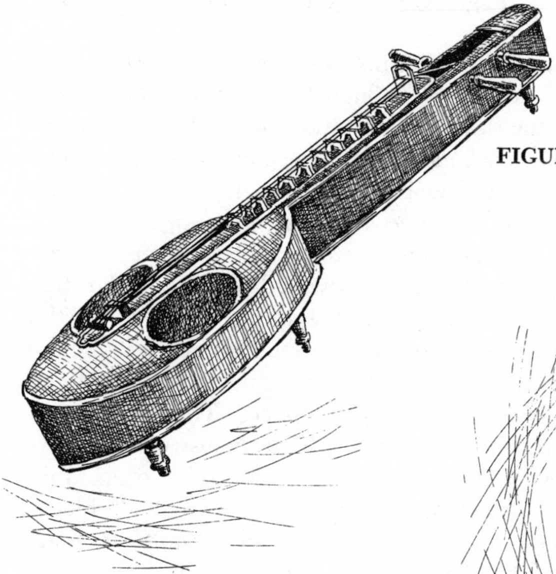

FIGURE 42. *Chakay* from Thailand.

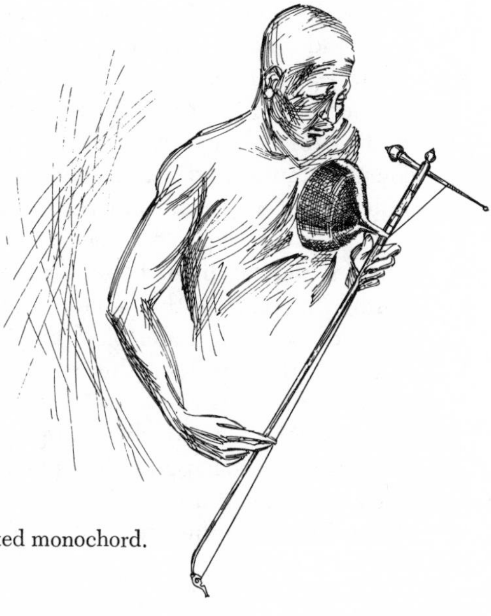

FIGURE 43. A chest-resonated monochord.

bells (*si*) and a clapper (*wa*), which keep the beat much as do the *talam* cymbals of India. Melodic differences in harp music can be found by studying the various principles of modes and modulations discussed earlier in this chapter as they apply to the two Burmese harp song traditions. Extended instrumental interludes in these songs reveal a great interest in melodic variation and extension.

The origins of the Burmese harp have been traced to ancient India, but a living Asiatic tradition of harp music is now unique to Burma. The audiences who sit all night in a Buddhist temple compound to hear it, as well as the rows of young ladies at the National Music Institute in Rangoon who diligently practice it in ensemble, are perhaps only faintly aware of how rare this music is. If it survives Burma's period of modernization, it will be one of the last classical harp traditions remaining from the ancient world.

Many of the instruments of the classical orchestras of Southeast Asia have a solo literature. The Mon *mi gyaun* and the Thai *chakay* and *grajappi* are good examples. Much of the solo and chamber music of this area, however, is really an arrangement of or accompaniment to vocal music.

One of the most exotic solo string instruments used to accompany the voice is the monochord called in Thailand the *phin nam tao* (Plate XV, Figure 43). As seen in the drawing, the resonance of the instrument is enhanced by placing the open back of its hemispherical body against the singer's chest. A similar instrument is found in Africa. In Vietnam there is a monochord called the *dan doc huyen* or *dan bau* that uses a standard wooden body as a resonator but stretches its string between the body and a flexible vertical stick. The pitch is varied by pulling the stick sideways to increase or lessen the tension on the string, somewhat in the manner one plays tunes on a rubber band. The monochords, plus many of the other strings of Southeast Asia, have their basic repertoire in the courting music and other social music of the villages. They have been joined in recent decades by the guitar and other Western instruments.

Outside the West, the borderline between orchestral and chamber music is very indistinct, for, as we have seen, many "orchestral" pieces can be played by rather small ensembles. One can find in Southeast Asia, however, separate repertoires of pieces created specifically for ensembles of two or three people; this can truly be called chamber music, although the relation of parts, as with the music for larger groups, is basically heterophonic. One lovely example is the Vietnamese trio consisting of a two-string pear-shaped guitar (*ty ba*), a flute (*dich*), and a sixteen-string plucked zither (*tranh*). This trio, like much of Vietnam's music, reflects a strong Chinese influence.

SACRED AND SECULAR VOCAL MUSIC

We have already noted that much Southeast Asian instrumental music is used for vocal accompaniment. In addition, there is a rich heritage of narrative musics not directly connected with theatricals. Some are purely vocal, such as the Thai *say pha,* in which the performer accompanies himself with four sticks clicked together like castenets. Other narrators use string instruments for ostinato-like backgrounds, and heterophony may also appear; it is found, for example, in survivals of *selampit* narrations in Malaysia, which reflect Moslem influence in their heterophony and their accompaniment by the *rebab* spike fiddle or sometimes the *serunai* oboe. Heterophony can also be found in certain Chinese-based forms, particularly in Vietnam.

Southeast Asian poetry may be recited in a musical fashion, although, as in the Near East, such performances may not be classified as music. From what was said in Chapter 3, one knows that "reading" the Koran in Malaysia is not music, though singing *hadrah* or *rodat* poems in praise of the Holy Prophet to the accompaniment of a *rebana* tambourine is a legitimate Malaysian Islamic activity. Unaccompanied praise poems sung by female attendants in Thai or other courts are considered music, as are survivals of earlier court musics such as the North Vietnamese *hat a dao* poems. *Hat a dao* singers remaining today play a rhythmic accompaniment with sticks on a *phach* related to the so-called Chinese wood block, while a long-necked three-stringed *dan day* plucked lute supplies a melody to which the singer adds refined ornamentations. Unison choral singing is heard in some *mahori* pieces and the *zikirbarat* or *dikirbarat* tradition of Malaysia, in which by call-and-response two groups are led by a soloist in matching the verses or retorts of their competitors. Such song contests are found in many forms in Southeast Asia. Perhaps the most unusual mass choral sound of the area is that of the Ma'yong drama of northern Malaysia. A highly melismatic, heterophonic duet between a singer and a *rebab,* accompanied by interlocking *gendang* drum parts and two gongs, is followed by a dance section in which all the performers on stage sing their own melismatic versions of the tune. The resultant massive proliferation of pitches and lines seems to be a unique form of disphony even in the context of mid-twentieth century European choral experiments. Southeast Asian singing in large groups is heard more often in religious chanting, generally in unison or organum-like forms. The majority of these chants are, like most liturgical music, *centric melodies;* that is, they center on one tone and use other tones to surround it. The styles of Southeast Asian religious musics usually reflect the cultural origin of the faith (Chinese Buddhism, Indian Hinduism, Near Eastern Islam, and Western Christianity), though there are many interesting mixtures, such as the *caodai* of Vietnam.[5] The most accessible indigenous religious music of Southeast Asia is perhaps the dream songs of village clairvoyants: personal problems of life and love being presented to these seers, they go into a trance and then through song relate the advice of the supernatural. With such music we touch on our next topic—folk music.

FOLK AND TRIBAL MUSIC

The dream songs mentioned above are found throughout Southeast Asia in the urban, rural, and back-country areas. Other forms of shamanism are equally widespread, their musical and ceremonial styles depending heavily on local influences. For example, a *put(e)ri* shaman of northern Malaysia villages may use instruments and tune names of Ma'yong drama while dancing with Thai-inspired movements before whirling his (or her) head in a Near Eastern style in order to go into a trance and become the spirit of illness.

The functions of other Southeast Asian folk songs are generally less complex, as in the many lullabies, love songs, and work songs. They often use the anhemitonic pentatonic scale. The kind of voice quality with which they are sung varies from a very high-pitched nasal sound to a rather soft, low crooning. In general, the higher, more tense voice qualities reflect classical influence; but folk songs and tribal musics are often no respecters of modern national boundaries, and little can be said at present about the many different styles of music that exist, particularly those behind the jungle walls. (This, however, reflects our lack of knowledge rather than a lack of variety.) Even the apparent functions of such musics may be deceptive. For example, among the Pwo Karen people of North Thailand, funeral songs are actually considered to be primarily social because they offer the best opportunities for young men and women to meet and flirt. In Vietnam, sets of bamboo tubes may be found activated by irrigation water, not only to scare away birds but also to clink out tunes entertaining to the gods and to the workers.

Bamboo and cane stamping-tubes, trumpets, panpipes, and flutes (including nose flutes) are as common in continental Southeast Asia as they are in New Guinea (cf. p. 15). The presence of these instrument

[5] Religious music in Southeast Asia is discussed in Volume 1 of *Encyclopédie des Musiques Sacrées* (Paris: Labergerie, 1968).

types, however, reflects the importance of local ecology in organological development more than indicating possible diffusions of cultures. By the same token, drums may be laced more often with rattan than rawhide, and the tension increased with wooden wedges rather than with metal screws. Southeast Asian jungle drums most often have single, laced heads and hourglass-form or extended, pot-shaped bodies, though there are two-headed barrel drums that seem related to the Indonesian *gendang*. Perhaps the most intriguing item of diffusionist potential is the knobbed bronze gong, which is as equally prized in tribal Southeast Asia as it is in the Indonesian archipelago (cf. p. 37). The origin of such an instrument is controversial, as is that of the Southeast Asian flat-surfaced gong with wide, slightly concave sides. Sometimes the latter has frog figurines or other animals etched into its surface or attached to its rim. It is played like a drum or suspended like a gong and seems related to a very ancient Chinese bronze drum. It may, however, be either a survival of that tradition or a predecessor of it, for later tenth-century Chinese military expeditions into Southeast Asia found such instruments quite "exotic" with their magical sounds of the bullfrog.[6] The *khaen* kind of mouth organ has already been mentioned as another historical mystery. Many plucked lutes in the northern tribes of Southeast Asia, by contrast, seem clearly derived from China. Obviously there is much to learn from Southeast Asian tribal music beyond its melodies and social functions. Some of its oral history and literature has been passed on to theater traditions.

THEATRICAL, RURAL, AND POPULAR MUSIC

Theatrical music in Southeast Asia has a long tradition going back to dance dramas depicted in ancient stone reliefs such as those of Angkor Wat in Cambodia. We have already shown that the *pi phat* and *mahori* ensembles can be used to accompany modern versions of these old classical dramas. Rural and urban theatricals such as the *lakon* tradition of Thailand deal with a variety of folkloric or topical events and use more modest accompaniments. Characteristic *lakon* ensembles include drums, gongs, and clacking bamboo sticks, the tunes being carried by an oboe, xylophone, gong circle, or bowed lute, alone or in combination. *Lakon* are often performed at temples, for their function is semi-religious, though their actions may become very secular and comic. The Ma'yong drama of northern Malaysia also seems to be based on religious needs,

[6] See Edward Schafer, *The Vermilion Bird* (Berkeley: University of California Press, 1967), p. 254.

but it is thoroughly secular now. Its musical style, mentioned earlier (p. 133), may imply a Moslem influence in this border area of Buddhism.

Music for the Southeast Asian puppet theater reflects further relations between music and theater and secular and sacred life. The major divisions of Burmese orchestral music, for example, are between *zat pwe* for secular entertainment and *yokthe pwe* for the puppet theater. In contrast to its Indonesian counterpart, the major melodic instrument for continental puppetry is one of the quadruple reed family. Most puppet ensembles include one or two drummers and some form of gongs. Drums and oboe are standard accompaniments for fight dances and cock fights as well. Very different sounds come from the theatricals supported by Chinese and Indian populations in Southeast Asia, while itinerant singers are found commonly discussing topical matters in patter songs often accompanied by a *khaen*-type mouth organ. Of course, standard popular and movie-industry musical products are ever–present, though regional compromises are found in Southeast Asia between indigenous and Western idioms like those mentioned in Chapter 3 (p. 81). In Malaysia, as in Indonesia (cf. p. 38), old forms of Portuguese popular music survive in a very localized style. Malaysian *dodang sayang* are sung in an Indonesian *kroncong* melismatic style to the accompaniment of a Western violin (or a *rebab*), an Arab tambourine and pot drum, and Southeast Asian knobbed gongs. Similar ensembles can be found accompanying Malaysian *ronggeng* and *joget* social dances. Such dances are often in quadrille or line form like those of the Philippines or rural Euro-America. The dances themselves differ from their Western counterparts in several ways. As in most Southeast Asian couple dances, the partners never touch, a preference adopted in Euro-American culture only since the 1950's. Unlike the Western preference for hip movements, the Malaysian and other Southeast Asian emphases are on movements of the feet and torso and on delicate hand gestures derived from classical Southeast Asian dance traditions. Urban dance halls, however, reflect whatever the latest Euro-American fad may be. Though national pride has sometimes aided regional traditions, it usually results in military bands and Western orchestras and choruses, along with an urban interest in jazz. Urban comic theater is dominated by Western and Chinese instruments, and the latest pentatonic popular tune may be played by saxophones and trumpets with chordal accompaniment. All this apparent potpourri reinforces the maxim that musical culture is never completely static. When one hears a piano played in the manner of a native xylophone (*Burmese Folk,* Folkways P 436, side 2, band 9), there is hope that all the foreign importations have not yet deadened the native to the charms of his own indigenous styles.

BIBLIOGRAPHICAL AND DISCOGRAPHICAL NOTES

Trân-Văn-Khê's *La Musique Vietnamienne Traditionelle* (Paris: Presses Universitaires de France, 1962) is recommended. Pham Duy's *Musics of Vietnam* (Carbondale, Ill.: Southern Illinois University Press, 1975) adds history and some song texts in translation. David Morton's translation of Dhanit Yupho's *Thai Musical Instruments* (Bangkok: Department of Fine Arts, 1960) is helpful, as are several brief studies by Jacques Brunet in *Traditional Drama and Music of Southeast Asia,* ed. Mohd. Taib Osman (Kuala Lumpur, Malaysia: Dewan Bahasa dan Pustaka, 1974). William P. Malm's "Music in Kelantan, Malaysia, and Some of its Cultural Implications," in *Studies in Malaysian Oral and Musical Traditions* (Michigan Papers on South and Southeast Asia, no. 8, 1974), may prove useful, as may Judith Becker's straightforward analytical study, "Music of the Pwo Karen of Northern Thailand," *Ethnomusicology,* VIII/2 (1964), and her more linguistic analytical approach to Burmese harp music in "The Anatomy of a Mode," *Ethnomusicology,* XIII/2 (1969). Becker's "Percussion Patterns in the Music of Mainland Southeast Asia," *Ethnomusicology,* XII/2 (1968), is brilliant. An informative study by Ms. R. C. Williamson is "The Construction and Decoration of the Burmese Harp," in *Selected Reports,* Institute of Ethnomusicology (U.C.L.A.), I/2 (1968), 45–77.

The UNESCO Musicaphon series of records edited by Alain Danielou is consistently useful for Southeast Asia; examples from the series include *Laos* (BM 30 L 2001), *Cambodia* (BM 30 L 2002), *Vietnam* (BM 30 L 2022), and *Malaysia* (BM 30 L 2026). Stephen Addiss has provided *Music from North and South Vietnam* (Folkways AHM 4219) and *Folksongs of Viet Nam* (Folkways FTS 31303), and Jacques Brunet has produced an *Anthologie de la musique du Cambodge* (Ducrete-Thomson DUC 20–22). Other Folkways offerings are *Folk and Traditional Music of Burma* (FE 4436), *Music from South Asia* (FE 4447), *Music of Thailand* (FE 4463), and, from Malaysia, *Temiar Dream Music* (FE 4460). William P. Malm produced *The Music of Malaysia* (Anthology AST 4006).

SIX
EAST ASIA

Geographically, "East Asia" in this survey will be restricted to the Asian mainland area from Tibet in the South to Mongolia and Manchuria in the north, with all of China proper in the center. The common bond shared by the many ethnic peoples of this vast area is that of Chinese culture or its strong influence. This is true of Korea and Japan as well, but they will be treated separately along with the most northern cultures in the subsequent chapter on Northeast Asia and the islands.

TIBET

Locked in its mountain fastness, Tibet has often seemed to Westerners to be the very symbol of an ancient, unchanging, Shangri-la world. Historically, however, the culture of Tibet has been altered periodically by influences from India, China, Mongolia, and perhaps even the West. Before the introduction to Tibet of Indian Buddhism in the seventh century, there seems to have been an indigenous religion called *bon,* whose music influenced the newer tradition and may still survive in Tibetan shaman traditions.

Although Buddhist writings are known to have existed in Tibet by the third century A.D., it was only in the seventh and eighth centuries that Buddhism began to have an impact on Tibetan rulers. Large monasteries were established in the eleventh and twelfth centuries, and by the seventeenth century Lamaistic Buddhism became a politico-religious force so dominant that Tibet's unique theocracy was able to remain intact until the Chinese invasion of 1950.

As does any large religious tradition, Buddhism has various sects, and within such sects in Tibet and among exiled Tibetan communities around the world there are different schools. The core of Tibetan religious music is chant (*dbyangs*), normally sung to a very low pitch. To the Westerner, the most astounding form is one used by some schools of the Gelgpa sect; in this chant the monks not only produce a fundamental tone some two octaves below middle C but at the same time reinforce the partials above, so that the tone is extremely "rich," and a note like E above middle C seems actually to be sounding at the same time.[1] Such a "throat" tone or "split" tone gives the impression that a single person is singing a chord. (We shall note related phenomena in Mongolia and Siberia.) The function of this unusual musical phenomenon is religious. In most world music cultures one finds that man does not communicate with God in the same voice he uses for his fellow beings. In Tibet, these seemingly non-melodic chants not only are intended to communicate with God and his helpers but to offer the performer a possible path out of the objective world towards inner transformation and eventual enlightenment. The challenging low pitch and the frequent clouding of the sung text with extra syllables serve as protection for these goals. The proper and safe use of such ritual material must be limited, in the Tibetan view, to those who truly understand its meaning and its power.

Since the function of Tibetan chant is obviously specific but esoteric, notated song books (*dbyangs-yig* or *yany-yig*) were evolved to help the singing master pass on the tradition with accuracy.[2] The form of notation is basically *neumatic*—that is, it uses single signs (neumes) to stand for a group of notes. This contrasts with the other two common forms of music notation in the world, the *graphic* and the *tablature.* A graphic system indicates the height of pitches (an example is Western

[1] This can be heard on *Tibet* (Anthology Records AST 4005).

[2] For details see Walter Kaufmann, *Tibetan Buddhist Chant* (Bloomington: Indiana University Press, 1975).

staff notation); this is found in Tibetan instrumental notation along with rhythmic signs, though much of this notation is more a graphic memory aid than a specific notation.[3] The tablature method indicates notes or fingerings on an instrument; it is more common in China or Japan and is found in the Western plucked-lute traditions.

Tibetan chant can be accompanied by a variety of instruments, the simplest being the *dril-bu* hand bell. This bell is found in all Buddhist countries, its shape remaining amazingly consistent from Ceylon and Bali to China and Japan. Another common Tibetan idiophone is a pair of cymbals (*sil-snyan* or *rol-mo*).[4] In some monasteries special signals for events of the day may be made by striking a wooden board (*gandi*) balanced on the left shoulder and struck with a wooden beater.[5] Although wooden "gongs" (*sumantran*) have been found in European Christian communities, and hanging wooden signalling devices are common in Buddhist temples of East and Northeast Asia, this portable form (with spiritual as well as functional connotations) seems unique to South Asian and Tibetan Buddhism.

Among the several membranophones of Tibetan religious music, two are characteristic. One is the *lag-rnga* (sometimes also called the *rnga-chung*), a large, two-headed tacked barrel drum set on the end of a pole which the player grips as he beats on one head with a curved stick. The other smaller, hourglass-shaped drum is also called the *rnga-chung* (which means "small drum") but the Indian name *damaru* is quite common; if the two attached hemispheres which form the body are made of human craniums, the drum may be called the *thod-dam*. This instrument is sounded by knobs or knots at the end of two strips of cloth that are attached to the waist of the drum so that the knobs strike alternate heads when the drum is twisted back and forth in the hand. Shamans often use this instrument.

The most spectacular Tibetan ritual instruments are long copper trumpets (*dung-chen*, "long trumpet," or *rag-dung*, "copper trumpet"). These straight, conical-bore natural horns vary in length from some 1½ to 70 meters. Many are made in sections that can be telescoped for portability. Each horn has a fairly shallow cup mouthpiece and, like the Western bugle, is capable of producing different tones. The basic use of

[3] The author is particularly grateful to Ivan Vandor for bringing this system to his attention and for further comments on the Tibetan musical traditions. Examples of the instrumental notation can be seen in Vandor's "La notazione musicale strumentale del buddismo Tibetano," *Nuova Rivista Musicale Italiana* VII/3, 4 (1973).

[4] There is considerable controversy over the romanization and pronunciation of Tibetan terms, depending on one's choice of monastic language or people's language. We use here one common monastic approach.

[5] For details and a photograph see Ivan Vandor, "The Gandi . . .," *The World of Music,* XVII/1 (1975).

these horns is not to play fanfares, but to be part of the instrumentation of ritual music. Smaller hand trumpets have dragon heads at the bell end; the players of these tend to concentrate on one note, from which they slide up and down. The shamans of Tibet use short trumpets made of human leg-bones. Criminals' bones are preferred because of their close connection with Tibet's many devils, which need to be placated. The conch-shell trumpet is also found in Tibet.

The only melodic instrument in Tibetan religious orchestras is the double-reed *surna,* called *rgya-gling* in the monasteries. It plays preludes and interludes to the chants, but not the chants themselves.

The best opportunity to hear Tibetan music in all its splendor is during the annual *cham* festival. For three days, actors in gorgeous costumes and fearsome *papier-mâché* heads perform an involved religious dance-drama to the accompaniment of a variety of instrumental combinations chosen from the instruments listed above. Whether a festival event is held in public or within the confines of a monastery, the music structure is generally percussion-accompanied singing alternating with instrumental interludes. The secular dances and historical plays of Tibet tend to use drums and cymbals for accompaniment. The influence of Tibetan culture on neighboring countries such as Sikkim and Nepal and the increase in expatriate Tibetan refugee communities since the middle of the twentieth century have naturally led to many variants on the traditions mentioned above; it may be, however, that through marginal survival many of the older forms of Tibetan religious music and Tibetan dance-drama can still be found in communities as distant as Switzerland.

So far, no Tibetan string instruments have been mentioned, because they are not used in Tibetan religious music. In secular music, one finds a four-string, bowed *gophong* modelled after the Mongolian horsehead fiddle (see p. 143). Example 6–1 shows the beginnings of two songs accompanied by the *dram-synan,* a plucked lute with five or six strings, tuned in thirds with some in double courses; the precise string arrangement and size varies among villages and districts. In these Tibetan folk dance examples, the *dram-synan* creates an isometric ostinato, against which the singers produce a stepwise heterometric melody.

While most Tibetan folk songs use the whole-step pentatonic scale, the two excerpts in Example 6–1 show that other, quite different tonal systems also appear. Example 6–1A makes striking use of the tritone (G to D♭) and exploits harmony in seconds at each cadence. Example 6–1B shows a melody built basically in a chain of thirds[6] (G to B♭ to D to F) in a manner quite different from Example 6–1A. In both songs the tonal vocabulary of the singers seems to be independent of that of the instru-

[6] For a discussion of melody-building with various interval chains, see Curt Sachs, *The Wellsprings of Music* (The Hague: Nijhoff) 1962, 143–67.

EXAMPLE 6–1. Two Tibetan folk dance excerpts from the recording *Songs and Music of Tibet* (New York: Folkways Record FE 4486), side 1, bands 5 and 2 (fourth entrance). By permission of Folkways Records and Service Corporation.

ment. This curious bitonality is common in many countries' folk dances accompanied by both voices and instruments. It may be that the rhythmic structure of the instrumental part is the clue to the existence of this bitonality (rather like the contour of some Indonesian *gamelan* melodies; see p. 47). With such a function, the relation of the instrument's pitches to those of the melodic line could be irrelevant, although the overall structure of the musical event is quite logical.

Since researchers have had to rely primarily on materials from border peoples, caravans, and refugees coming out of Tibet, little can be said about idiomatic aspects of Tibetan folk style. There seems to be frequent use of antiphonal singing in dance pieces, as in Example 6–1. But as yet the space age still knows little about the music of the land nearest the sky.

MONGOLIA

If we move down from the mountains of Tibet and out onto the steppes and deserts along China's western border, we find the tribal remnants of the Mongol Empire. In ancient times, these hardy horsemen made their fame in the art of war rather than music; but even in war, drums and bugles were used for signalling. In the thirteenth century Marco Polo mentions a battle before which both sides sang. The signal for the start of the battle was given on a large kettledrum with the familiar name of *nagarah* (see *naqqara*, p. 62).

Although the Mongolian nomadic people were strong militarily, they were always susceptible to outside cultural influences. Today their western tribes are influenced by Islamic culture, while Lamaistic Buddhism and Chinese culture dominate in the East. An indigenous shamanistic tradition survives in a few songs found in present collections, though the shaman and his drum can best be found further north in Manchuria and Siberia, as well as across the Bering Straits in Alaska and Canada (see p. 209).

The musical legacy of the Mongols is found today primarily in their folk music, known generically as *duun*. This music can be divided into several types of songs according to subject matter, such as spiritual songs, songs about the heroic deeds of the days of the great Khans, contemporary political songs, and epic narratives (*uliger*). While the political songs tend to be sung by unison chorus, the most common Mongolian performance practice is for one singer to accompany himself on the *khil-khuur* bowed lute. This fiddle has a flat trapezoid body with sheepskin covering both the front and back. It has two strings tuned in fifths. The pegbox is often topped with the carving of a horse's head in a manner similar to the carving on the *gusle* fiddles of the Yugoslavian epic singers.

There seem to be two common styles of folk singing in Mongolia. One is in an even *tempo giusto*, usually isometric; the other is in a *parlando-rubato* style. In both styles, the relation of the voice to the accompaniment tends to be heterophonic. The *parlando-rubato* pieces make extensive use of melismatic improvisations in both the vocal and instrumental parts. Thus, though the songs tend to be strophic, there is considerable variation between each strophe. In the study of such variant strophic music it is often useful to construct a comparative score;[7] in this

[7] Such a score can be seen in the Indian excerpt of Example 4–6. Mongolian songs in comparative scores are found in Ernst Emshiemer, *The Music of the Mongols*, Publication 21, VIII, Part 4 of *The Sino-Swedish Expedition*, Dr. Sven Hedin, director (Stockholm: Thule, 1943), 22–35.

way one can quickly see the areas of similarity and difference. No notation, however, can successfully symbolize the low yodel (ululation) that is characteristic of the Mongolian manner of singing these songs.

In Mongolia one finds another version of the split-tone singing noted earlier in Tibet. Since this fascinating tradition is found also among other Central Asian and Siberian groups such as the Tuvinian, Oirats, and Bashkirs, we shall discuss it for all of them at this time.[8] The use in the secular music of these peoples of a fundamental tone plus various partials tends to follow two methods. From the few examples heard from Mongolia, it would seem that a melody is sung in a rather low, rough tone, and then prolonged cadence notes are "split" so that arpeggios can be performed by reinforcing such partials as the sixth through tenth and the twelfth. This would mean that, if the fundamental were C two octaves below middle C, the arpeggio could use G above middle C plus B♭, C, D, E, and G above that.[9] The second method seems to concentrate on melodies growing directly out of the overtones, which can be enriched by moving the fundamental to a different pitch. Though some twentieth-century European composers have tried this kind of sound production, it is only in Central and North Asia that it has been established as a popular musical style.

Returning to Mongolia, one finds a few Central Asian plucked lutes, plus Chinese-style violins and flutes. With the increase of government controls in both China and Outer Mongolia during the mid-twentieth century, there has been a tendency to form State Folk Ensembles whose music seems more reminiscent of Rimsky-Korsakov than of the great Khans. However, there are still Mongolian bards practicing their solo art. Though they may now sing about the new ponies on the collective farm, there is much of the Asian steppes tradition left in their performance style.

CHINA

Organized civilizations of Mongoloid peoples have occupied the Chinese mainland continuously since at least 3000 B.C. By the time of their first verified dynasty, the Shang (1766–1122 B.C.), they were already using a writing system that, unlike the ancient scripts of the Egyptians and the Sumerians, related directly to the system used by their modern

[8] For more detail see A. N. Aksenov, "Tuvin Folk Music," *Asian Music,* IV/2 (1973), translated by Mark Slobin.

[9] Though neither a Mongolian nor a Tuvinian, I find that placing the tone in the throat, curling the tongue against the roof of the mouth, and shaping the mouth cavity and lips correctly seems to generate most of the pitches described.

descendants. Thus, one finds in China a tradition of amazing age and continuity which, with a great interest in history and respect for the written word, has left a vast legacy of information about the ways of Chinese civilization over a period of some three thousand years of actual history, plus another two or three thousand years of legend and pseudo-history. Within the thousands of volumes of ancient Chinese history, philosophy, and literature that have survived to the present day, there are many scattered references to music. A composite of these sources gives us many details concerning the history, theory, instrumentation, and uses of music throughout the ages. Unfortunately, it tells us nothing about the sound of ancient Chinese music. Thus, both Western and Oriental scholars tend to concentrate on the history of Chinese music to the neglect and often the disparagement of its living tradition. The present survey, reflecting the historical orientation of available material, is organized into four general periods: the formative (third millennium B.C. through the fourth century A.D.); the international (fifth century to the tenth); the national (the tenth through the nineteenth centuries); and the period of world music (the twentieth century). The first section deals primarily with the theoretical foundations of Chinese music; sections of the second and most of the third periods will concentrate on history; only in materials since the seventeenth century will we begin to say something about the actual music. Compared to the scope of Chinese history, this last section is a tiny period, though in relation to the history of Western music it covers the time from Bach to the present. An overview of Chinese music is obviously a study for a lifetime, but perhaps some of the grandeur of its history and the richness of its surviving traditions can be discerned in the discussions that follow.

The Formative Period (*Third Millennium* B.C. to *Fourth Century* A.D.)

The earliest musical artifacts in China date from around 1000 B.C.; they consist of rounded clay ocarinas and stone chimes. Instruments of less durable material no doubt existed before this time, but the oldest Chinese writings list only a few of the instruments of the early Chou period (1122–221 B.C.). These writings also mention folk festivals, for ancient China seemed always to be interested in ceremonies, particularly those dealing with divination and the honoring of ancestors. Thus it is not surprising that one of the first extensive discussions of music is found in the second-century B.C. *Book of Rites*. The other famous Chinese classics of this period that deal with history and court activities also contain scattered references to music, while the poetry collection, the *Book of Odes*, has many texts that seem, originally, to have been sung. The teachings of

Confucius (551–479 B.C.) likewise make frequent mention of music, primarily because, like the philosophers of other ancient civilizations, Confucius considered the performance of music to be an ethical as well as pleasurable experience. From all these sources four basic kinds of information emerge: (1) the mythological origins of music; (2) the theoretical basis of Chinese music; (3) the instruments of the court; and (4) the relation of music to court life and ritual in the Chou and later the Han (third century B.C. to 220 A.D.) dynasties. These four areas will form the basis of our discussions of the foundations of Chinese music.

The most famous legend concerning the origin of Chinese music says that around 2697 B.C. a certain Ling Lun was sent by an emperor, Huang-ti, to the western mountains to cut bamboo pipes (*lü's*) from which the fundamental pitches of music could be derived. The legend is interesting in three respects. First, it places the origins of music at the western borders, where so many other new ideas have crossed over into China. Secondly, the concern of the emperor to secure proper fundamental pitches reflects indirectly the close relationship of early Chinese music to ritual and to the extra-musical, for, in China, setting a proper pitch meant literally putting music in tune with the various forces of the universe. Further proof of this relationship is seen in the fact that a new emperor traditionally ordered his musicians and astrologers to work together on re-calculating the length of the imperial pitch pipes so that his reign would harmonize with all the elements of nature and supernature. This reflection of the natural order of the universe in the arts remained fundamental to Chinese music speculations until very recent times.

The third point of interest that stems from the legend of the *lü's* is that Chou and Han dynasty writers used these pipes as the basis for an elaborate tone system that still strongly influences Chinese music. The Near Eastern and Indian tone systems studied earlier were *divisive*, that is, they were based on the divisions of a vibrating string (on the *'ud* and *vina* respectively). The Chinese system, by contrast, was *cyclic*. It was created from a cycle of tones generated by blowing across the tops of a set of tubes closed at one end (like a bottle), whose lengths were arranged in a set mathematical proportion.

The pitch produced by the first tube was called the Yellow Bell (*huang chung*). This does not mean it was played on a bell; it was merely a name for that pitch—as, for example, the pitch vibrating 440 times a second is called in the West "A." For the sake of comparison with other material in this book, we shall call the Yellow Bell pitch middle C, though traditionally it is placed on the F above that. Additional tones are produced by constructing tubes that are alternately ⅔ and 4/3 the length of their previous tube. The acoustical basis for this method is the principle of the *overblown fifth*—that is, by blowing hard on the first tube, a tone

one fifth higher (G in our series) is produced. A tube ⅓ shorter than the first one will produce this G without overblowing. If this second tube is overblown, the note D appears in an upper register, as shown in Example 6–2. The note D is played more easily an octave lower on a pipe ⅓ longer

EXAMPLE 6–2. The Chinese *lü* system.

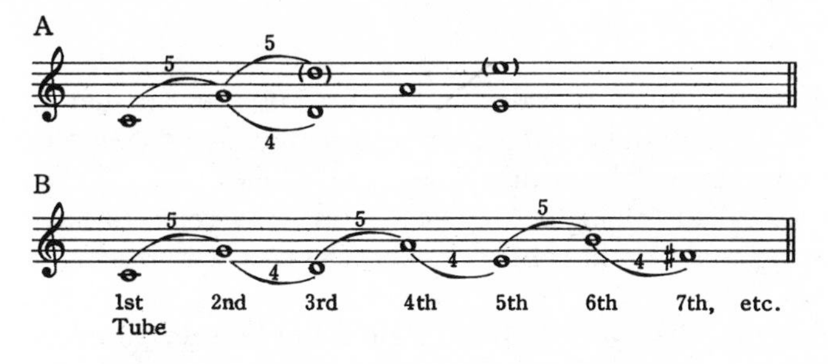

than the second pipe. A pipe ⅓ shorter than the D pipe produces an A, and a pipe ⅓ longer than the A pipe produces an E at the lower octave. When these tones are written in the manner in which they were generated, one sees that they follow a pattern going up a fifth and down a fourth, as shown in Example 6–2. Chinese theoreticians first carried this process through twelve tubes, but only the first five were needed to illustrate the fundamental five tones (*wu sheng*) of Chinese music. This pentatonic scale—which no doubt existed in China long before Chinese science found a way of explaining its origin—is shown in Example 6–3, along with the Chinese names for each scale degree. These names—like the Western *do, re, mi*—indicate positions in the scale rather than specific pitches (such as middle C or *huang chung*). The actual pitches produced by the full set of twelve *lü's* have specific names (like Yellow Bell, Forest Bell, and the like).[10] When the Chinese arrange them in ascending order

[10] The various names attached to pitches by the Chinese may have had specific acoustical-scientific meanings. See Fritz Kuttner, "A Musicological Interpretation of the Twelve Lüs in China's Traditional Tone System," *Ethnomusicology,* IX/1 (1965). The romanization of Chinese terms in this chapter is the so-called Wade-Giles system most commonly used in Western publications. The non-specialist reader cannot be expected to respond to those tonal aspects of the language that appear in this system. Readers should note, however, that an apostrophe before a consonant maintains its general English-language sound, but that without the apostrophe some of the pronunciations are as follows: ch = j, k = g, p = b, and t = d. The new romanization system adopted by the government of China reflects these and other pronunciation differences more clearly but is not yet seen frequently in European-language publications. At the end of this chapter there is a comparative list which may prove helpful in pronunciation and in the reading of future publications. The author is particularly grateful to Professor James Dew and James Crump of the University of Michigan Far Eastern Language Department for assistance in this and other technical aspects of the section of this book on China.

EXAMPLE 6–3. The basic Chinese scale system and its changing tones.

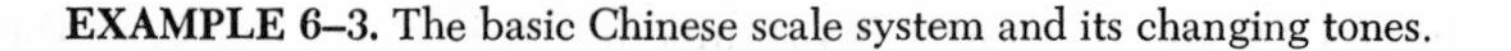

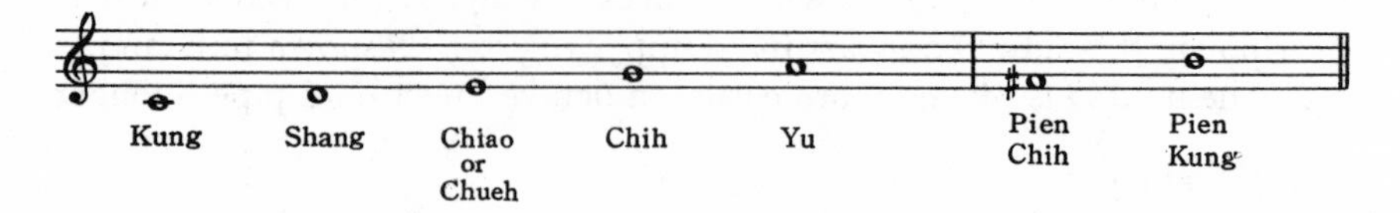

they look like a Western chromatic scale, but they are not; they are merely a listing of all the tonal material available for constructing five-note scales or modes within these scales. The sixth and seventh *lü* tones (F♯ and B in Example 6–3) were called "changing" (*pien*) tones; they seem to have been used as passing tones or to achieve modal changes within a basic five-tone framework.

As implied above, the five-tone basic scale could be transposed by putting the note *kung* on any one of the twelve *lü* pitches and thence constructing a five-tone scale in the proper interval sequence. It was also possible to construct modes within each one of these transposed pentatonic scales. Chinese music theorists, like their Near Eastern and Indian counterparts, continued over the centuries to create ever more elaborate systems. The fact that the *lü* system created acoustically perfect (untempered) but musically inconvenient pitches caused other Chinese scholars to struggle with the problem of tempered tuning. Some attempts seem to date from as early as the sixth century A.D., and the system later adopted in the West first appears in China in the writings of the sixteenth-century Prince Chu Tsai-yü (*circa* 1596). All these noble experiments seem to have had little effect on the actual condition of Chinese music. It remained untempered and pentatonic even though the diatonic seven-tone scale was described in the fifth-century *History of Later Han* and in T'ang period (618–907) sources, and tempered tuning was introduced in the Ch'ing period (1644–1911).

It is important to keep the basic pentatonic scale in mind, for many studies list notes in larger scale-like orders, either for the sake of theoretical speculations or to illustrate extra-musical, nonscalar relationships. For example, the twelve chromatic *lü* tones have been divided into two six-tone series according to whether they are generated by going up a fifth or down a fourth (see Example 6–2). The main function of such a listing is to organize the tones of Chinese music along the lines of the female-male (*yin* and *yang*) principles of Chinese metaphysics. Thus, the legends explain that the notes of the upper series are those sung by the male phoenix bird, the lower series those of the female. The influence of such symbolic structures is seen in some of the imperial panpipes (*p'ai hsiao*) in which the male and female pipes are arranged separately, outward from the middle of the instrument rather than in ascending order. *Yin* and *yang* tones also tended to be arranged separately in the racks of sixteen bronze bells (*pien chung*) and similar sets of stone chimes (*pien ch'ing*) so popular in Chou court orchestras.

The twelve tones themselves were supposedly created in order to provide a cosmologically correct *kung* tone for the proper scale to be used in each of the twelve months or the twelve hours. The five tones, in turn, were connected with the five directions, the five elements, and many other qualities in a manner that reminds us of the other great musico-philosophical constructs of Asia and the Near East.

The importance of music as a reflection of the natural philosophy and orderly penchants of Chinese thought has been much emphasized in the writings on ancient Chinese music. This plethora of legendary analogies, however, has combined with the pictographic nature of the Chinese language to cloud the fact that the ancient Chinese were skilled, knowledgeable acousticians. Many of the fanciful legends and terms are actually ancient ways of reporting important scientific and musical findings derived from controlled, empirical experiments. At least two thousand years ago, Chinese scientists knew as much about soundproof research laboratories, the laws of vibrations, and tuning as did Western scientists at the turn of the present century.

Like the Greek theoretical foundations of Western music, many of the early Chinese concepts concerning music have faded away, while others remain as the subliminal heritage of modern musicians. Besides the usual pentatonic scale, many of the structural principles of Chinese music today can be traced to the grand syntheses created in an age that parallels the era of Aristotle and Pythagoras but predates Al Farabi or Pope Gregory by several centuries. Thanks to the literacy of Chinese and Greek civilizations, we can still savor some of the wonders of the ancient theoretical foundations of music, though the concomitant practical musics of both the East and West are lost. However, there are descriptions of musical instruments which, in China, give us tantalizing hints of the flavor of a musical cuisine as exotic as even the most romantic Westerner could imagine.

The Chinese genius for orderly systems appears again when we study musical instruments. These were classified under the so-called "eight sounds" (*pa yin*) system, which differentiated instruments by the main material from which they were made—earth (pottery), stone, metal, skin, wood, bamboo, gourds, and silk. This system often relates to the design of the Chinese characters used to write the names of Chinese instruments. For example, the character for the clay ocarina (*hsuan* 塤) has the symbol for earth at the left; the stone chime's character (*ch'ing* 磬) has the stone symbol on the bottom; and the idiogram for metal appears in the word for the bronze bells so often seen in books on Chou dynasty art.

The ancient lists contain wonderful legends about instruments as well as much accurate information. For example, the same Huang-ti who "ordered" the invention of music is said to have had a drum made from the skin of a one-legged monster which, when struck with a huge bone, could be heard for hundreds of miles. This fabulous drum is listed under the "skin" category along with several types of drums that we know to have existed in ancient times. An exotic entry in the "wood" category is the *yü,* a model of a crouching tiger with a serrated ridge or a set of wooden slats along its backbone; it is seen in its surviving Korean form in Plate XIX, Figure 55. A split bamboo whisk is swept along its back to indicate the end of a piece in Confucian ritual music. Another ancient Chinese instrument surviving in Korea is a box (*chu*) that is thumped with a pole stuck through a hole in the top.

Under the "bamboo" category one finds the *lü* pipes bound together as a panpipe (*p'ai hsiao*). Both the vertical notched *hsiao* flute and the horizontal *ti* flute are in this category. The *sheng* mouth organ (Plate XVI, Figure 46), although using seventeen bamboo pipes, is classified as a gourd instrument because of the gourd-like wind chest in which the pipes are set. We have explained earlier how chords may be played on the Southeast Asian relatives of this instrument by closing the hole on the side of each pipe, thus activating the free reed that is placed at the windchest end of each pipe. The *sheng* uses the same system, though the pipes are much shorter (compare Figure 40 and Figure 46). The placement of the pipes in a circle around the edge of the wind chest facilitates the performance of chords as well as melodies. The ancients say that the *sheng* sound is an imitation of the cry of the phoenix bird and that its shape is that of a phoenix with folded wings. The facts of history say that it is the oldest known instrument in the world based on the organ principle and that it was apparently responsible for the introduction of the reed organ into Europe in the seventeenth century. We shall meet it again in modern Chinese music and in the court ensemble of Japan.

The "silk" category contains a surprisingly large number of multiple-stringed zithers[11] with movable bridges, such as the twenty-five-stringed *se* and the thirteen-stringed *cheng*. The most famous of the "silk" instruments, however, is the seven-stringed *ch'in* (Plate XVI, Figure 44). This instrument and its music have long been associated with Confucius and the life of the intellectual in China. A look through any collection of Chinese landscape paintings as they survive from later periods will inevitably reveal a bearded scholar either seated behind his *ch'in* while viewing the scene or followed by an apprentice carrying this lovely

[11] Compare this with the emphasis on harps and dulcimers in the ancient Near East.

PLATE XVI. China

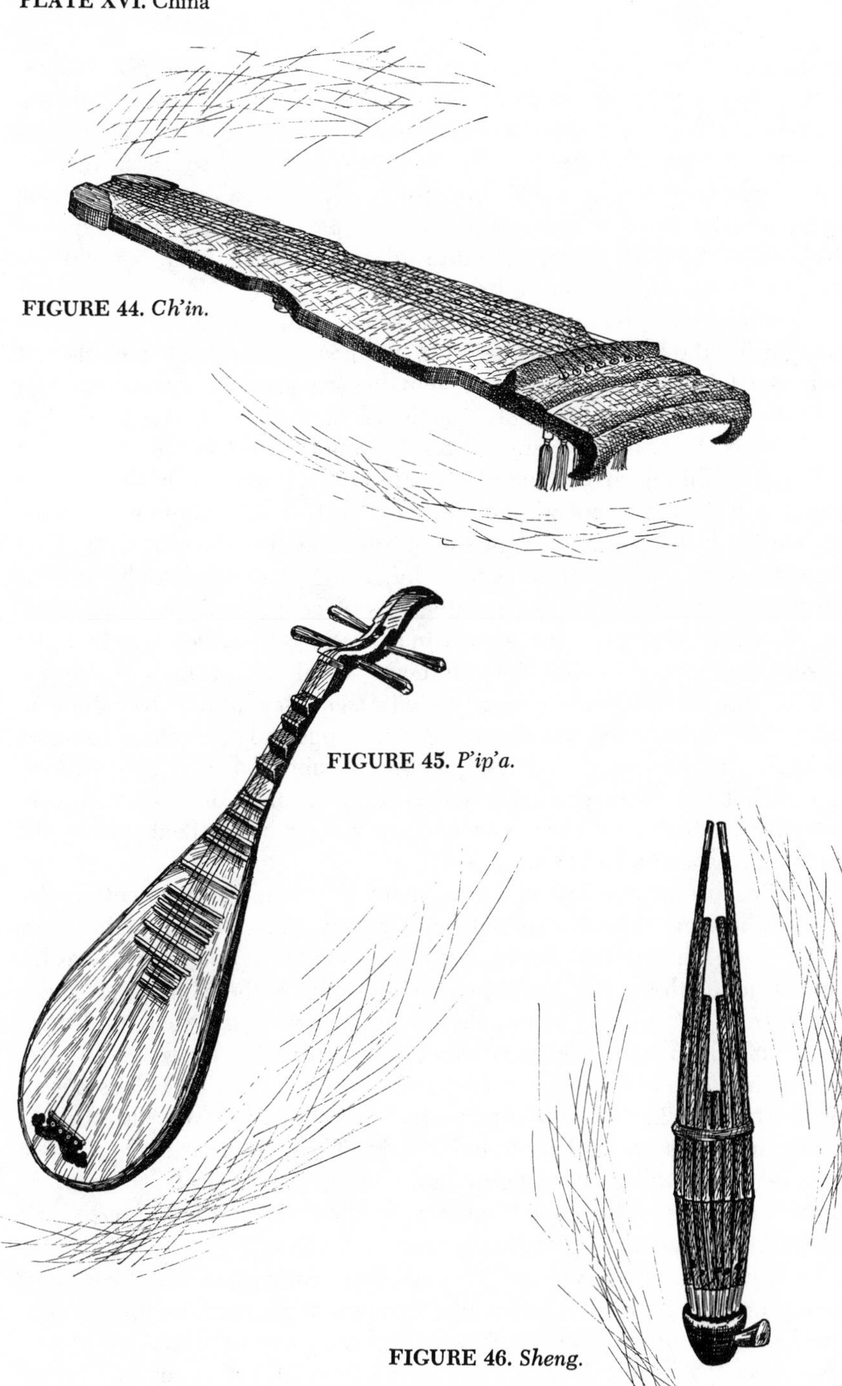

FIGURE 44. *Ch'in.*

FIGURE 45. *P'ip'a.*

FIGURE 46. *Sheng.*

instrument. Unlike the other zithers of China, the *ch'in* has no bridges. Rather, it is played by touching the strings along and between thirteen positions marked by ivory dots inlaid on the side of the instrument. Although the *ch'in* is played in this divisive manner, its seven strings are tuned according to the cyclic principles (C, D, E, G, A, c, d). Some scholars claim that the many sliding effects, harmonics, and other special strokes used by both hands were derived in the international period from the *gamaka* ornamentations of India.

Though no *ch'in* music survives from Confucian times, the notation used during the Sung dynasty (960–1279) shows a system of symbols that look like Chinese characters but actually are artificial constructs that indicate simultaneously the note, the fingering, and the stroke to be used.

Since the classics were written by scholars in Confucian-oriented courts, they do not give a complete picture of the musical life of ancient China. For example, outside of the few folk festivals mentioned above, the music of the peasants went unnoticed, though it is said that many ancient poems were court versions of folk songs. Nevertheless, by at least the third century B.C. the basic categories of court music were codified. The two principal divisions were ritual music (*ya yueh*) and banquet music (*yen yueh*). Within the Confucian ritual were found six dances, divided into military (*wu wu*) and civil (*wen wu*) forms. Over the centuries there were changes in the precise meanings and contents of common and court music, ritual and banquet music, and the civil and military dances, but the distinctions themselves survived until the twentieth century. We shall discuss them first as they were systematized during the Han dynasty (202 B.C.–120 A.D.).

Because of the destruction of many books and instruments under Ch'in-shih-huang-ti in the short Ch'in dynasty (221–206 B.C.), the court music of the Chou period disappeared; but the idea of court music was far from dead in the great intellectual revival under the Han ruler Wu-ti (140–87 B.C.). A governmental office of music (*yueh fu*) was established, the job of which was to set the correct pitch of the *lü's*, supervise all ceremonies, and also collect regional popular and folk music as well as poetry for court songs. The basic *lü* pipe preserved in this office was also used as a standard measure for length and weight. Thus, the music office was a bureau of the Office of Weights and Measurements and remained so through many dynasties even though, in the later Han period, bronze bells were used as a standard for pitch in place of the *lü's*.

The orchestras used in the Han official court rituals and banquets were quite large and, somewhat like Western symphony orchestras, consisted of large numbers of string and wind players plus a backing of percussionists. (The instruments, of course, were of the types mentioned earlier; thus their sound was totally different from their modern Western counterparts.) The ritual dance troupe was also generally large. In both cases the number of participants was governed by Confucian numerology.

Non-Confucian musics were found in certain warrior dances (not the *wu wu* mentioned above) whose accompaniment relied heavily on stone and metal instruments, and in the banquet music of the women's quarters. In the latter the sound of strings and winds prevailed. The ladies sang songs based on folk texts to create a light-hearted mood. Theatricals had already been known in the Chou dynasty and continued to find a place in the court, though the great flourishing of Chinese drama was centuries ahead.

By the end of the Han period, the Chinese Empire had reached its maximum size and surpassed its contemporary giant, the Roman Empire, in territory, population, and power. As Chinese armies and foreign traders returned from Central Asia and Northern India, they brought with them many exotic items, including "barbarian" instruments such as a crooked-neck relative of the *p'ip'a* lute (Plate XVI, Figure 45) around the second century B.C. and, in the first century A.D., a new religion, Buddhism. When the Han dynasty began to break up and the barbarians themselves invaded the borderlands of China with renewed vigor, the effects of this new religion and the new musics began to change the surface of Chinese music. It was the Six Dynasties period (222–589 A.D.) that saw the struggle of the old ways against an ever-increasing influx of new ideas. In music, however, as in many other basic Chinese attitudes, the foundations laid in the more insular formative period remained essentially the same during the international period that followed.

The International Period (Fifth Century to Tenth Century)

The two major areas of cultural and political vulnerability in China were its western and northern borders. During the Six Dynasties period the Chinese heartland was no longer unified; hence we find that the North China kingdoms were heavily influenced by music from both border areas, while the southern kingdoms held as best they could to the old court and popular traditions—though they also were affected by the flood of new ideas coming over the Western trade routes. The influences from the north consisted primarily of militaristic drum, trumpet, and oboe music, including Tartar cavalry bands. The western influences included Indian music theory, particularly as it related to Buddhist chanting. The main streams of Western music came from the Central Asian Gandharan, Iranian, and Tokharian cultures. These traditions came into China by three main routes: via the trade cities of Khotan to the south (third to fifth centuries), Kucha in the center (fourth through eighth century), and Turfan to the north (fifth through ninth centuries). Though all these towns are now only dust mounds in the deserts, their artifacts and cave paintings, along with the larger Buddhist cave paintings in China proper, reveal a host of new instruments, including cymbals, the Assyrian angle harp (*k'ung hou*), and a variety of plucked lutes, some of which have been traced back as far as ancient Egypt.[12]

It was the short Sui dynasty (589–618) that began to reunify China. In the process, court music was revived, this time with many of the new instruments added or with entirely new music ensembles imported from outside China. All these national musics were organized by the government into seven (and later nine) kinds of music. The codification and flourishing of international music in China, however, occurred in the brilliant T'ang dynasty (618–907) which followed.

Some idea of the international scope of the T'ang musical world may be gleaned from a listing of the ten kinds of music (*shih pu chi*) found in the government music bureau at the time of the famous ruler Hsuan-Tsung (712–756). The most distant musics were those of a band of five instruments from Samarkand, beyond the Pamir mountains, and of another group from Bokhara, still farther west. Kashgar, at the doorway of the Western world, sent yet another music. The trade centers of Kucha and Turfan each had orchestras at the court (Khotan by this time was destroyed). A sixth music came from India to the southwest, while another came from Korea to the northeast. One group of musicians specialized in a music that combined Chinese and Kucha styles. Indigenous Chinese folk music from earlier periods was yet another category, and finally, a large orchestra using 25 different kinds of instruments was dedicated to performing Chinese court music. In addition to these ten official kinds of music, there are records of musical tribute coming from Tibet and the kingdoms of Southeast Asia. Each of these groups maintained its own repertoire, instruments, performers, and dancers. Even the color of their costumes varied. Truly this was an international period, and the fads for various "western" musics and manners that ran through the populace were the subject of many essays and reproving poems by classical scholars of the time.

This host of foreign and native musicians resided primarily in the capital city of Ch'ang-an, supported out of tax funds as government slaves. But even slavery had its ranks, and many musicians rose to comfortable positions by way of their musical or political talents. In addition, there were a great many musicians and dancers dedicated to purely secular

[12] The most persistent claimant for an Egyptian origin is Professor Hisao Tanabe, whose writings (in Japanese) present the theory in detail. West-to-East migrations are seen in Shigeo Kishibe's "The Origin of the P'ip'a," *Transactions of the Asiatic Society of Japan,* Second Series, XIX (1940), 259–304.

entertainment. In the days of Hsuan-Tsung, the section of Ch'ang-an called the Pear Garden (*Li Yuan*) was a huge school for the training of such personnel. Its music was a synthesis of foreign and Chinese secular styles, and it is said that the emperor himself taught there.

Since the days of Kao-tsu (618–626), selected girls (*kung nü*) had been taught music in a special school inside the court (the *nei chiao fang*). One of the earliest extant pictures of Chinese secular music shows a group of these ladies entertaining the emperor.[13] In another school outside the court (the *wai chiao fang*), professional female musicians were trained; these became a source for the teahouse girls in the later T'ang dynasty and are distant ancestors of the famous Japanese geisha.

To the basic distinction between court music (*ya yueh*) and common music (*su yueh*) of previous eras, the T'ang dynasty added the category of foreign music (*hu yueh*). While we can see each of these as a separate style in some of the musics listed above, the important characteristic of the period was the manner in which the three musics exchanged idioms and instruments. This adventuresome spirit resulted in new instruments as well, such as a set of sixteen iron slabs (*fang hsiang*) used in imitation of the bell and stone chime-sets of before. The greatest changes instrumentally, however, came in the chordophones.

We have mentioned the appearance of harps and plucked lutes. The former are the only harps to play any significant role in Chinese music. Among the lutes, the *dram-snyan*—still used in Tibet (see Example 6–1)—is of interest not only because it is mentioned in T'ang documents but also because it may have led to the better-known three-stringed lute tradition of later Chinese and Japanese times (see Figure 48 and Figure 54). The four-stringed, pear-shaped *p'ip'a* (Plate XVI, Figure 45) was the dominant lute of T'ang times and was used extensively in ensembles. It also had a repertoire of descriptive solo pieces and was used to accompany songs. In T'ang sources we begin to learn the names of pieces, their composers, and the events for which specific pieces were written. In the repertoire of the court ritual music, for example, there are titles and descriptions of eight pieces played without strings as "standing music," probably outside in the courtyard, and six pieces played as "sitting music" inside the palace halls. Famous emperors and empresses are credited with the composition of such hit pieces as "The Lion Dance of the Five Directions" or "The Battleline–Smashing Music." The choreography of the dances required from four to 180 dancers. The larger groups sometimes formed letters in a manner familiar to viewers of American football half-time extravaganzas.

[13] See Shigeo Kishibe, "A Chinese Painting of the T'ang Court Women's Orchestra," in *The Commonwealth of Music,* ed. Gustave Reese and Rose Brandel (New York: The Free Press of Glencoe, Inc., 1965), 104–17.

A few T'ang documents give general descriptions of the manner in which pieces were performed. Useful detail about performance practice, however, is lacking except as it is implied by the imitations of T'ang music found in the surviving court orchestras of Korea and Japan. There have been attempts in China to revive certain T'ang popular melodies,[14] primarily as they appear in collections of later dynasties. At present the closest we can come to the spirit of such T'ang dance pieces as "A Night of Flowers and Moonlight by the Spring River" is to read the poetry of Li Po or gaze at T'ang clay figurines with their flying sleeves, curved bodies, and aristocratic heads encased in *haute coiffure*.

Since the huge and complicated art-music establishment of the T'ang period was supported by tax funds, it declined rapidly as soon as the imperial fortunes began to wane. The singing girls of the court (*chi nü*) became teahouse singing girls (*chi kuan*), while male musicians from the court found themselves at liberty to starve or to find new audiences. Theaters and brothels, both of which had always been present in some form in China, began to absorb more of the governmental musicians and dancers, and the center of Chinese musical interest shifted from Confucian rites and courtly life to the demands of the public stage or the homes of wealthy merchants.

During the chaotic Five Dynasties and Ten Kingdoms period (907–979), a few more "barbarian" instruments such as the two-stringed Mongolian fiddle were adopted in China (the *hu ch'in,* Plate XVII, Figure 47), but this time such additions are first noted in the theater rather than in the court. China had passed its peak as a land of cosmopolitan taste and as a pace-setter for the Asian world. Out of the new Chinese society, however, came the standard practices of a national style that are still in effect today.

The National Period (Tenth through Nineteenth Centuries)

The Sung dynasty (960–1279) brought to China a new stability and prosperity that were based primarily on military and mercantile activity. The court periodically refurbished Confucian music, though its main musical contributions came through new theoretical studies and indirectly through its support of huge encyclopedic and historical compilations and the fostering of new poetry forms. The latter developed along two lines, each of which reflected important factors in the further development of Chinese music. One form was chanted in such a way as to exploit the basic

[14] One document of T'ang melodies has survived and has been transcribed, though its lack of rhythm and orchestration leave us ignorant about how it was performed. See Laurence Picken, "Twelve Ritual Melodies from the T'ang Dynasty," in *Studia Memoriae Béla Bartók Sacra* (London: Boosey & Hawkes, 1959), 145–71.

PLATE XVII. China

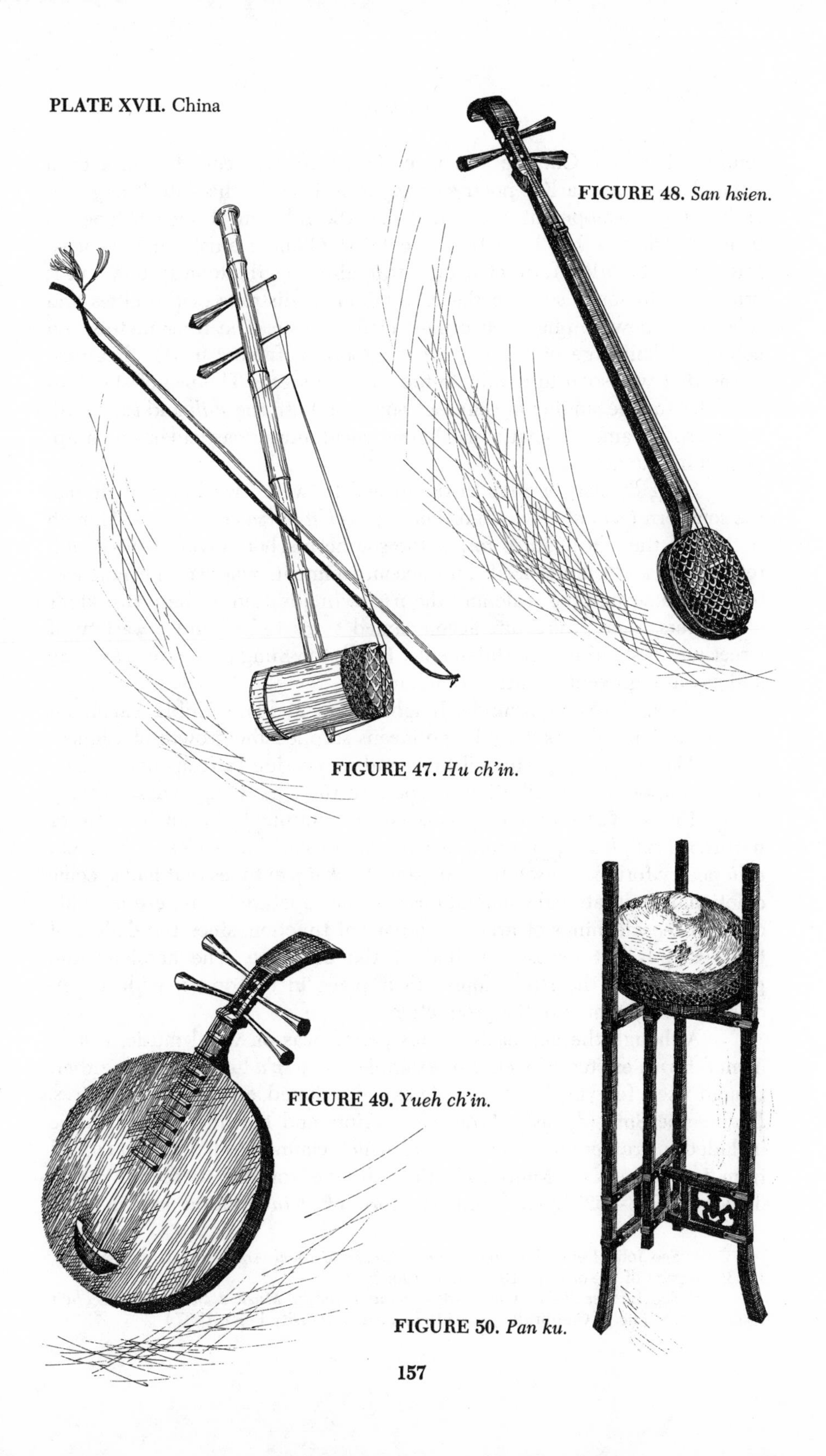

FIGURE 48. *San hsien.*

FIGURE 47. *Hu ch'in.*

FIGURE 49. *Yueh ch'in.*

FIGURE 50. *Pan ku.*

tone levels of the Chinese language. This form was called *shih,* a term applied to many earlier poetry styles as well as to this late T'ang and early Sung development. Some feel that the relation of speech tones to melodic structure has been fundamental to Chinese music since at least this era.[15] The other form of poetry, *tz'u,* also uses the tone system, but it originated in songs sung in the entertainment districts of the cities and reflected a new emphasis on urban secular music. The freer meters and colloquial language of the *tz'u* were important factors in the theatrical music that was soon to dominate the Chinese scene. The use of standard melodies for the singing of different poems in both the *shih* and *tz'u* traditions also became idiomatic of Chinese vocal music, particularly as it appeared in drama.

Sung dynasty writers distinguished between two kinds of drama, the southern (*nan ch'ü*) and northern (*pei ch'ü* or *tsa chü*) styles. Though both used the *tz'u* poetical forms, the southern school favored the pentatonic scale and emphasized flute accompaniment, whereas the northern one used a seven-tone scale and the *p'ip'a.* In addition to these two kinds of theaters, there were lute-accompanied story tellers and a variety of street and restaurant entertainments. In all, the Sung cities were as lusty and gay as eighteenth-century London.

When the Mongols under Jenghiz Khan, and later Kublai Khan, put an end to Sung glories, they by no means stopped the growth of Chinese opera. The infusion of Mongol lutes and percussion instruments, in fact, was an important contribution to opera in the succeeding Yuan dynasty (1279–1368). Yuan drama (*Yuan ch'ü*) continued the distinction of northern (*tsa ch'ü*) and southern (*hsi wen* or *nan hsi*) styles. A freer *san ch'ü* poetry form was used for texts sung to *ch'ü p'ai* tunes that had specific emotional or situational connotations and thus operated as repertoire-wide clues to the meanings of aria—an important function, since the dialect of the text was not necessarily that of the audience. The acrobats and pantomimists of the street found their place in the opera, with a concomitant brightening of the productions.

Although the emphasis of this period was on vocal music, instrumental forms existed as well. For example, the *p'ip'a* lute and *ch'in* zither, though used for vocal accompaniment, developed extensive repertoires. During the Sung dynasty, both manuscripts and the first printed music included instrumental pieces, some of which claimed to have been copied from T'ang sources.[16] Many collections survive from the succeeding Ming dynasty (1368–1628). The composite form of *ch'in* notation used in these

[15] See John Levis, *Foundations of Chinese Musical Art* (New York: Paragon, 1963; a reprint of the original 1936 publication).

[16] See further Rulan Chiao Pian, *Song Dynasty Musical Sources and Their Interpretation* [*sic.*] (Cambridge, Mass.: Harvard University Press, 1967).

works has already been discussed (see p. 152). Other instrumental notations used a symbol for each note in a five- or seven-note scale and named at the start of the piece the type of scale or mode desired. Tempo and meter markings also appeared, but rhythmic details of the melodies were lacking, leading to a variety of interpretations over the centuries. Nevertheless, the two basic types of instrumental solo music found in Sung and Ming times have remained dominant to the present day. The first type is the descriptive or impressionistic piece. The *p'ip'a* is particularly famous for its battle pieces, in which the clash of armor, zinging of arrows, and cries of the wounded are all depicted; the *ch'in* tends more towards impressionistic scenes like "The Drunken Fisherman."[17] The second type of solo instrumental music is the abstract piece, best–known in a kind of variation form played on the *ch'in.* The social context of instrumental music was still the court, but the moneyed merchant class could also enjoy such music. This led in the Ming and Ch'ing (1644–1911) periods to a kind of bourgeois chamber music using the *p'ip'a* plus newer theater instruments such as the two-string fiddles (the *erh hu* and *hu ch'in,* Figure 47), the three-string plucked lute (*san hsien,* Figure 48), and the "moon" guitar, with four strings in double courses (*yueh ch'in,* Figure 49). Flutes included the end-blown *hsiao,* with six finger holes. The *hsiao* is noted for its three extraneous holes: the two at the end of the instrument are used to tie a long silk tassle, which adds a decorative touch to the performance; the third, just below the mouth hole, is covered with thin rice paper, which adds a gentle buzzing quality to the instrument's tone. Some of the chamber music using these various instruments is purely instrumental, while other pieces have a vocal part. In either case, much of the chamber music repertoire is derived from the all-pervading style of Chinese opera.

The generic term for Chinese opera is *hsi ch'ü.* A survey of its history since the fading of Yuan drama reveals some 300 regional popular theatricals which go under the generic term *ti fang hsi.* Most of these are small theatricals amounting to folk dramas, while others are urban professional theatricals. Many of these forms survive today and are generally known by the name of the location of their origin. Since Peking opera (*ching hsi* or *ching ch'ü*) is the best-known form in the West and the dominant form in China today, both our historical and musical discussions will concentrate on that genre.[18]

[17] Both instruments can be heard on the recording *Chinese Classical Masterpieces* (Lyrichord LL 82).

[18] The author is particularly grateful for the historical information concerning this topic found in the works of the Australian scholar Colin P. Mackerras, such as his *The Rise of the Peking Opera* (Oxford: Clarendon Press, 1972) and "The Growth of the Chinese Regional Drama in the Ming and Ch'ing," *Journal of Oriental Studies,* IX/1 (1971).

Four major regional theatricals set the stage for the rise of Peking opera; *k'un ch'ü, i yang ch'iang, pang tzu chi'ang,* and *p'i huang. K'un ch'ü* was a form of theater popular with the aristocracy in the sixteenth century and derived its name from the city in which it is said to have begun, K'unshan in the northeast coastal province of Kiangsu.[19] Its texts and musical style reflect the preferences of the class of its patrons. Delicate, falsetto voices are usually accompanied by a flute of the horizontal (*ti tzu*) or end-blown (*hsiao*) type, though the *p'ip'a* plucked lute, *sheng* mouth organ, and even the plebian *san hsien* plucked lute can be found in regional forms of the genre. The term *kuan,* which usually refers to a double-reed aerophone of the type surviving in Korean and Japanese court music, is used for a free-reed pipe that sometimes accompanies *k'un ch'ü.*[20] Since a *k'un ch'ü* text is in classical Chinese and thus is (and was) not understood by many listeners, the vocal line often treats one syllable melismatically (like the coloratura tradition of Italian opera) without concern for communicating the meaning of the words.

In the early sixteenth century *i yang ch'iang* opera appeared in I Yang, a city in Kiangsi province. It attempted to clarify its classical text by inserted passages called *kun tao,* which were in colloquial local languages. The singing was in a more syllabic style in order to communicate better to general audiences. *I yang ch'iang* orchestras were bombastic and more filled with percussion instruments than those of *k'un ch'ü,* and a unison chorus (*pang ch'iang*) was added, a tradition that still survives in some regional operas in Kiangsi, Hunan, and Szechwan. Perhaps the Ming-period theatrical that was most influential on the later developments of Chinese opera was the so-called clapper opera (*pang tzu ch'iang*), which seems to have originated in the northwest province of Shensi. Its name relates to wooden clappers that are part of its accompaniment, as well as to certain "slapstick" qualities which may appear in its productions. Although clappers are used by the leader of the accompanying ensemble, the *yueh ch'in* plucked lute (Figure 49) is basic to the string section.

By the middle of the Ch'ing dynasty period (1644–1911) some regional theatricals (particularly those from Canton) included in their ensembles a "western zither" (*yang ch'in*). This is called by some writers a "butterfly harp" because of its shape, but it should be noted that it is not a harp but a hammered dulcimer—a Chinese version of the Near Eastern *santur,* which was imported into China in the eighteenth century. In that

[19] The student of European opera history will recognize such a tradition of nomenclature, for we speak of Venetian or Neapolitan opera for the same reason. The parallels between Chinese and European opera history become more evident as one delves deeper into both fields.

[20] The closest relative to the single-reed form of the *kuan* is the *pi saw* mentioned in our Southeast Asian study, page 130.

same period many regional theatricals became classified not as clapper operas but rather as *p'i huang,* an abbreviation of the two terms *hsi p'i* and *erh huang.* These terms refer to two styles of singing which will be discussed later. The origin of the terms is unknown and a direct translation of their meaning is of little help (*hsi p'i,* 西皮 , means "western skin" and *erh huang,* 二黃 , is "two yellows"). Interpretations vary from opinions that they may be regional musical jargon to other views that see them as shorthand references to various cities or as attempts to reproduce in Chinese character form the sounds of pronunciations in local dialects. Whatever their historical origin, they did become basic nomenclature in Chinese opera, and the *p'i huang* musical syndrome joined the host of other theatrical traditions in a migration to the more lucrative, metropolitan world of the capital. There, all styles combined in the eighteenth and nineteenth centuries into *ching hsi,* Peking opera.

If our historical introduction has seemed full of names of places and genres, it must be realized that we are dealing with a tradition that developed in a period longer than that of the entire history of European opera and involved the regional preferences over some 500 years of peoples from many Chinese provinces, most of which contained larger populations than that of Europe. In that context our introductory remarks have been brief indeed. They must serve our goal, however, which is to prepare us for a discussion of the musical aspects of this vast tradition.

Though Chinese opera includes instrumental music for dances, pantomimes, and interludes as well as vocal recitatives, its characteristic musical styles are found in arias. There are two general approaches to the settings of arias. The first, called *lian ch'ü,* selects from a body of standard pieces a set of works that are appropriate to the moods of a given drama. This kind of structure is only possible when the text uses a rather rigid poetical form. Hence the *lian ch'ü* were used in the oldest opera forms, like those of the Sung dynasty around the twelfth century and the *k'un ch'ü* Ming opera form mentioned earlier. While this standard-piece approach is linked to the court poetry tradition, it has a basis as well in the structure of folk theatricals.

The second approach, called *pan ch'iang,* uses stereotyped melodies rather than complete pieces. These melodies are subject to extensive variation, depending on the dramatic situation. Rhythm plays a very important role in determining how these tunes are used. This approach began in the Ming dynasty but prevailed most strongly during the Ch'ing, when the clapper opera tradition flourished. A unique and extreme example of rhythmic emphasis is found in the *kao ch'iang* opera of the Szechwan and Hunan provinces, which originally used only gongs and drums as accompaniment. (Modern productions of such operas have added complete songs in the *lian ch'ü* style accompanied by winds and strings.) In truth, both basic approaches, the complete-song and the stereotyped-tune-and-rhythm methods are found within one opera genre today. It is the mixture of these approaches, along with various features of the northern and southern styles, that make traditional opera interesting. Peking opera, as the cumulative tradition in the capital of the country, offers the greatest variety of sights and sounds—from deafening preludes of crashing cymbals and stages filled with sword-swinging acrobats to pathetic arias sung by a comely girl or a female impersonator standing before a set consisting of only two chairs and a cloth-covered table. In discussing its music, we will start with the orchestra.

Two basic kinds of instrumentation are used in Peking opera. The first is used for battles or military entrances and consists of a battery of gongs, cymbals, and drums, plus the double-reed *sona,* already familiar to us from the Near East and South Asia (see Plate IX, Figure 24). The other ensemble is used for all civil and domestic scenes and is, therefore, heard more often. Its instrumentation varies with each number according to the mood; however, two kinds of instruments are basic, a time-beater and a bowed lute.

The most common time-beater is a *pan ku* or *tanpi ku* (Plate XVII, Figure 50). It consists of a skin stretched over a set of wooden wedges bound in a circle and so hollowed out that only a small part of the skin covers a cavity at the center of the drum. The sharp, dry, cracking sound produced by this instrument penetrates nicely through the other instrumental sounds—as it should, since the *pan ku* player is the leader of the orchestra. The rhythm he plays (see Example 6–4) often determines the nature of the piece. Additional time-beaters used in conjunction with or in substitution for the *pan ku* include wooden blocks, thick wooden sticks, and various sets of wooden clappers often played in the manner of castanets. The generic term for most of the clappers is *pan* 板 (a term using a different Chinese character from that of the *pan* 木邦 in *pan ku*).

The standard bowed lute of Chinese opera is the *hu ch'in* (Plate XVII, Figure 47), the barbarian fiddle borrowed from the Mongols around the time of the Yuan dynasty. Its pegs are in the back of its neck so that the two strings, tuned in fifths, are aligned vertically over the snakeskin soundboard. This position allows the bow to pass between them rather than over them in the manner of Near Eastern bowed lutes. The *hu ch'in* is played with the finger along the string like the *rebab,* rather than pressed against the finger board like the Western violin. The *hu ch'in* leads the ensemble in performing the stereotyped melodies as set in the matrix of the time-beaters. It is often doubled by a larger, two-stringed *erh hu* fiddle, which sounds an octave lower and is similar to the *hu ch'in* in appearance, except that its body may be either hexagonal or round. There is also a four-string, *szu hu* fiddle that may appear.

The plucked lutes most commonly found in opera orchestras are the *p'ip'a* (Figure 45), the *yueh ch'in* (Figure 49), and the *san hsien*

(Figure 48). The *yueh ch'in* has a thin metal plate suspended inside its wooden body to add resonance. A similar metal strip is suspended inside the neck of the larger northern form of the *san hsien,* although this is not found in the smaller southern form. Either form may appear in the opera.

The double-reed *sona* has already been mentioned as the aerophone used in ensembles accompanying military scenes. In other types of scenes the only melodic aerophone is the *ti* (or *ti tzu*) flute mentioned earlier. Besides its use in the older *k'un ch'ü* style, it can still occasionally be heard in other opera traditions in a solo or duet backing for an aria. Normally, like all other melodic instruments listed so far, it plays a heterophonic version of the main melody. The *sheng* mouth organ is also occasionally used melodically in opera, though it usually adds harmony in fourths or fifths.

Various sizes of cymbals (*po*) and thin knobless gongs (*lo*) appear in most Chinese opera ensembles. Their most important uses are in the long percussion overtures that begin most scenes, or as accompaniment for recitatives. At the end of each phrase in a recitative, the time-beater will signal it with short clashes on cymbals and gongs. These sounds are functionally rather like the chords plunked on the harpsichord in eighteenth-century Western opera recitatives.

The voice quality and range used in a Peking opera depend on the character portrayed. Heroines may use a high, thin tone derived from the stylizations of the female impersonators who dominated the feminine roles until the mid-twentieth century. Military heroes, by contrast, may emphasize a powerful voice quality that would damage the vocal cords of a Western singer. Such vocal styles are like those of Western opera in one important respect: they are artificial; that is, they are the result of deliberate training. They require years of rigorous practice and, when brought to perfection, they are capable of portraying a wide range of emotions. In this the singers of Chinese opera are aided by the specific connotations of the stereotyped melodies they perform.

In terms of vocal music, traditional Chinese opera consists of recitatives with percussion interjections followed by appropriate arias. In Peking opera there are some 30 different standard aria melodies, of different moods, to which the text of a given opera situation can be attached. Poetically, the texts of almost all arias are based on a series of rhymed couplets with seven or ten syllables in each line, though they may be divided between two singers or split into dialogue, which can even leave the first line of a couplet in one aria and the second in the aria that follows, with poetically unrelated dialogue in between. Melodically, arias are usually classified under the two basic types mentioned earlier, the *hsi p'i* and *erh huang.* In musical analysis these two types can be distinguished by their tonal emphases and certain melodic or rhythmic conventions. (Similar criteria could be applied to eighteenth-century Italian opera, although the specific results would certainly be different.) The average Chinese opera enthusiasts are not scholars, however; they learn the distinctive characteristics of an aria subliminally by hearing it used in fairly consistent conventional dramatic situations. (Just as, even without knowing musical theory, let alone the language, one can recognize a love duet or a vengeance aria in traditional Italian opera.)

The dramatic function of an aria is most directly implied by the style and tempo of its rhythmic accompaniment. Thus, Example 6–4

EXAMPLE 6–4. Two Peking opera aria excerpts transcribed from the recording *The Ruse of the Empty City* (New York: Folkways Record FW 8882), side 2, bands 1 and 6. By permission of Folkways Records and Service Corporation.

shows two seemingly different arias that are both classified as *hsi p'i.* What they share is a tonal emphasis on G, which along with C would be characteristic preferences for *hsi p'i* arias if they were written on the pitch level of these two examples.[21] (An *erh huang* aria on this pitch level would have emphasized a B♭ or the E♭ above it). The two arias also share a rather heterophonic relation between the string accompaniment and the vocal line and time-beater's clear rhythmic signals which prepare for a cadence climaxing with crashing cymbals. These musical features do not help the listener distinguish one aria from another, for they are common to most performance practice. The total rhythmic accompani-

[21] Against the background of our earlier discussion of the Chinese tone system (page 148) we should note that, although both pieces in Example 6–4 have a pentatonic core, they also use the pitch as A♭ *pien* tone.

ment, however, is of the greatest value in guiding the average Chinese listener into the nature of a given aria. For instance, he would know that Example 6–4A is a narrative aria because its rhythmic accompaniment is in a style called *yuan pan* ("Steady or level clapper [rhythm]"). Example 6–4B is recognizable as a dramatic aria because of its *yao pan* ("unsteady or wavering clappers") accompaniment. A *hsi p'i* aria indicated in a libretto as *hsi p'i man pan* ("slow clappers") would be lyrical; a highly animated aria would have its rhythm marked as *liu shui* ("flowing clappers") or *k'uai pan* ("rapid clappers"); and, if there is to be a sung interjection on a different topic in the middle of one aria or between two arias, the interjection would be accompanied by *tao pan* ("guiding or inverted clapper [rhythms]"). One can double the variety of choices in the Chinese opera tradition by applying such rhythmic accompaniments to *erh huang* melodies instead. There are, of course, further arias and rhythmic patterns that are used in special dramatic situations.[22] On the level of this brief overview of the tradition, however, one need realize only that all these aria forms are not specific melodies but rather combinations of tonal, melodic, and rhythmic conventions that make distinctions possible in the ears of Chinese opera fans. Because of this, individual performers can sing a well-known aria in a way that may differ not only from renditions of other performers but also from previous performances by the same artist.[23]

Our preliminary remarks and the two short excerpts from *hsi p'i* arias can give us only an inkling of the organization of Peking opera's music, but we may now know enough to be able to recognize the musical and theatrical validity of the tradition. The use of connotative melodies is of great importance in the appreciation of a given situation; and the use of rhythm to demarcate melodies and give them a sense of progression is as valid here as it is, in different forms, in the time-cycles of Indonesian *gamelan* music and the *tala* of India. Add to these elements the gorgeous costumes and a troupe of acrobats, and you have good theater by any standards. It is our contention that it is also good music.

The Chinese narrative tradition does not always require such an elaborate setting. In addition to many kinds of small regional theatricals, there are hand and shadow puppet plays that use small ensembles of opera instruments backstage to accompany the narrator-manipulator. There are

[22] For rhythmic examples see Rulan C. Pian, "The Function of Rhythm in the Peking Opera," in *The Musics of Asia,* ed. Joe Maceda (Manila: National Music Council of the Philippines, 1971).

[23] Variations in a melody sung by the same singer at different times can be seen in Liu T'ien-hua, *Selections from the Repertoire of Operatic and Terpsichorean Melodies of Mei Lan-fang* (Peiping, 1929). See also Rulan Pian, "Aria Structural Patterns in the Peking Opera," in *Chinese and Japanese Music-Dramas,* Michigan Papers in Chinese Studies, no. 19 (1975).

also at least two major traditions of solo narrators. The first, sometimes called *t'an tz'u,* is that of one performer who accompanies his own songs, which are usually strophic, with a *p'ip'a* lute that plays a steady stream of melody heterophonically related to the narrator's own short melodic phrases, in a manner somewhat like that of the melodic aspects of Example 6–4B. The other narrative tradition is called *ta ku tz'u* after the name of a small flat drum (*ta ku*) that is usually used as accompaniment. The singer often plays a castanet with his left hand and the drum with his right. A *san hsien* may also accompany him in his strophic songs. Though both these traditions have their professional performers, musical storytelling as such, since at least the Sung dynasty, has belonged to the itinerant street musicians whose appeal was to the peasant and the passerby. The roles of both the singer and his audience have changed in the contemporary scene.

The World Music Period (Twentieth Century)

In 1911 the last of the Chinese dynasties fell and a republic was declared. The stormy years that followed witnessed sporadic attempts at Westernization that were compromised by internal strife and external pressure. Western music, which had appeared in China as early as the Ming period, still found little favor with the general public, but the Chinese elite accepted it along with men's suits and automobiles as symbols of Western culture. Western music teachers began to appear in the cities of China, and Chinese students went to Western conservatories. Orchestras were formed, musicales were given, and talk of a synthesis of Chinese and Western music was heard from both Asian and Western writers and musicians.

The search for a new East-West art was not particularly successful in either world. On the peasant level in China, however, a new tradition of unison singing arose as greater numbers of Chinese became involved in civil construction, civil wars, and the struggle against the Japanese. At the same time, the harmonic tradition of Christian hymns became part of the learning of a new rising educated class. Perhaps the most famous and most appropriate symbol of the musical spirit and style of the times is the patriotic march shown in Example 6–5. It was composed in 1934 by Nieh Erh to a text by T'ien Han, a modern Chinese playwright. The piece was motivated by increasing confrontations between China and Japan (much as "The Star Spangled Banner" was one result of British intervention in the United States), and in 1949 it became the national anthem for the Peoples' Republic of China on the mainland. In the example, the first line of the melody has had added to the Western five-line notation the standard

EXAMPLE 6–5. The national anthem of the Peoples' Republic of China.

modern Chinese form of number notation, which was derived from the French Chevé system. The style of this first line seems quite Western, with its four-bar phrases, major-mode implication, and a leading tone, G♯. Thereafter, however, the melody becomes intriguingly Chinese, with a pentatonic scale, varying phrase lengths, and different rhythmic patterns.

The Communist victory on mainland China in 1949 is of special interest to us because it made a Marxist-Leninist doctrine of music the national policy for a country that contains one third of the world's population. Chairman Mao Tse-tung of the Chinese Communist party explained that the function of the arts is to serve the whole mass of the nation's people and to reflect the class struggle as well as the triumphs of socialism.[24] The musical results of this admonition are most easily noted in modern Peking operas. Many of the arias are quite traditional in their melodic and rhythmic names, but now the characters who are to sing them are workers or soldiers rather than members of the nobility or mythological characters.[25] At the same time, larger orchestras are used,

[24] See Mao Tse-tung, *On Literature and the Arts* (Peking: Foreign Language Press, 1960).

[25] For librettos and polemics concerning the new Chinese operas, see *The Drama Review,* XV/3 (1971). See also the controversy over reconstructed Peking opera in *A Great Revolution on the Cultural Front* (Peking: Foreign Language Press, 1965).

including Western instruments and new families of traditional stringed instruments that have been constructed to reflect the communal spirit of Chinese society. Large choruses now appear frequently and sing spirited unison or harmonized pieces that grew out of the protest tradition of previous decades mentioned earlier. Acrobats remain popular in Chinese opera, though their costumes are modern peasant or military clothes, and the influence of Russian ballet is frequently evident. In a word, Chinese opera on the mainland has continued in its tradition of creative adoption and adaptation of topics and materials that are socio-economically viable in the period in which they were created. To see and hear traditional Chinese opera, one must follow the marginal-survival principle and seek out performances in Taiwan, Hong Kong, Singapore, or New York. The latest socialist-realist forms of Chinese opera are to be found in the peoples' palaces of culture on the mainland.

In the midst of this musical reconstruction period one should note the position of the composer, whose duties now are to serve the people in a new society. A study of earlier Chinese (or even Italian Neapolitan) opera traditions shows that the composer was seldom given special attention as compared with the prestige of the singer. (One could also make this comparison in most popular music in the world.) In modern communist societies such as China's, one often finds that the creation of an opera or some other large work is assigned to a composition committee rather than to an individual. Thus, the person employed to create the music (known in the West in the singular as *the* composer) is placed in the position of other skillful artisans in other trades, whose rewards are judged according to their talent for serving, together with others, the needs of the people, rather than by demonstrating special "genius" or "originality." Such a position for a composer returns him to a role not unlike the one noted in our earlier studies of tribal or village musicians in Oceania and thus gives him a strong sense of sociological function in an ever-changing world, though it also places external restraints on the idioms in which he may work.

The nature of compositions themselves in contemporary mainland China reflects the goals of the new system, as is suggested by the titles of such works as "The Sacred War Symphony," "The Yellow River Concerto," and "The Ming Tombs Reservoir Cantata," or of the opera "Raid on the White Tiger Regiment" and the ballet "The Red Detachment of Women." Ballet has become particularly useful as a new idiom because it easily communicates social messages without the operatic problems of the many dialects of China. The challenge of so many languages and minority peoples in mainland China was met musically with energetic attempts to reconstruct or newly compose the idioms of the peoples involved. As we noted in Soviet Central Asia (p. 91), the soloistic and traditional instrumental traditions of various areas in China were reconstructed through a new emphasis on communal choral training and the creation of folk orchestras. The new families of different sizes of traditional instruments noted earlier not only reflect the communal spirit but allow the composition committee to create vertically balanced sounds with materials which grew in earlier times out of a basically horizontally-oriented line. Given the potentially rich sources of musical materials found in the many ethnic groups of China, it has been possible for some composer-arrangers to create quite original compositions by combining basically Western-style pieces with the sound ideals and tone qualities of indigenous musics. Because of the rather tonally conservative dogma of national policy, much modern Chinese music at this stage sounds somewhat like Russian choral music—Rimsky-Korsakov in his "oriental" moments—or light opera with loud sounds. However, functional music that serves the people need not be "great" music, and the cult of compositional personality and total originality, which is still found in some Western traditions, remains anathema in mainland China. One must always remember when hearing new Chinese music that its goal is to sell or reinforce national or regional ideas. In the West such music is used only to sell material goods, though there have been a growing number of popular singers who have become concerned with communicating with the masses on important social issues. It is in context of the Chinese national goals that such songs as "Socialism is Good," "I'm So Happy on the Collective Farm," or the new Tibetan "folk song" entitled "Gifts from Chairman Mao" make sense. Some of these seemingly trite songs may be as valuable to their singers as are athletic-team "fight songs" in Western schools, or as are "We Shall Overcome," "Stand Up, Stand Up for Jesus," and "Hare Krishna" to other groups of involved people. In all these situations the functional value of the music must be considered to be more important than the sonic event itself. It will be educational to see the styles and directions that music will follow in the decades ahead along the paths of socialist realism in China.

Overseas Chinese communities have shown an equal interest in furthering native Chinese traditions in the light of idioms from other parts of the world of music. There has been a tendency to emphasize music for ensembles that often include Western instruments, thus allowing tempered tuning to make strong inroads into Chinese idioms. The traditional arts of opera and solo instrumental music are still patronized, and Confucian rituals have occasionally been revived on Taiwan, somewhat in the spirit of Western collegium musicum revivals of old European traditions. In all expatriate Chinese communities there are forms of popular and film music which combine foursquare strophic forms and international social dance rhythms with singers using hybrid vocal qualities and a mixed orchestra playing harmonized accompaniments.

Some say that Chinese music will never return to its former greatness until its theoretical-philosophical base is restored. The same has been said, of course, of Western music. It seems unlikely that the *lü's* and their cosmological significance will ever return to China, any more than the ethical power of the ancient Greek modes will ever affect the European scene again. Nevertheless, the overwhelming past and brilliant present of Chinese traditional music provide ample material for an appreciation of the musical genius of the Chinese people. Their impact on world music has been strong; and it is still evident in our last remaining area of study, the music of Manchuria, Korea, and the Asian Islands.

BIBLIOGRAPHICAL AND DISCOGRAPHICAL NOTES

Peter Crossley-Holland writes extensively on Tibetan music and has provided an annotated bibliography of Western studies of it in *Ethnomusicology,* XI/2 (1967). Lobsang P. Lhalungpa's "Tibetan Music: Secular and Sacred," *Asian Music,* I/2 (1969), gives a lama's view of the topic, while Ivan Vandor is opening up the world of Tibetan instrumental music in publications such as those listed in footnotes 3 and 5. Walter Kaufmann's *Tibetan Buddhist Chant* (Bloomington: Indiana University Press, 1975) is a paragon of detail. Ernst Emshiemer's work listed in footnote 7 is the first extensive study of Mongolian music. Further transcriptions are found in *Dix-huit chants et poèmes mongoles,* First Series, IV, of the *Bibliothèque Musicale du Musée Guimet* (Paris: Geuthner, 1937). Recordings include Vogue *Chants mongols et bouriates* (LDM 30138-Collection Musée de l'Homme) and Le Chant du Monde *Mongolie Sin-Kiang* (LDY 4039). Tibetan examples are heard in *Songs and Music of Tibet* (Folkways FE 4486), *Musique tibetaine du Sikkim* (Contrepoint MC 20.119); *The Music of Tibet: The Tantric Rituals* (Anthology AST 4005), and *Tibet* in the UNESCO series (Musicaphon BM 30 L 2009–2011).

Fredric Lieberman's annotated bibliography *Chinese Music* (New York: Society for Asian Music, 1970) lists 1483 items in Chinese and European languages; Laurence Picken's important scholarly works are included. See also Picken's and Peter Crossley-Holland's articles on Chinese music in *Grove's Dictionary of Music,* 5th ed. (1954); the 6th edition promises to cover Asian musics in more detail. The chapter on China in vol. I of *The New Oxford History of Music* (1957) and Fritz Kuttner's "The Music of China," *Ethnomusicology,* VIII/2 (1964) are interesting starting points, as is William P. Malm's article "Music, East Asian" in the *Encyclopaedia Britannica,* 15th ed. (1974), XII, 669–691. J. A. Van Aalst's *Chinese Music* (1884) has been reprinted by Paragon Book Store in New York. R. H. Van Gulik's *The Lore of the Chinese Lute* (Tokyo: Sophia University, 1940) is a classic combination of scholarship and evocative writing, as are the works of Edward Schafer, such as *The Golden Peaches of Samarkand* and *The Vermillion Bird* (Berkeley: University of California Press, 1963 and 1971), which discuss the exotica of the Chinese T'ang and Han dynasties China. Shigeo Kishibe's major studies of T'ang music are in Japanese, but selections can be read in English in his "On the Origin of the P'ip'a," *The Transactions of the Asiatic Society of Japan,* Second Series, XIX (1940), and "A Chinese Painting of the T'ang Court Women's Orchestra," in *The Commonwealth of Music,* ed. Gustave Reese and Rose Brandel (New York: The Free Press of Glencoe, Inc., 1965). Chinese excerpts from historical sources are found in *Chung-kuo ku-tai yin-yueh shih-liao chi-yao* (Peking: Chung-kua, 1962). Notations and evaluations are available in Rulan Chiao Pian's *Song Dynasty Musical Sources and Their Interpretation* [*sic.*] (Cambridge, Mass: Harvard University Press, 1967). Among her studies of Chinese opera music are the two important items listed in footnotes 22 and 23. Many opera pieces are notated and analyzed in Gerd Schönfelder, *Die Musik der Peking-Oper* (Leipzig: Deutcher Verlag für Musik, 1972), and much information is found in the *Chinoperl News* printed periodically by the Conference of Chinese Oral and Performing Literature and issued through The China Program, Franklin Hall, Cornell University, Ithaca, New York. A study of instrumental music is David Liang's *Music of the Chinese Ch'in* (Taiwan: Chinese National Music Association, 1972). Practical details on *ch'in* performance are found in the two articles by the performer Tsun-yuen Lui in *Selected Reports,* Institute of Ethnomusicology (U.C.L.A.), I/1, 2 (1968). Articles in *The Drama Review,* 15/3 (1971), present the mainland Chinese view of opera and ballet. Publications of the Foreign Language Press of Peking, such as those listed in footnotes 24 and 25, are readily available around the world.

Chinese recordings include *The Music of China,* ed. Fredric Lieberman (Anthology AST 4000 and 4002), and, on Lyrichord, *Chinese Classical Masterpieces for the Pipa and Chin* (LL 82), *China's Instrumental Heritage* (LL 92), *Chinese Drums and Gongs* (LL 102), *Shantung Music of Confucius' Homeland* (LL 112), and *Chinese Classical Music* (LL 72). Peking opera is heard on two Folkways records, *The Ruse of the Empty City* (FW 882) and *Beating the Dragon Robe* (FW 8883). Modern Chinese operas and much reconstructed music are readily available on mainland records now sold all over the world; similar material is found on *China Today* (Bruno 50115). Popular music is heard on *China* (Capitol T 10087).

MUSIC TERMS IN CHINESE CHARACTERS AND TRADITIONAL (WADE-GILES) AND MAINLAND ROMANIZATIONS

箏
cheng = zheng

妓 官
chi kuan = jiguan

妓 女
chi nü = jinu

角
chiao = jiao

徵
chih = zhi

琴
ch'in = qin

磬
ch'ing = qing

京 劇
ching chü = jingju

京 戲
ching hsi = jingxi

柷
chu = zhu

朱載堉
Chu Tsai yü = Zhu zaiyu

曲 牌
ch'ü p'ai = qupai

角
chueh = jue

二 胡
erh hu = erhu

二 黃
erh huang = erhuang

方 響
fang hsiang = fangxiang

戲 曲
hsi ch'ü = xiqu

西 皮
hsi p'i = xipi

戲 文
hsi wen = xiwen

簫
hsiao = xiao

壎
hsuan = xuan

玄 宗
Hsuan tsung = Xuan Zong

胡 琴
hu ch'in = huqin

胡 樂
hu yüeh = huyue

黃 鐘
huang chung = huangzhong

黃 帝
Huang -Ti = Huang Di

弋陽腔
i yang ch'iang = yiyangqiang

高 腔
kao ch'iang = gaoqiang

高 祖
Kao - tsu = Gaozu

快 板
k'uai pan = kuaiban

管
kuan = guan

崑 曲
k'un ch'ü = kunqu

滾 道
kun tao = gundao

宮
kung = gong

箜 篌
k'ung hou = konghou

宮 女
kung nü = gongnu

聯 曲
lian ch'ü = lianqu

流 水
liu shui = liushui

鑼
lo = luo

律 or 呂
lü = lu

慢 板
man pan = manban

南 曲
nan ch'ü = nanqu

南 戲
nan hai = nanxi

內 教(房 or 坊)
nei chiao fang = neijiaofang

八 音
pa yin = bayin

排 簫
p'ai hsiao = paixiao

板
pan = ban

幫 腔
pang ch'iang = bangqiang

班 鼓
pan ku = banku

梆子腔
pang tzu ch'iang = bangziqiang

北 曲
pei ch'ü = beiqu

皮 黃
p'i huang = pihuang

變
pien = bian

編 磬
pien ch'ing = bianqing

編 鐘
pien chung = bianzhong

琵 琶
p'ip'a = pipa

鈸
po = bo

散 曲
san ch'ü = sanqu

三 絃
san hsien = sanxian

瑟
se = se

商
shang = shang

笙
sheng = sheng

詩
shih = shi

十部伎
shih pu chi = shibuji

哨 吶
sona = suona

俗 樂
su yueh = suyue

四 胡
szu uo = sihu

大鼓詞
ta ku tz'u = daguci

弹 詞
t'an tz'u = tanci

地方戲
ti-fang hsi = difangxi

笛 子
ti tzu = dizi

導板 or 倒板
tao pan = daoban

單皮鼓
tan-pi ku = danpigu

雜 劇
tsa chü = zaju

詞
tz'u = ci

外 教(房 or 坊)
wai chiao fang = waijiaofang

文 舞
wen wu = wenwu

五 聲
wu sheng = wusheng

武 舞
wu wu = wuwu

陽
yang = yang

洋 琴
yang ch'in = yangqin

搖 板
yao pan = yaoban

宴 樂
yen yueh = yenyue

陰
yin = yin

雅 樂
ya yueh = yayue

羽
yu = yu

敔
yü = yu

元 曲
yuan ch'ü = yuan qu

原 板
yuan pan = yuanban

月 琴
yueh ch'in = yueqin

樂 府
yu eh fu = yuefu

SEVEN
NORTHEAST ASIA AND THE ISLAND COUNTRIES

MANCHURIA AND KOREA

We noted in the last chapter the pervasive influence of China on all the areas surrounding it. Manchuria and Korea are part of this Sinicized belt, yet their cultures present very different mixtures of foreign and domestic elements.

The nomadic tribes of Manchuria have at various times been vassals of Chinese or Mongolian dynasties as well as the conquerors and rulers of China itself. Russian and Siberian influences have also been felt. The resulting musical culture displays features of each external area. Both Lamaistic and Chinese Buddhism exist in Manchuria, as do Mongolian- and Siberian-style shamans with their pan drums. Russian-style folk choruses, in which a rhythmically free, melismatic solo is sung over a sustained chordal background, can also be heard. At the same time,

Chinese puppet plays and operas are a main source of entertainment. Finally, one can find, in mid-twentieth century Manchuria, remnants of court orchestras playing music derived from the lost court traditions of China, now preserved primarily as Manchurian Confucian ritual music. While the names of many of the pieces played can be found in very ancient Chinese sources as well as in the repertoire of the T'ang dynasty-inspired orchestras remaining in Korea and Japan, the instruments used in Manchuria derive from around the time of the Manchu conquest of China (1644). Moreover, the storerooms of Jehol and other Manchurian centers of culture have produced several unique instruments of great importance in the tracing of the movement of musical ideas and materials over Asia.

Although Korea was also subject to long periods of Chinese domination and Mongolian intrusion, it maintained its own kingdoms which, though based on Chinese models, contained many native elements. The basic types of surviving Korean court orchestral music reflect this. They are Confucian ritual music (*a-ak*), Chinese T'ang and Sung dynasty pieces (*tang-ak*), and Korean court music (*hyang-ak*). The instrumentation of each differs. The basic melodic instruments include some form of double-reed aerophone (*piri*) and a flute. The *taekeum* flute is of particular interest for its considerable length (74 centimeters) and its membrane-covered "buzzing hole," which produces a tone of unusual richness.

The basic zither in both Korean court and city music is the *kayakeum*, seen in Plate XVIII, Figure 51 (with its courtly player). Its 12 movable bridges allow the pitch of each string to be changed. Pushing on the strings beyond the bridge with the left hand while plucking the notes with the right hand (as in Figure 51) gives further tonal variety to each string. The relative thinness of the instrument's body (when compared with the resonance chamber of the *koto* in Plate XXII, Figure 59) allows one to produce percussive sounds by snapping the strings. Thus there is excellent dynamic contrast in *kayakeum* music. The *kayakeum* is claimed as an indigenous instrument, as is the *komungo* (Figure 52). The latter, credited to the seventeenth-century court musician Wang San-ak, is indeed a unique zither, for although three of its outer strings are placed on movable bridges, three in the middle pass over sixteen tall frets. The strings are plucked by a wooden stick (seen lying on the strings in Figure 52) that is clenched in the right hand with the thumb stretched along the top of it. An equally unusual Korean court zither is the *a'chiang;* its seven strings pass over movable bridges like those of the *kayakeum,* but it is played by bowing it with a resined wooden dowel.

The Korean *haekeum* bowed lute (Plate XIX, Figure 54) also seems "exotic" when compared with its Chinese relatives such as the *hu*

PLATE XVIII. Korea

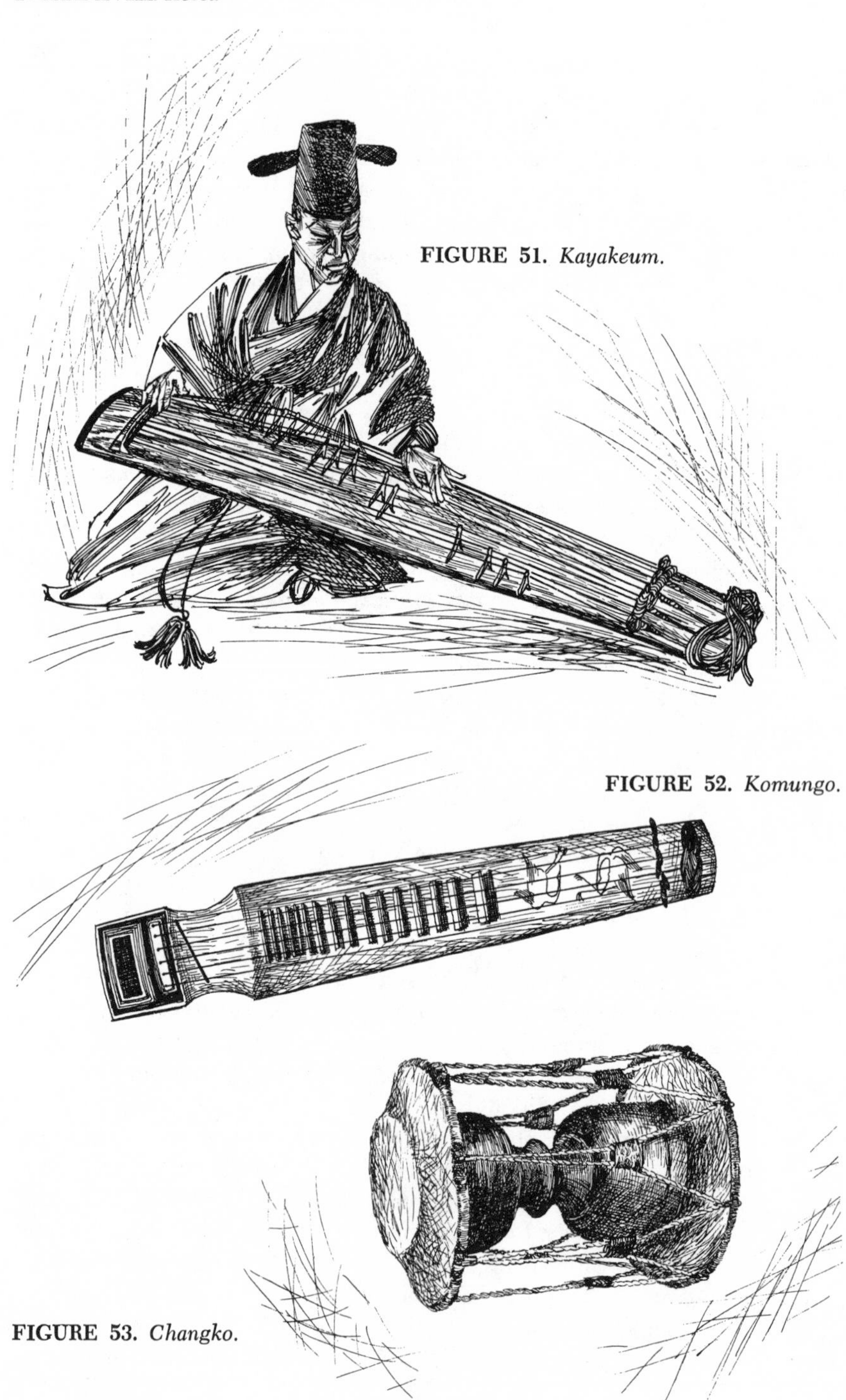

FIGURE 51. *Kayakeum.*

FIGURE 52. *Komungo.*

FIGURE 53. *Changko.*

FIGURE 54. *Haekeum.*

FIGURE 55. *O* or *Yu.*

ch'in (Figure 47) or other bowed lutes like the *kamanchay* (Plate VIII, Figure 21). The curve of its neck, the insertion of the pegs, and the attachment of the strings to the pegs seem to be unique in the world. When it is used in court music, a cloth is hung from its pegs so that the movements of the fingers on the strings are hidden.

The main percussion instrument in all kinds of Korean music is the *changko,* shown in Plate XVIII, Figure 53. The right-hand skin is played with a stick, the left-hand skin with the hand.

We have already noted some fairly exotic instruments in Korean court music, but its greatest historical treasures are China's most ancient idiophones—racks of 16 tuned bells (in Korean *pyonchong*), tuned slabs of iron (*panghyang*), and stone chimes (*pyongkyong* or *teukkyeng*). Only in Korea can one still hear their simple but sonorous sounds. A musical curiosity of old China survives in Korea in the form of the *o,* the crouched wooden tiger in Figure 55 of Plate XIX. Its serrated backbone is scratched with a split bamboo whisk at the end of Confucian ritual pieces. Another Chinese survival is the *pak,* a clapper made of six slats of wood held together at one end like a folded fan. The director of the orchestra begins and ends each piece with the sound of this instrument. Globular flutes (*hoon*) and the Chinese mouth organ (in Korean *saing*) are also found in Korea.

The ancient traditions of the Korean courts survive now primarily through the efforts of the National Music Institute in Seoul and its North Korean counterpart. In attempting to restore some of the old traditions, they have been aided not only by oral tradition but also by early notation books and historical sources. The earliest notations are in Chinese styles, but a Korean mensural notation (one that shows time as well as pitch) was developed in the fifteenth century. In its modern form it uses columns of six or twelve squares which represent beats. Pitches, rhythms, and tempos are easily recognized once one learns the meanings of the notational symbols. Like the Korean phonetic system that was invented about the same time, Korean notation is one of the clearest notations known.

The most famous Korean historical document on music is the *Akhak kwebon* ("Handbook of Music"), which first appeared in 1493.[1] It is a compendium of instrument tunings and fingerings, theoretical tone systems, choreographic patterns and orchestral seating arrangements, and ceremonial costumes and paraphernalia.

As performed today, Korean court music is played in a rather slow tempo, often beginning in a free rhythm. There is a florid heterophony

[1] For a discussion of an even earlier work see Robert C. Provine, Jr. "The Treatise on Ceremonial Music (1430) in the Annals of the Korean King Sejong," *Ethnomusicology,* XVIII/1 (1974).

between the melodic instruments, except for the bells and chimes, which play melodies devoid of rhythmic variety, primarily because their surviving ancient notations are still in the Chinese system, which shows only pitches without rhythm. The mode systems in which court music is set are based on the ancient Chinese pentatonic discussed earlier (p. 148), though their Korean interpretations have varied greatly over the centuries. Earlier theorists seemed to want to consider each of the five tones as a potential "tonic" within the Chinese scale with its fixed *kung* tone in Example 6–3. Using C as a *kung* tone for the sake of comparison, the Korean *u-jo* mode would be as shown in Example 7–1A. Transposed up a fifth

EXAMPLE 7–1. One interpretation of the Korean mode system.

into *akshi-jo,* it is as in Example 7–1B. The *kyemon-jo* uses a different pentatonic arrangement which, if built from the same fundamental pitch as the *u-jo,* appears as shown in Example 7–1C. The meaning of the term *pyong-jo* remains controversial, but later theorists tended to consider it as a transposition of *u-jo* up a fourth, as shown in Example 7–1D. By now, our discussions of various mode systems in other cultures will have made it clear that the tonal vocabulary of any mode is only a small part of its real musical meaning; we must await further musicological research to discover the "real" meanings of the Korean mode system, but even a comparison of the basic Chinese and Japanese (Example 7–7) ancient scales with those of Korea demonstrates the uniqueness that seems so characteristic of Korean music in its East Asian context. At the same time, the court music of Korea, though little known or appreciated in its own country, is of considerable historical importance in East Asia, for it was the primary link between the Chinese and Japanese ancient traditions, and it remains one of the very few living clues to the glories of the musics of the Orient in former times.

Chamber music for strings (*pungnyu*) and classical vocal forms (*norai*) have also been preserved from the dynastic periods of Korean history. The *norai* include *kasa,* narrative songs, as well as *kagok,* long suites of instrumental accompaniments and interludes. *Sijo,* songs to shorter classical poems, are sung to the accompaniment of the *changko* drum. In many of these older forms the syllables of the text are drawn out to such an extent that the meaning is lost unless one can actually see the poem. A more active and communicative narrative form is the *pansori,* which is sung by a fan-carrying narrator-dancer to the accompaniment of a *puk* barrel drum or a *changko*. The most popular and widespread Korean narrative songs are the *japka* ballads, sung primarily by professional artists or *gishang* entertainment girls. Accompanied by the driving syncopation of a *changko* drum playing in a triple meter, the singers produce startling effects through sudden changes in style, from intense throaty renditions of low, tone-centered lines to high, steel-edged tones which may turn into dynamic vibratos seldom heard elsewhere in the world's vocal traditions. The tonal systems also vary, and songs may include extended slidings as well as passages bordering on heightened speech. Such a form of Korean music, like Korean food, seems spicy and rather unoriental. This exciting vocal art and its compelling rhythmic accompaniment almost seem closer to the Spanish Flamenco or pan-Islamic traditions than to the surrounding Oriental styles. Perhaps further music studies would shed light on the possible continuities between East and West caused by the constant moves of ancient Asian hordes. At present, all that can be said is that such Korean singing deserves special attention for its unique qualities. The transcription of Example 7–2 is only a pale reflection of its true sound.

EXAMPLE 7–2. A Korean ballad song transcribed from the recording *Japan, The Ryukyus, Formosa, and Korea* (New York: Columbia Masterworks Records KL-214), side 2, band 3, item 29. Used by permission.

EXAMPLE 7–3. A Korean entertainment song transcribed from the recording *Japan, The Ryukyus, Formosa and Korea* (New York: Columbia Masterworks Record KL-214), side 2, band 3, item 31. Used by permission.

Korean folk, dance, and entertainment songs use the same characteristic triple rhythms, as shown in Example 7–3. When combined with the sleeve-swinging dances of Korea, the total effect is very gay. Even the music of the Korean shaman (*mudang*) maintains this quality. This tradition and various folk festivals (*nong-ak*) and masked theatricals were noted in Chinese sources as far back as the third century. Korean shamanism is particularly interesting when placed in the context not only of the Central and North Asian examples mentioned earlier (p. 143) but also in relation to the other arctic traditions with which this chapter will end.

TAIWAN AND THE RYUKYU ISLANDS

Within the various musical cultures of the islands off the East Asiatic shore, we can find reflections of traditions already surveyed in this book as well as unique regional solutions to the standard musical problems of function and structure. On Taiwan (Formosa), for example, one is first struck by the predominately Chinese styles of music heard in the cities. Japanese and Western occupations of the island have also left their musical marks. Tribal traditions reminiscent of Borneo and Indonesia are more evident in the jungle. Harmonic singing, like that we noted in Oceania and Borneo, and instruments like the musical bow point to a very different world from that of the urban Sino-Japanese society. In a word, when in Chapter 2 we turned from the Philippines south and westward toward Indonesia and the African–Near Eastern world, we were arbitrarily choosing one of two cultural tracks. The other moves northward through the aboriginals of Taiwan and beyond. It is difficult to say how far one can continue to trace the influence of Oceanic and Indonesian cultures beyond Taiwan, but the Ryukyu or Loochoo Islands, lying between Taiwan and Japan off the coast of China, seem to be the point at which the myriad cultures of Asia have their last clear confrontation.

The oldest forms of Ryukyu music are the *umui* religious chants, sung primarily by priestesses (*nuru*), and the *kwena* songs. Both are sung either unaccompanied or with a drum. Two basic styles of *umui* (or *omoro* in the Japanese pronunciation) survive. The first, apparently a courtly style, consists of variants on a single-centric melody—one centered on a single pitch (like that in Example 7–4A)—sung in a slow litany fashion. The second style, used in regional shrines, retains the same sliding vocal technique and short strophic form of the first, but it uses many different melodies, some of much wider range, as seen in Example 7–4B.

EXAMPLE 7–4. Ryukyu *umui* songs transcribed from tapes accompanying Seihin Yamanouchi, *Ryukyu ocho koyo himitsukyoku no kenkyu* (Tokyo: Private edition, 1964). Used by permission.

This style may begin with a nonsense syllable such as *heya, o,* or *e.* Either style may end in a pitchless drop reminiscent of techniques used in Oceania and the Philippines. Occasional examples in triple meter are found.

Other ancient forms can be found in the Ryukyus, but the predominant ones of today are songs and dances accompanied by the three-stringed plucked lute with a snakeskin head called the *sanshin* or *jamisen.* This instrument first appeared on Okinawa, the main island of the Ryukyu chain, in the fifteenth century. It is derived from the Chinese *san hsien* (Figure 48). It is plucked with a talon-like pick attached to the right forefinger. As seen in Example 7–5, the *sanshin* plays a rather straightforward tune against which an off-beat vocal line is performed. This syncopation makes it easier to hear the words against the percussive sound of the accompaniment.

EXAMPLE 7–5. An Okinawan song "Mo-Ashibi" transcribed from the recording *Japan, The Ryukyus, Formosa and Korea* (New York: Columbia Masterworks Record KL-214), side 2, band 1. Used by permission.

While much Ryukyuan music uses the Chinese pentatonic scale, there are pieces more reminiscent of Indonesia, with their use of half steps and their rising lines. Japanese influence is reflected in the use of the 13-stringed *koto* zither (Plate XXII, Figure 59), although many of the *koto* pieces common to both countries are played in different tone systems, the Ryukyuan versions preferring the standard pentatonic over the Japanese *yo* and *in* scales (see p. 188).

Ryukyuan music is most commonly heard today as dance accompaniment. A *sanshin* player, singers, and a stick drummer provide the background for dances of which the hand movements often look Indonesian, the costumes Chinese, and the choreographic floor patterns Japanese. The quick-stepping feet are Okinawan, however, and the overall combination is unique to Ryukyuan culture.

JAPAN

Folk Music

Japan is a country of many islands. This geographical fact has combined with a long history of feudalism to create strong regional folk traditions. Nevertheless, these traditions have certain points in common. Japanese folk song tends to be sung in a high, tight-throated, melismatic fashion. Much of it tends toward the *parlando-rubato* style, although dance songs are, of course, in regular rhythm. It is usually duple, although, as seen in Example 7–6, it can have a triple tendency as well. The standard dance accompaniments are handclaps or barrel drums with two tacked heads played with sticks, which usually strike only one head. The generic term for such drums is *taiko*. Festivals (*matsuri*) usually use drums and bamboo flutes (*takebue*) plus occasional small brass gongs (*kane*). The generic term for these ensembles is *hayashi*. In urban festivals like those in Tokyo, these ensembles may play sets of pieces in varying tempos and moods, rather like Western dance suites. While improvisation hardly exists in Japanese music, the festival music often seems improvisatory because of the ornamentation (*ashirai*) of the melody by the flute and because different groups seem to play the same piece in a very different manner. Actually, each group plays the piece with little internal variation from performance to performance, but the version of each may differ from those of the others among the guilds (*ryu*) of players, to distinguish it from the others' and keep it "secret" from them. Though the flourishing of recordings in Japan now makes this sonic control impossible, the attitude reflects well the guild tradition that is typical of Japanese music in its older forms and, at least in principle, in modern idioms as well.

The festival ensemble (*matsuri bayashi*) music itself produces a strong sense of driving forward through the time continuum of each piece

EXAMPLE 7–6. An excerpt from the student version of the *matsuri bayashi* piece "Yatai." The transcription is based on oral lessons given the author by Fumio Wakayama, director of the Edo bayashi troupe in Tokyo.

by frequently exploiting a rhythmic technique that may be called the *slide-rule effect:* the actual phrase lengths of various instrumental lines are not the same, so that, while they seem quite symmetrical by themselves, they sound out of synchronization when performed together. Example 7–6 shows how this method creates a tension that drives the music forward towards a release at the cadence.[2] Since all such music is learned orally by mnemonics, the conflicts that might be revealed by a written score do not exist for the student or the professional performer.

Japan has many folk theatricals (*minzoku geino*) that appear during festivals. These include a variety of animal dances, from Chinese-inspired lions to fearsome bands of deer with large horns and bamboo "antennae" projected high in the air. Elaborate flowered hats and grotesque masks can also be seen. Many of the pantomime theatricals and ritual dances are related to the ancient theatricals of the court or to the surviving professional traditions, in which folk variants of more aristocratic instruments may be used instead of the usual flutes, drums, and gongs.

The three-stringed plucked *shamisen* or *samisen* lute (Plate XXII, Figure 58) did not enter Japan before the sixteenth century and thus does not tend to be used in older theatricals. However, it is frequently used to accompany regional and occupational folk songs. As seen in Example 7–7, it sometimes plays an ostinato against the vocal line.

EXAMPLE 7–7. A Japanese folk song, "Sado Okesa," transcribed from the recording *Traditional Folk Songs of Japan* (New York: Folkways Record FE 4534), side 2(B), band 7. By permission of Folkways Records and Service Corporation.

[2] Phrase marks have been used in Example 7–6 to show the different lines of the "slide rule." The example is an excerpt from a student version of the piece; professional recordings contain more elaborate renditions of the patterns shown, though the basic organizing principle remains the same. For details concerning another piece see the author's article "Shoden . . . ," *Yearbook of the International Folk Music Council* (1976).

The two basic scales of Japanese folk music, as well as most other music after the appearance of the *shamisen,* are the *yo* and *in* (A and B in Example 7–8). While they both reveal a pentatonic core with two possible

EXAMPLE 7–8. Four basic Japanese scales.

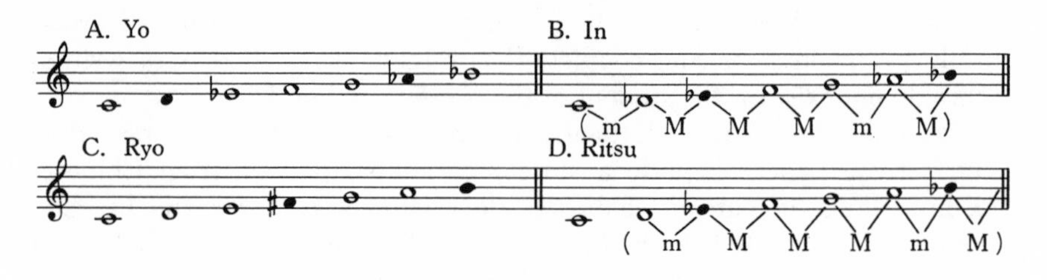

additional tones (shown as black notes in Example 7–8), they differ particularly in their use of half steps. The *yo* scale is basically an anhemitonic pentatonic, relating to the ancient scales of the Japanese court (C and D in Example 7–8), while the *in* scale produces a more obvious Japanese-like sound by its frequent use of half steps above the root and fifth of the scale (Example 7–7 uses the *in* scale).

In modernized Japan, folk traditions are kept alive by local chambers of commerce, Shinto shrines, and Buddhist temples. The ability to sing or perform a folk dance has also become as much a part of a businessman's qualifications as his skill at golf or cost accounting. Thus, folk song has managed to keep contact with modern life by assuming new functions and appealing to new audiences while maintaining its position in the vestiges of rural society. The folk revivals common among the youth cultures of the mid-twentieth century are found in Japan as well.

Japanese Art Music—Ancient Traditions

Artifacts and Chinese references inform us of indigenous Japanese musics as far back as the third century B.C., but historical information does not surface until much later, when Japan gradually adopted and adapted the Chinese writing system (from the fourth century A.D. on). The first major importation of continental court musicians is traditionally dated as 453 A.D., when eighty Korean musicians were sent to perform at the funeral of a Japanese ruler. In the sixth century, Chinese Buddhism joined the indigenous Shintoism as an official religion in Japan. Thus it was that Buddhist chant (*shomyo*) and continent-derived court music (*gagaku*) became the two foundations of Japanese classical music.

The nomenclature and tone systems of Buddhism bear the same relation to Japanese art-music traditions as the Catholic Gregorian chant theories do to the growth of Western musical styles. Selected Japanese converts were sent to the international centers for Buddhist studies in China, whence they returned with treasures of enlightenment and information, including music theory and practice. The major surviving source for the Japanese interpretation of such material in the Tendai sect of Buddhism is the *Shomyo yojinshu* by Tanchi (1163–1237). It is paralleled in the Shingon sect by *The Great Collection from Fish Mountain* (*Gyosan taikaishu*, 1496), which takes its name (*gyosan*) from the Japanese equivalent of the name of the center in China where so much of such information was taught. The notations of Buddhist chant, like those of Tibet discussed earlier (p. 139), are generally neumatic. However, since Sino-Japanese writing is ordered in vertical columns rather than horizontal lines, the shapes and styles of Japanese neumes are quite different from those of Tibet. Perhaps the most interesting (and historically controversial) system is the *go-in hakase*, said to have been invented by Kakui (b. 1236) of the Shingon sect. In this system the five notes of each set of three octaves of pentatonic scales are indicated by short angled lines (like the hands of a clock). Starting with the fourth note of the lowest pentatonic as G, the pitches G, A, C, D, E, G would be notated as o—, o\, ♀, ρ, —o, \o . This system contrasts with most Western neumatic notations, especially in that the graphic direction of the line has no necessary relation with upward or downward motion from one pitch to the next (for example, low G up to C is o—, ♀). An interesting comparison has been made between this system and the ritual hand gestures (*mudras*) and oracle stick placements of earlier Indian Buddhism.[3] Whatever its origin, it provides for the professional singer an equally logical but different memory-aid system, as well as a means of preserving the "secret" traditions of his sect. Within the traditions of each sect are found not only different notation systems but also the names of stereotyped melodic patterns that require aural memory rather than notation for their performance. This principle of named stereotyped patterns is characteristic of many of the Japanese musics that developed in later historical periods. Of equal influence was the tone system of early Buddhism and music of the court.

Example 7–8C and 7–8D are the two basic scales of ancient Japanese court music, the *ryo* and *ritsu*, here built on the note C for convenience in comparing them with Example 6–3. The *ryo* scale conforms to the traditional view of East Asian pentatonicism, but the *ritsu* seems to imply something that may be indigenous: the greater use of half steps. It is possible to think of *ritsu* as some ancient theoretical attempt to explain

[3] See Walter Kaufmann, "The Mudras in Samavedic Chant . . . ," *Ethnomusicology*, XI/2 (1967).

the *in* scale of folk song (Example 7–8B) in terms of a more "classical" Chinese system. In this view, the *in* scale is seen as a "hidden" mode in the *ritsu* scale; such a relationship is shown in Example 7–8 by the parenthetical listing of major and minor seconds beneath the *ritsu* scale (starting from its D instead of C) and beneath the *in* scale. Such an interpretation is conjectural, however, and is not part of traditional Japanese music theory.

In traditional theory the two scales may be constructed on three pitches each. These tone systems (*cho*) are normally listed in modern writings on the following Western pitches: D (*ichikotsu*), G (*sojo*), and E (*taishiki*) for *ryo;* E (*hyojo*), A (*oshiki*), and B (*banshiki*) for *ritsu,* the two names of E appearing in order to distinguish between the two *cho* that can begin on that pitch. Note that the five different pitch centers put together would create an anhemitonic pentatonic scale, which is the core of so many East Asian scale systems.

The scales and transpositions mentioned above represent only a small part of the essential differences that actually distinguish one *cho* from another. As in Near Eastern *maqamat,* Indian *raga,* Catholic chants, or negro blues, there are melodic units, ranges, and, in the case of *cho,* even accompaniment figures that may play equally important roles in the aural definitions of the sonic whole. Modes as such are not discussed in the writings on *cho,* although *cho* is often mistranslated as "mode." There are, however, a few compositions that appear in two *cho.* In such "crossed over" examples (*watashimono*) one finds that the piece is not merely transposed but is, in fact, modal; that is, the melody in one *cho* uses a different pitch in the scale as its tonal center, i.e., the pitch on which it ends (in Western terms, the *finalis*), than it does in the other *cho.*[4]

Although the modal aspect of *gagaku* may not be clearly stated, there is no lack of documentation concerning the general tradition. In 735 a Japanese ambassador, Mabi Kibi, brought back from China a ten-volume *Digest of Music Matters* (in Japanese, *Gakusho yoroku*) which still survives. A Japanese court dancer, Chikazane Koma, produced a similar ten-volume set, the *Kyokunsho,* in 1233, and the extensive *Taigensho* was written by a court musician, Sumiaki Toyohara, in 1512. But perhaps the most powerful source of information about and symbol of the *gagaku* tradition and its performance practice is the Shoso-in storehouse, built in 756 as a repository for objects from the Todai-ji temple and the household goods of the late Emperor Shomu. When it was opened in 1872, among its thousands of items was found a marvelous set of 45 musical instruments plus one fragment of lute notation and sets of dance masks and accessories, as well as a catalogue of most of the contents of

[4] See Example VII in the article, "Music, East Asian," *Encyclopaedia Britannica,* 15th ed., XII, 683.

the storehouse listing the origins of many items.[5] Inlays, etchings, and masks show lions, Bactrian camels, and palm trees as well as Chinese acrobats and bearded, big-nosed Westerners—that is, traders from Central Asia and the Near East. Figure 56 in Plate XX, taken from a *biwa* lute in the Shoso-in, shows a scene appearing on the cover (*bachikawa*) of the *biwa*, which protects part of its face from the strokes of a plectrum (*bachi*). End-blown and side-blown Chinese flutes are seen joining an hourglass-shaped drum played by a big-nosed "foreigner" in the accompaniment of a dancer who cavorts on the back of a white elephant. We show this one scene from one instrument in an attempt to suggest some small part of the excitement of the historical and musical treasures of ancient Japan in general and of the Shoso-in collection in particular.

Perhaps Figure 57 in Plate XXI is an even more powerful example. It shows a *kugo*, the best preserved example of the kind of angle harp that is seen elsewhere only in bas-reliefs in Babylon or in painting and statuary from Egypt, Persia, Central Asia, and China. Though the *kugo* has not been played in Japan for centuries, it is still, thanks to the Shoso-in storehouse, our most striking example of marginal survival. It is an excellent and beautiful symbol of Japan's cultural-historical position as a kind of cul-de-sac into which a rich stream of ancient Asian traditions flowed. Some of the sonic remnants of their musics are heard in *gagaku* performances today.

The term *gagaku* ("elegant music") is actually a Japanese reading of the same characters (雅楽) that are pronounced *yen yueh* in China and *a-ak* in Korea. *Gagaku* flourished in Japan during the Nara (710–784) and Heian (794–1185) periods, which correspond with China's "international period" (cf. p. 154). Japan's musical imports at that time were quite exotic: in addition to China, Korea was always an important source, and there is some evidence of South and Southeast Asian materials as well. Official court music was administered through a music bureau (*gagaku-ryo*) established in 702, and by the early ninth century a "Big Sound Hall" (*outadokoro*) was added to handle Japanese compositions. *Gagaku* is called *kangen* if it is an instrumental performance and *bugaku* if it accompanies dance. Historically, the many types of *gagaku* were organized, in the best Confucian style, into two categories; the music of the right and of the left. Music of the right was called *komagaku*. It contained Korean- and Manchurian-based music, and the costumes of its dancers emphasized green. Music of the left was called *togaku;* it contained music from China and India and featured red costumes. Japanese com-

[5] Photographs, measurements, and an English summary of these objects in the collection are found in two handsome Japanese volumes, *Shosoin no gakki* and *Shosoin no men* (Tokyo: Nihon keizai shimbun sha, 1967).

FIGURE 56. Figures on the face of a *biwa*.

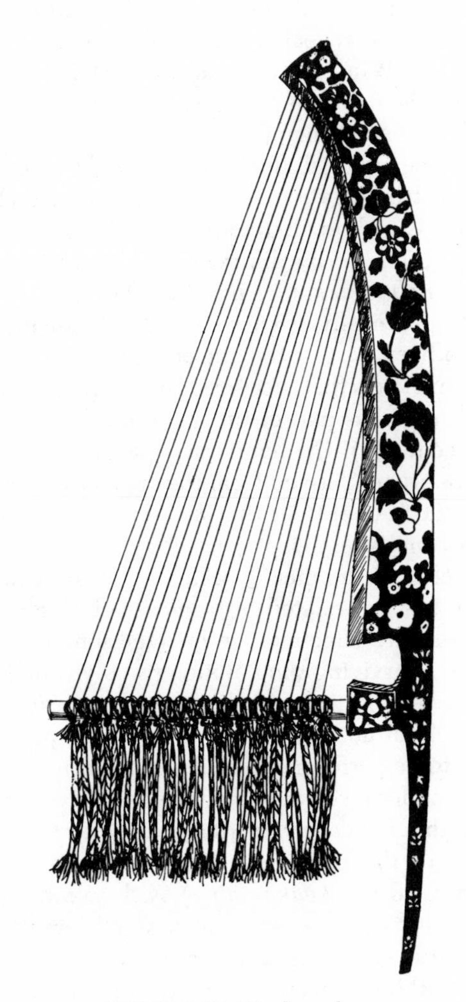

FIGURE 57. The *kugo* harp.

positions are said to have appeared in *komagaku,* though it is possible that they occurred in both categories, since composers are not listed nor are the repertoires further differentiated. The titles of compositions, however, often at least reveal continental origins: for example, "The Barbarians Drinking Wine" (*Konju* or *Koinju*) is obviously a Chinese composition, while the dance of *Genjoraku* can be traced to an old Indian Veda story about the exorcising of a snake.

The major means of differentiating *togaku* and *komagaku* today is through their instrumentation. The basic *gagaku* melodic instrument, in both categories, is a short double-reed aerophone called the *hichiriki.* It is joined in performance by different side-blown flutes, the *ryuteki* in *togaku* and the *komabue* in *komagaku.* In either case, the melodic instruments play heterophonically. (These differences in interpretations of a melody may have been part of the ancient tradition, but also may reflect unyielding discrepancies that occurred when musicians from separate ensembles were merged as part of the modernization of Japan during the late nineteenth century.) Contemporary performance practice on the 17-pipe *sho* mouth organ, derived from the ancient Chinese *sheng* (Figure 46), is also a puzzle.[6] At present the *sho* provides a handsome harmonic matrix for *gagaku* melodies by playing chords (generally tone clusters) built on basic pitches of the melody. Such a performance style has never been found in any of the related instruments of East or Southeast Asia, though tone clusters are effectively interjected into some melodies of the *khaen* (Figure 40). Surviving *sho* notation usually contains only one pitch name for about every four beats, like a guitar lead-sheet in Western popular music; in both notations there is little except tradition to tell us how it actually is to be performed. Whatever the original sound of the *sho* may have been, modern versions of its music have provided a special texture in *gagaku* that has captivated many a Western listener.

The center of the percussion section of a *gagaku* ensemble is a large hanging barrel drum (*gaku-daiko*) with two tacked heads, one of which is played with two beaters, and a small hanging gong (*shoko*). Their entrances are so spaced that they seem to function in a manner suggesting the time-marking concept originally noted in Indonesian music by Jaap Kunst (see p. 43). For example, in an eight-beat phrase the gong marks off the second and sixth beats while the *gaku-daiko* sounds on beats four and eight. The leader of the ensemble performs more actively, on a small barrel drum (*kakko*) in *togaku* or on a larger hourglass-shaped drum (*san no tsuzumi*) in *komagaku.*

[6] See Laurence Picken, "Tunes Apt for T'ang Lyrics from the *Sho* partbooks of *Togaku,*" in *Essays in Ethnomusicology: A Birthday Offering for Lee Hye-ku* (Seoul: Korean Musicological Society, 1969), 401–420.

Today, stringed instruments are not used in *komagaku,* nor are they used in *togaku* when it serves as dance music (*bugaku*). Concert *togaku,* however, uses the 13-stringed *koto* zither (Plate XXII, Figure 59) and a pear-shaped *biwa* lute similar to the one shown in Figure 60. As used today, these instruments do not play the melody but, rather, short stereotyped melodic phrases or arpeggios which, while influenced by the melody and its tone system, function in a colotomic fashion through the regular spaces that exist between their entrances. This performance practice is based upon a literal translation of traditional notations, which originally may have been merely "lead-sheets" from a much richer tradition. From the novels and memoirs of the Heian period (794–1185) we know that both the *koto* and *biwa* were frequently used in accompanying courtly songs or in instrumental solos. Today all that survives of this tradition is the poetry and some descriptions of romantic performances, plus a small repertoire of vocal music performed with great solemnity by musicians of the court or of large Shinto shrines.

From the few surviving genres of vocal music sung today, one can gain insights into the spirit of the past. *Roei* songs show an inspiration from Chinese poems. *Saibara* seem to be derived from songs of pack-train drivers. *Imayo* are of particular interest because they were apparently derived from popular songs and texts of the day, often set to well-known courtly tunes.

The Shinto vocal music performed in the palace or in a large temple falls into two types, songs of praise or petition for aid (*torimono*) and songs to entertain the gods (*saibari*). These songs are sung by a unison chorus usually accompanied by a *hichiriki,* a *kagura-bue* flute, a *sho,* and a six-stringed board zither (*wagon*) that resembles the Korean *kayakeum* (Figure 51). The leader may mark the start and finish of a piece or its verses with the sound of a pair of long, thin *shakubyoshi* clappers (cf. the *pak* of Korean Confucian music, p. 180). Shinto music and dance for the palace is called *mi-kagura,* that for the large shrines *o-kagura;* the local shrine events mentioned earlier are *sato-kagura.* Together, they reflect an ancient agricultural sense of time that remains as fundamental in modern Japan as it does for most of the West.

The vocal and instrumental traditions of Japanese ancient music have all been preserved not in scores but in part-books. In instrumental music these combine fingering indications with mnemonics that (unlike Western and Indian systems) do not necessarily represent pitches in a scale but, rather, help the reader recall the melody with its contour and ornamental nuances. Rhythmic aspects of the melody are not indicated, though beside each column of notation dots appear; these correspond to the moments when each time-marking instrument plays. Though pieces are arranged in such books according to their *cho,* the various pitches

PLATE XXII. Japanese Chordophones

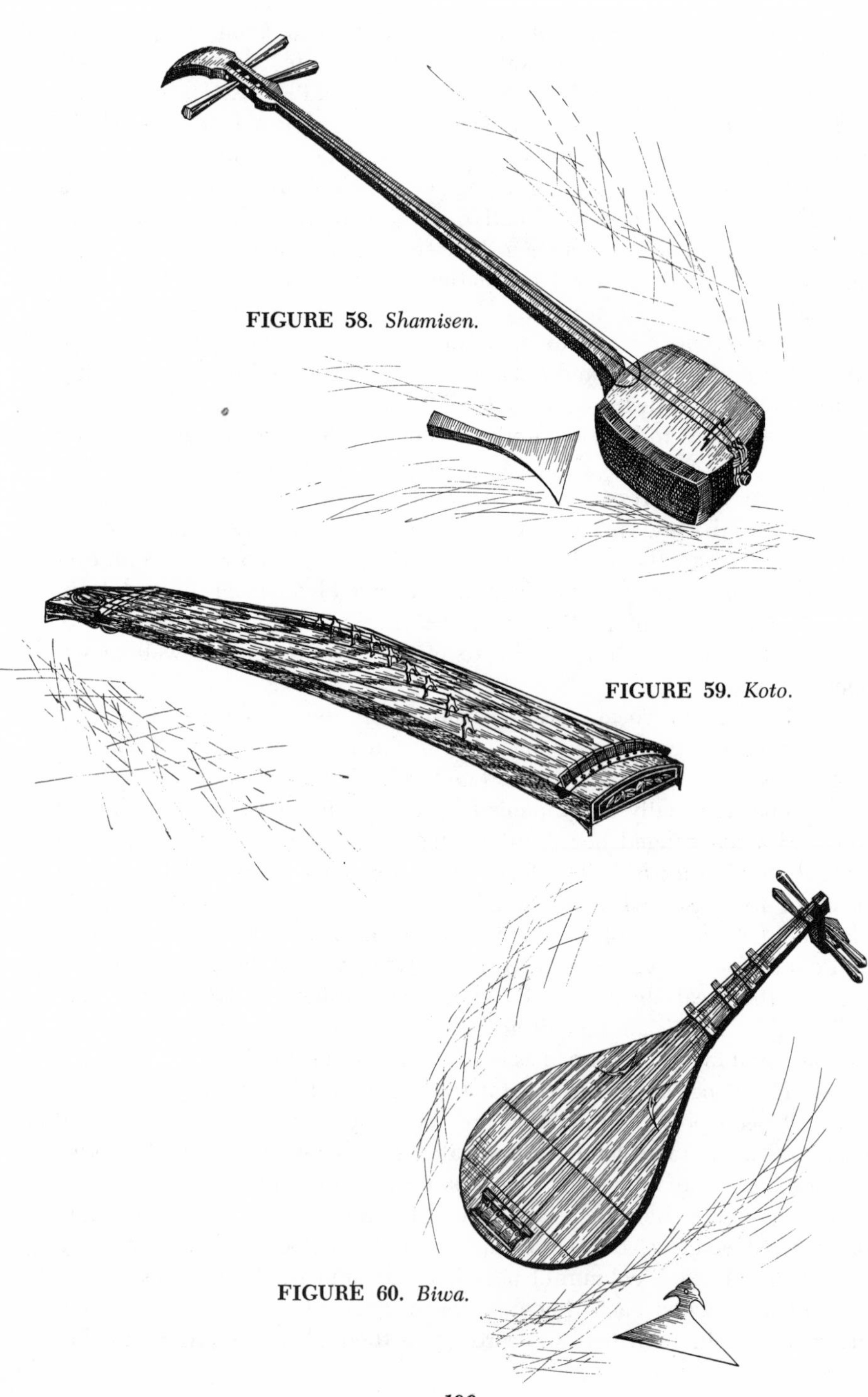

FIGURE 58. *Shamisen.*

FIGURE 59. *Koto.*

FIGURE 60. *Biwa.*

available from a single fingering on the main melodic instruments make it difficult to determine what the actual tune is. Originally this was no problem, since the music was first taught orally—by singing the mnemonics while beating out the rhythmic divisions—and then learned on the instrument. Whatever the relation of modern practice may be to the original product, however, Japanese *gagaku* is still one of the rarest and oldest orchestral musics in the world.

We have intimated that many of the principles found in these ancient musics are basic to Japanese music in general. One of these is the concept of getting the maximum effect from a deliberately restricted amount of material. For example, the many techniques possible on various *gagaku* instruments are generally not all exploited. Rather, there is a concentration on only a few basic sounds in order to enhance their effectiveness. At the same time, one can observe in *gagaku* performance the Japanese principle that instruments are to be played in a graceful manner, so that the music provides an aesthetically pleasing sight as well as sound.

Both *gagaku* and Buddhist chanting make use of a common Japanese principle of *elastic* or *breath rhythm*. There are, of course, many steady, metronomic beats in Japanese music, but one also finds sections—like the opening of any *gagaku* piece (the *netori*)—in which the beat simply cannot be conducted. The melody moves from beat to beat in a rhythm more akin to that of a breath taken deeply, held for an instant, and then expelled. In ensembles, such a rhythm can only be coordinated when the performers listen to each other and feel the music together. This is the kind of attitude Westerners associate with chamber music, and much Japanese music has this chamber-music quality regardless of the size of the ensemble. It also is chamber-like in the sense that the individual instrumental lines are designed to be heard separately, rather than merged as they are in the Western orchestral sound-ideal.

We have noted—in the string parts of *gagaku* as well as in Buddhist music—the important principle in Japanese music of using stereotyped patterns that are aurally perceptible. This will become even more evident as we look at later theatrical traditions.

Early Japanese Narrative and Theatrical Traditions

During the twelfth and thirteenth centuries a tradition arose called *heike-biwa*, in which a famous war narration was sung to the accompaniment of a *biwa* lute. The music consisted of lines of poetry chanted to named, stereotyped melodies separated by pitch-giving notes or stereotyped interludes played on the lute. Many of the names of both the vocal and instrumental patterns were derived from Buddhist chant nomencla-

PLATE XXIII. Japanese Membranophones

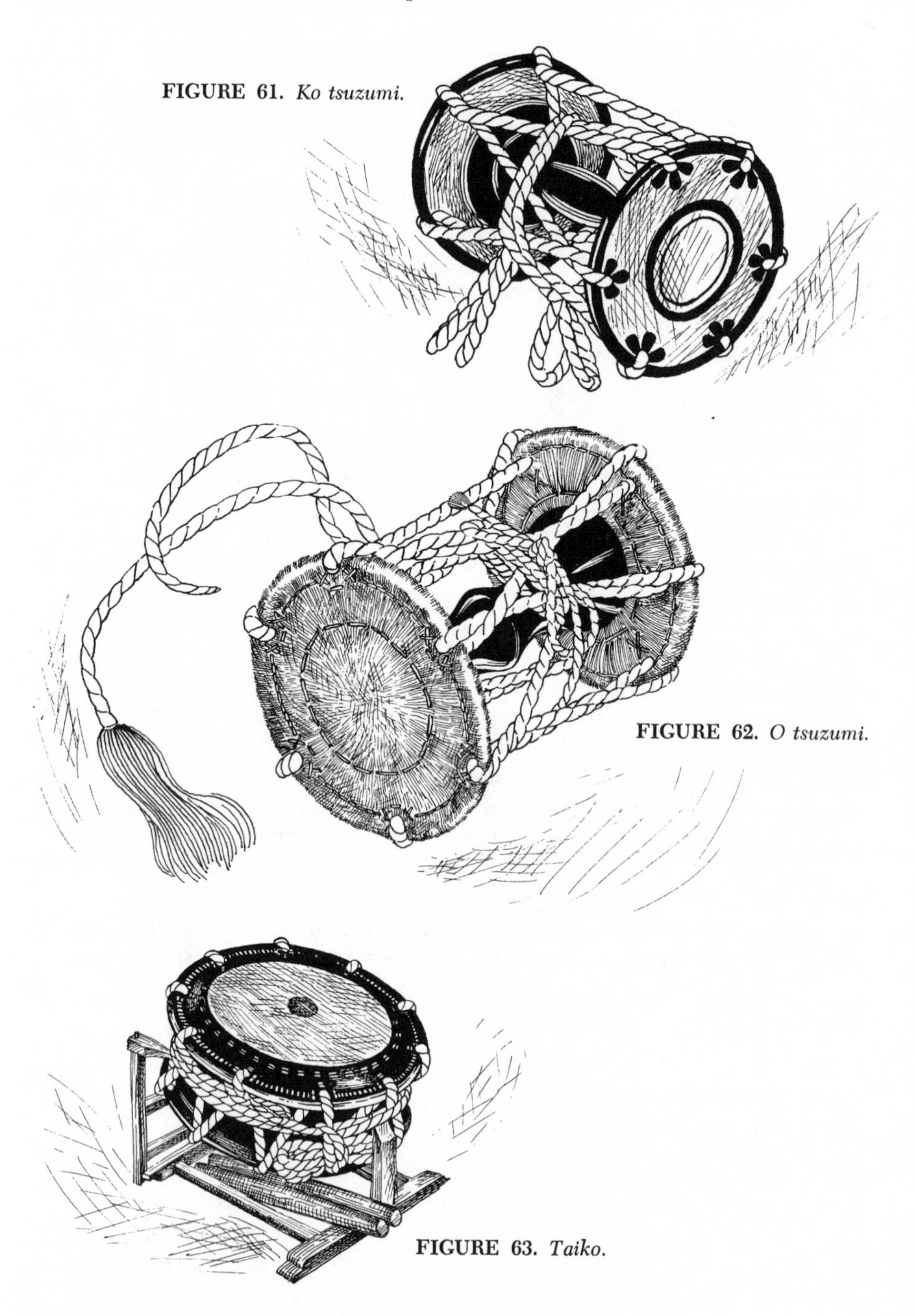

FIGURE 61. *Ko tsuzumi.*

FIGURE 62. *O tsuzumi.*

FIGURE 63. *Taiko.*

ture. This style of narration became very popular and, though *heike-biwa* itself is rare today, its tradition is carried on in a similar if more flamboyant style by modern *biwa* and *shamisen* narrators. The *Satsuma biwa* shown in Figure 60 is only one of several styles of *biwa* used today, but the music of all tends to continue the tradition of alternating vocal and instrumental sections. In such a tradition, the notation need only show the text plus the name of the particular pattern to be played or sung. The individual performer must interpret these patterns according to the requirements of the particular piece, as well as those of the style of the specific guild of performers to which he belongs. This does not mean that he improvises. As mentioned earlier, in Japan there is variation but not improvisation. Whatever the version of a piece, it must be played as accurately as a Mozart sonata, despite the existence of other versions of the same composition.

Our earlier references to festivals and to dance materials in court imply that theatricals have been a part of Japanese music for a long time. Continental theatricals are believed to have been brought into Japan in 612 by a Korean musician, Mimashi. Throughout the subsequent centuries there are many records of street entertainments, folk festivals, and pantomime plays in Shinto shrines and Buddhist temples. Through a skillful combination of such materials, Kiyotsugu Kanami (1333–1384) and his son, Motokiyo Zeami (1363–1443), created a major theatrical genre that became known as *noh* (or *nō*, "accomplishment"). *Noh* combines music, dance, poetry, design, costume, and a Buddhist world-view in a manner that remains meaningful to this day. The music of *noh* consists of singing, known generally as *yokyoku* or *utai*, by the main actors or a unison chorus with or without instrumental accompaniment. In *noh* the term *hayashi* is used for an ensemble of four instruments: a flute (*nokan*), a shoulder drum (*ko tsuzumi*, Plate XXIII, Figure 61), a side drum (*o tsuzumi*, Figure 62), and a floor drum played with sticks (*taiko*, Figure 63). The last is seldom used except in dance sections of a play, in which case a full ensemble is the normal accompaniment. The flute also serves primarily as the melodic element for dance accompaniment, though its sounds are very important for marking off sections throughout a play as well as for creating special moods. However, it is seldom related tonally (and never thematically) with the vocal part. It is the *ko* and *o tsuzumi* drums that are most intimately linked with the singing, for they provide an essential rhythmic framework into which the music for each line of text must be set. Example 7–9 shows one way in which the vocal and percussion parts might relate to each other. Each unit of text, influenced by the conventions of much Japanese poetry, consists of a seven- and a five-syllable line set in a normal *noh* framework of eight beats. The total twelve syllables

EXAMPLE 7–9. A *noh* drama excerpt transcribed from "Hagoromo" in *Noh: Two Major Dramas* (New York: Caedmon Records TC 2019), side 2, the first entrance of the chorus. Used by permission.

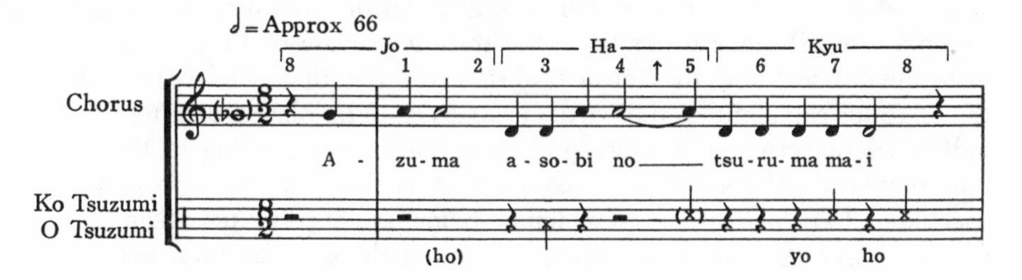

and their framework are conceived in terms of a three-part subdivision: *jo,* the introduction; *ha,* the scattering; and *kyu,* the rushing towards the end. Beneath this vocal line the drummers play a named, stereotyped rhythmic pattern which, with the aid of the drummers' calls (*kakegoe*), helps mark the subdivisions of the line. Thus, in Example 7–9 the "yo" of the *o tsuzumi* player prepares for the first sound of the drum on beat three which, in turn, marks the end of the *jo* section and start of the *ha;* the division between the *ha* and *kyu,* which occurs on beat five in this setting, is frequently marked by a "ho" from the *ko tsuzumi* player followed by the sound of the drum on the fifth beat, somewhat like the *ko tsuzumi* part at beat eight which, here, marks the end of the *kyu* and preparation for the next *jo.* There are, of course, many other possible solutions to the musical needs of this given phrase, just as one line of a Western tune may be set in different ways. The relatively simple solution seen in Example 7–9 is heard frequently, however, and does illustrate the basic principles upon which more complicated structures are built.

For Western listeners the most puzzling sounds in *noh* music are often the drummers' calls. It is possible that they were originally teaching aids in drum lessons, though there are no historical data to support this theory. As used today, however, they have several truly musical functions. Since the principle of elastic rhythm is very prevalent in *noh,* drummers' calls are an important means of controlling and signalling the progression from one beat to another in a manner that all participants and listeners can understand. They also function as an aid in identifying aurally a named pattern, for the calls are specific for each pattern and often specific to the guild of the drummers who are performing it. Thus, the particular arrangement of drummers' calls and drum sounds in Example 7–9 is "correct" for the drum pattern *uke mitsuji* as performed by members of one guild of drummers in the context of this one phrase of one *noh* play; they will never appear in quite the same manner in another pattern of a different name, though renditions of *uke mitsuji* by drummers from a different guild may be the same or very similar to the version shown in Example 7–9.

Named drum patterns are not only internally identifiable but also fall into predictable orders of progression; that is, after a given pattern is played there is a strong likelihood that another specific pattern will follow it. This kind of progression will continue until a specifically cadencing pattern appears. Similarly stereotyped patterns appear in Western music. For example, after a C major and then an F major chord, there is a strong possibility that the next chord will be on G. Of course, other chords are possible—just as other rhythm patterns are possible in our Japanese example. The important point is that both systems involve sets of aurally identifiable, stereotyped patterns that tend to move in predictable succession so that the forward motion of the music is enhanced. The only significant difference between the Western and the Japanese system is that one involves vertical stereotyped sonorities called chords while the other involves horizontal rhythmic patterns. Here is one answer to the lack of harmony in much non-Western music; it is not needed, for its forward-moving function is served by a different concept of rhythm. How many times in this survey have we not seen similar "strange" uses of rhythm which put a third dimension into the music beyond those of melody and rhythm as they are understood in the West? The lack of the development of an involved concept of harmony in non-Western music may be because its functions had already been supplanted by special uses of rhythm. The Japanese *noh* drama certainly illustrates one such use very clearly.

The *jo-ha-kyu* concept mentioned above applies to more than just a single phrase. It may be applied to large sections of a play, the entire play, or the arrangement of an entire day of plays. In a word, it is an aesthetic view of music, much as the concepts of question and answer or of arsis and thesis often are found to permeate thinking about form in Western music. The bi-partite form is also common in Japan, but the *jo-ha-kyu* concept is the one most used by Japanese musicians when they are called upon to explain their music.

Music During Japan's Edo Period (1615–1868)

In Japan, as in the West, the major kinds of traditional music heard today arose in the period from the seventeenth through the nineteenth centuries. This is called the Edo or Tokugawa period in Japan because the Tokugawa clan controlled the country and moved the government to a new center called Edo, known today as Tokyo. It was during this period that Japan became isolated from outside contact and thus was able to develop her own artistic resources without extensive foreign influence. It was a period marked by the rise of a merchant class and an emphasis on city life. Music reacted to the needs of this new audience.

One of the first theatricals to flourish in the new society was the puppet theater (*bunraku*), which found its greatest audience in the business town of Osaka. The three-string, plucked *samisen* (in the Tokyo dialect *shamisen,* Figure 58), adapted from the Ryukyuan *sanshin* in the sixteenth century, was used to accompany a singer-narrator. This music became known as *gidayu-bushi* after the name of its most famous singer, Gidayu Takemoto (1651–1714). It was one of many such *shamisen*-accompanied narratives, known generically as *joruri,* that flourished during the Edo period.

The musical style of *gidayu* developed from the previous *biwa* lute narratives with extensive use of stereotyped patterns and interludes. As these were connected with a theatrical art aimed at a bourgeois rather than a courtly audience, their style became more flamboyant and intricate. Specific melodic phrases took on dramaturgical meaning in much the way that emotions and situations could be portrayed in Western baroque music and in Wagnerian operas through the use of special tunes. As performed today, *gidayu* music has all the melodrama and pathos of Italian opera, though a *gidayu* performer must be as great an actor as singer, since he (or in some concert performances, she) not only sings all the music and provides comments and narrations in the story but also speaks the dialogue for *all* the roles, masculine, feminine, hero, and villain.

The other basic Edo Period theatrical was the *kabuki.* Traditionally an all-male theatre (though it began as all-female), *kabuki* has pleased Japanese audiences for over 200 years with a combination of melodrama and colorful dancing. Three basic kinds of music were developed to accompany these actions, the on-stage ensemble, the narrative music, and the off-stage group.

The first on-stage (*debayashi*) ensemble in *kabuki* was the *hayashi* group of three drums and a flute mentioned earlier in connection with the *noh* drama. Next were added *shamisen*-accompanied songs derived from several genres popular in the adjacent brothel districts. Eventually the *shamisen* and singers were combined with the *hayashi* to form a new Japanese ensemble. While several different types of *shamisen* music are still played with this combination, the basic genre used today is called *nagauta*—"long songs." In keeping with the bright spirit of *kabuki,* the drums borrowed from the *noh* developed rhythmic patterns directly related to the rhythms of the *shamisen* part. These patterns are called *chiri-kara* by the *tsuzumi* drummers, after the mnemonic with which they are learned. However, the drummers also use *noh*-derived patterns, which produce an even greater dynamic, forward progression when set against *shamisen*-vocal lines. It is common for the *taiko* drum and the *noh* flute to play in *noh* style while the *tsuzumi* drums support the *shamisen* line with direct rhythmic imitations. When they do, one can sense the forward drive of the music created by the "slide-rule" effect mentioned earlier, since the phrases of the flute and *taiko* do not coincide with those of the *shamisen* and *tsuzumi* drums. In this music, then, there are three distinct musical units: the melodic, held by the voice and *shamisen;* the rhythmic, in the *tsuzumi;* and a third "dynamic" unit consisting of a flute and *taiko* performing many of the functions Western musicians normally associate with harmony.[7] Since the *noh* flute does not operate as a melodic unit, it has no tonal or thematic relation to the *shamisen* part. In *kabuki,* the *noh*-flute player may also use a folk bamboo flute (*takebue*) if lyrical support of the melody is required. Such changes in instrumentation and in the relations among the various instrumental parts are guided by the choreography of the dance as well as by principles of form. The formal implications of changes in style and orchestration are important in such a through-composed music. Because of them, an experienced listener has a strong sense of formal progression without reference to or development of specific themes.

The major influence on the melodic structure of *shamisen* music is the text. There are many subtle reactions or even word–paintings to be found behind its modulations or turns of phrases.[8] This became particularly true after the mid-nineteenth century, when compositions began to be written for concert performance rather than theatrical accompaniment. Another result of this development was the appearance of famous composers and performers, such as Rokuzaemon Kineya XI (1829–1877),[9] and the building of a cadre of concert-goers and amateur practitioners. Thus, economically and sociologically the *shamisen* tradition developed aspects similar to those of the Western concert world or, later, to the world of Western-music concerts in Japan.

The second basic *kabuki* music is the narrative (*joruri*), as derived

[7] For further details see William P. Malm, *Nagauta: The Heart of Kabuki Music* (Tokyo: Tuttle, 1963).

[8] For specific examples see Malm, "On the Nature and Function of Symbolism in Western and Oriental Music," *Philosophy East & West,* XIX/3 (1969).

[9] In the Japanese music guild system a member receives a professional name (*natori*), and by heredity or talent certain names are passed on through generations. In this example, Kineya is the guild name; by the mid-twentieth century the title Rokuzaemon had been given to its 14th bearer.

from the *gidayu shamisen*-singer combination from the puppet tradition. *Gidayu* musicians usually sit downstage left, as they would in the puppet theater. The various musics used in the *kabuki* often appear onstage at the same time, so that a given performance consists of interjections by two or three different groups of musicians.

The third kind of *kabuki* music (*geza*) is the offstage music. Its basic purpose is to provide mood, set scenes, and give musical clues as to action or location. Singers, *shamisen,* flutes, drums, and a battery of special gongs and bells are used singly and in combination. They are able to assist the drama by playing named patterns or melodies that have specific dramaturgical meaning. For example, the large *o daiko* barrel drum with two tacked heads can be made to symbolize the ocean, various degrees of rainfall, battles, or soft snowfall through the choice of the proper pattern. A given tune on the *shamisen* may indicate the weather, the time of day, or perhaps the specific location of the scene that is to follow. (Similar, less codified techniques are used in Western movie music.) In the *kabuki,* the *geza* combines with the onstage ensembles to provide a varicolored accompaniment for one of the Orient's most enjoyable theatricals.

Not all the music of the Edo period is theatrical. In addition to many kinds of intimate *shamisen*-vocal forms, there developed other vocal-instrumental traditions, such as those using the 13-string *koto* (Figure 59). Movable bridges allow for several different tunings, while three picks attached to fingers of the right hand and varying pressures on the strings with the left hand provide a variety of timbres and pitches. While much *koto* music is vocal, there is an important genre of variation solos (*danmono*) that is very popular. In addition, the *koto* may be combined with a singer, a *shamisen,* and a five-hole end-blown flute (*shakuhachi*) to form a chamber music (*sankyoku*) ensemble. The particularly soft sound of the *shamisen* in this ensemble is caused by the use of a heavy bridge, a thin plectrum, and strings of a special weight. Actually, each kind of *shamisen* music requires an instrument of different size as well as different accessories in order to produce a particular tone color. The *shakuhachi* also comes in various sizes; however, the choice of length is determined not by tone color but by the tuning of the other instruments in the ensemble, since Japanese music is played heterophonically. The *shakuhachi* is best heard when performing its solo literature, for a good player can produce a beautiful variety of tone colors and ornaments on this deceptively simple-looking bamboo tube.

Music in Modern Japan

The modernization of Japan, begun in 1868 under the Emperor Meiji, has drawn special interest from the West because of the swiftness with which it proceeded. Actually, Western materials (including music) were known in Japan as early as the sixteenth century through merchants and Catholic missionaries,[10] but the suppression of Christianity and foreign trade in the Edo period left only one trade center as a source of what became known as "Dutch learning." In the Meiji era (1868–1912), Western music developed in Japan primarily through two channels, the military and the educational. Through them Western music was introduced, at first not out of any special interest in the music itself but rather as part of a desire to reproduce various foreign systems accurately. Thus bands were formed because they were included in the standard table of organization for military services; and music was made part of the newly formed public schools because it was included in the foreign models. Foreigners were brought to Japan as instructors, among them Luther Whiting Mason (1828–1896) who, along with Shuji Izawa (1851–1917), helped found a music teachers' college and form a curriculum for the public schools that was to affect Japanese musical life for generations. Their original intent was to combine the best of East and West, and both Western and Japanese instruments were taught at the college; similarly, songbooks for schools tried to include the best of the Boston public school tradition plus harmonized Japanese tunes. Unfortunately, only the Western style instrumentalists from the college went into public school teaching, the Japanese-style players returning to their own traditional world. At the same time, the children found the new military songs composed for the Chinese and Russian confrontations to be of greater interest than the old Japanese tunes. To capture the children's interest, many of these songs were reworked with suitable words. The net result of these various factors was that a child in school heard only Western instruments, Western children's songs, or heavily Westernized Japanese military-style music. Indeed, not until the late 1950's was Japanese traditional music to be found on music appreciation records issued for public school use. Today even the songs of Stephen Foster can be claimed as part of the Japanese musical tradition, since they have been sung by at least three generations.

Another interesting result of Japan's American-based public school music system has been that young people are trained to sing in harmonized choruses, unlike the monophonic style of traditional music. Various political and religious groups have taken advantage of this training and have organized workers, students, or co-religionists into choral societies. These have proven to be very useful in recruiting new members as well as in unifying large bodies of people in public demonstrations.

[10] A survey of the first Christian music in Japan is found in Eta Harich-Schneider, *A History of Japanese Music* (London: Oxford University Press, 1972), Chapter 14.

Readers of other chapters in this book will assume—correctly—that throughout its history Japan, like other parts of the world, has always had some form of popular music. Thus the so-called *hayari uta* of the Edo period became the *ryukoka* of the Meiji era simply by giving a different reading to the characters used for the term "popular" and changing the character for "song": (流行歌 became 流行唄). In some ways, popular music of the early modernization period was more creative than its military, educational, and religious competitors because it had no firm dogma. Its major rule was (and probably always will be) that it had to sell. Thus, bugle songs (*rappa-bushi*) were all the rage during the time of military events in the Meiji era, while patter songs (*oppekepe-bushi*) in music halls became well-known outlets for commentary on Japanese developments and problems.[11]

During the subsequent years Japanese popular music, like that of most of the world, has developed with the following general characteristics: it is evanescent (a hit today, gone tomorrow); eclectic (a good pop writer may mix any idioms or textures without concern for being either original or authentic); international (a Japanese mountain-yodel song is as good as a Swiss oriental piece); and egalitarian (there is some kind of popular music for every class and age). With such a sociologically viable base, a burgeoning mass-communications system, and some talented composers and performers, popular music continues to flourish and exchange ideas throughout the world, including Japan.

If we turn our attention to "serious" music in Japan over the past 100 years, traditional Japanese music (*hogaku*) and Western music (*yogaku*) will be seen to have continued to develop, but along basically separate if parallel lines. We will discuss traditional music first.

During the Meiji restoration, the monopolies of Japanese guilds were declared illegal, and traditional musicians thus lost control over an important source of income. One positive result of this action, along with the growth of concerts mentioned earlier, was the increase in music lessons for amateurs and therefore an increase in appreciation and support for traditional music. Many traditional composers naturally became concerned with and curious about the strange sounds of Western music. From a Japanese standpoint it seemed that Western music, when first heard, differed from indigenous idioms in the following ways: it used "exotic" tone systems (the major and minor); it preferred large ensembles; it was

[11] Examples are found in the author's "The Modern Music of the Meiji Era," Chapter 7 of *Modernization and Japan in the Humanities*, ed. D. Shively (Princeton: Princeton University Press, 1971). See also his "Layers of Modern Music and Japan," *Asian Music*, IV/2 (1973).

louder; it seemed based on the idea that playing faster meant playing better; and it was thicker, its melodies clouded by chords, though undernourished rhythmically. On the basis of these insights "new" traditional music (*shin-hogaku*) was attempted. The establishment of orchestras of traditional instruments was matched by new works with virtuoso parts and much plunking of chords. Perhaps the most successful of all such compositions were those of a *koto* musician, Michio Miyagi (1894–1956) of the Ikuta guild. His modern pieces, written before World War II, are now part of the standard repertoire.

In the field of Western classical music in Japan one finds several pioneers who had no experience in Japanese traditional music at all and who sought their training abroad, particularly in Germany. Among them is Koscak (né Kosaku) Yamada (1886–1965), who founded Japan's first major orchestra and opera organizations and who composed many works in a European style, usually based on Japanese ideas. For example, his 1940 opera *The Black Ships* (*Kurobune*), which deals with the first visit of the American fleet to Japan in 1853,[12] is composed in a style reminiscent of Wagner's *The Flying Dutchman* and the late operas of Puccini. In general, one finds interesting parallels between the solutions by composers in Japan and those in developing countries (and in America in the 1930–40's) to the problems of using national materials in Western-style concert idioms. Regional folk songs and folk tales are the standard source for such attempts.[13]

Japan's international reputation is even greater for the efficiency with which it has produced both performers of Western music and, in addition, instruments and a teaching-method industry. The last is exemplified by Shinichi Suzuki, whose violin method combines some elements of the Japanese traditional rote-learning system with a business organizational acumen.

The many efforts by traditional and Westernized Japanese musicians and by foreign composers of "oriental" taste are sometimes quite pleasant, but they seldom accomplish any real meeting of East and West. The problem is not that there is any lack of talent; rather it has been that there has been no composer to have really understood both musics on an equally deep level. It was not until the second half of the twentieth century that the "anational," transcendental idioms of the times—and talent along with supranational understanding—could be combined to provide

[12] A very different approach to the same topic was made in America in 1976 in a musical titled *Pacific Overtures*.

[13] The record *Tokyo: 1918–1942* (Victor VX-116–8) provides an excellent selection of such materials.

musical abstractions that were international in appeal but still evocative of indigenous music. In Japan as of the 1970's, the most frequently successful composer in this manner seems to be Toru Takemitsu (b. 1930).

It should be obvious from our discussion that almost any kind of music is available in Japan today. In the modern mass-communication world this is somewhat true for any part of the world if one is willing to find the right radio band or search out the special record store. Under the international pressure of a uni-cultural world, Japanese youth has joined that of other countries in seeking national roots, even though it may accompany its folk songs with guitar and accordion rather than *shamisen*. In any case, it would seem that for some time to come one can listen to the best of several musical worlds in Japan.

THE NORTHERN ISLANDS AND BEYOND

On Hokkaido, Japan's most northerly island, and the Russian-occupied Shakalins beyond that, one finds the remnants of several ethnic groups quite unrelated to the general East Asiatic traditions. The best known of these are the Ainu, a Caucasoid group, possibly with some racial affinity to the Australian aborigines. Much of the Ainu's music seems equally remote from its surroundings. The Ainu two- to five-string *tonkori* plucked zither, for example, has few parallels outside of Africa, while the singing in canonic and disphonic style of the Ainu has not been mentioned in this book since we left Melanesia! Though none of these facts necessarily has any historical connections, some things do imply more logical and possible cultural relations between the Ainu and other parts of the world. Ainu shamanism and, more specifically, its bear cult have relatives in Korea and in many cultures of North Asia. The Ainu jaws harp (*mukkuri*), which is sounded by jerking a string, is common also among such peoples as the Yakuts of Siberia. Similarly, one is tempted to compare the quavering, half-spoken Ainu voice quality and the short iterative melodies of Ainu narratives (*yukar*) with vocal styles heard among the Lapps of Sweden. More intriguing and tempting in comparative musicology is an Ainu style of singing (*rekkukara*) in which two women use each other's mouths for resonance while chanting a quick iterative refrain; similar techniques have been found among Alaskan and Canadian Eskimos, while Eskimo children have been heard panting quickly into empty oil cans to make a similar sound.

Research has only just begun; but it would seem that much might be learned about possible human cultural relations or about ecology and culture if one studied *circumboreal* music, that is, music produced by cultures that live around the arctic world in regions that view most closely the aurora borealis. Plate XXIV, Figure 64, shows a style of performance from the North American area of that region. The type of pan drum shown is often made of bone and seal skin because these are basic raw materials in the circumboreal world. Of greater cultural interest is the position in which the drum is used. If one traverses the circumboreal region from Alaska, Canada, and Greenland to Siberia other positions will, of course, be found, but this "backward" stroke on the drum is in the majority. The way in which the drum is held and struck from the "outside" is the opposite of the method that most Euro-Americans would use "naturally." It begins to make sense only when one notes that the drummer is also singing into the face of the drum. This enhances his tone in an acoustical world often muffled by snow and ice blocks or animal skins.

Slowly but surely one begins to find in the seemingly barren tundra world (as in other areas we have surveyed) a logical (if different) system of music enriching human life. The circumboreal chants themselves, with their short texts surrounded by meaningless syllables, may seem "primitive" outside their cultural context. To correct this error in understanding, one must place the chants in a world where survival depends on sensitivity to minute differences (for example, in one dialect there are a dozen words for the various kinds of snow) and a patient view of time. Only then can one realize that the Eskimos with their drums in Figure 64 may be communicating with their audience as powerfully as Mozart and his symphony or Art Tatum and his jazz piano do with theirs. And all three musicians would be evaluated as critically by their listeners as the *dijeridoo* player in Figure 1. Our first drawing, from Australia, along with the last one, from Alaska, have been used to enclose the text of this book partly as symbols of the fact that a musical event is most meaningful when it is heard in its own cultural context. Because music is *not* an international language, such meaning and functionality can seldom be enjoyed more than vicariously by an outsider. If this were not true, lecturers would not have to explain Beethoven to modern Western music-lovers, nor would uninformed persons speak of the "tuneless ditties of the natives." Fortunately, music *does* seem to be a universal *need.* Thus, there has been much to study and appreciate musically in our journey from Australia to the myriad cultures of Asia and finally across the northern frontiers of human society.

PLATE XXIV. Circumboreal Membranophones

FIGURE 64. Eskimo pan drums.

BIBLIOGRAPHICAL AND DISCOGRAPHICAL NOTES

Bang-Song Song's *Korean Music* (Providence: Asian Music Publications, 1971) is an annotated bibliography of 1,319 items, most of them in Asian languages. Lee Hye-ku, a leading Korean scholar, has a few article summaries in English, as in his *Topics in Korean Music* (Seoul: Korean Musicological Society, 1967). *Essays in Ethnomusicology* (Seoul: Korean Musicological Society, 1969), written to honor Lee, includes some European-language articles, among them "Notes on the Yongsan Hoesang Source" by Donald Sur. Alan Heyman's "Pansori," *Essays on Asian Music and Theater* (New York: Asia Society, 1971), and his "Comparative, Critical Study of Korean Traditional Music Today," *Korea Journal,* II/9 (1962), are more easily available, as is the Coralie Rockwell study *Kagok* (Providence: Asian Music Publications, 1972). The article by Robert C. Provine cited in footnote 1 (p. 180) is a promising beginning to new Korean music scholarship. Excellent recordings of Korean music are available through the Korean Broadcasting Corporation (KBC). Barbara Smith has edited the record *Music of Korea,* vol. 1, *The Kayakeum* (East-West EWM 1001). Lyrichord has produced *Korean Court Music* (LLST 7206), the Collection Musée de l'Homme provides *Musique bouddhique de corée* (Vogue LVLX 253), and Nonesuch produced *Pansori* (H 72049).

Jan LaRue's "Native Music on Okinawa," *The Musical Quarterly,* XXXII (1946), and his "The Okinawan Notation System," *Journal of the American Musicological Society,* IV (1951), are to be followed by a book on the topic (Harvard University Press).

An early general introduction to Japanese music is Francis T. Piggott, *The Music and Musical Instruments of Japan* (1909, reprinted New York: Johnson Reprints, 1971). For more recent studies, see William P. Malm's *Japanese Music and Musical Instruments* (Tokyo: Tuttle, 1963) and the items cited in footnotes 7, 8, and 11, plus his "Practical Approaches to Japanese Music," in *Readings in Ethnomusicology* (New York: Johnson Reprint, 1971). Eta Harich-Schneider's *A History of Japanese Music* (London: Oxford University Press, 1972) is an excellent source for Buddhist and court orchestra studies, as is her *Roei: The Medieval Court Songs of Japan* (Tokyo: Sophia University, 1965); Hans Eckardt's *Das Kokonochomonshu* (Wiesbaden: Harrassowitz, 1956) and Robert Garfias's *The Music of a Thousand Autumns, The Togaku Style of Japanese Court Music* (Berkeley: University of California Press, 1975) are scholarly studies. The musical form of *noh* is best described in the translation by Frank Hoff and Willi Flindt of Mario Yokomichi's work *The Life Structure of Noh* (Tokyo: Nogaku shorin, n.d.), and studies by William P. Malm are found in *Ethnomusicology,* II/3 (1958) and IV/2 (1960), and in *Chinese and Japanese Music-Dramas,* ed. James Crump and Malm, Michigan Papers in Chinese Studies, No. 19 (1975). Malm's studies of *kabuki* music found in the book cited in footnote 7 and in Chapter 3 of *Studies in Kabuki* by J. Brandon, D. Shively, and Malm (Honolulu: University of Hawaii Press, East-West Center Series, 1976). On *koto* music, see Willem Adriaansz, *The Danmono of Japanese Koto Music* (Berkeley: University of California Press, 1973), and on *shakuhachi,* articles by Donald Berger, *Asian Music,* I/2 (1969), and Elliot Weisgarber, *Ethnomusicology,* XII/3 (1968). Unpublished at the time of writing are some promising articles on Japanese music for the 6th edition of *Grove's Dictionary of Music* (London: Macmillan, 1978?).

Basic Japanese recordings are listed in the appendix of the 1973 printings of Malm's *Japanese Music and Musical Instruments* (cited above) and are reviewed in *Ethnomusicology,* XI/1 (1967). The UNESCO series on Japan (Musicaphon BM 30 L 2011–2016) demonstrates basic genres, as does Shigeo Kishibe's English-language release, *Traditional Music of Japan* (Japan Victor JL 52–54). The article on Alaskan Eskimo dance by Thomas F. Johnston in *Dance Research Journal CORD,* VII/2 (1975), includes circumboreal comparisons and Beverley Cavanagh's annotated bibliography on eskimo music is in *Ethnomusicology,* XVI/3 (1972).

EPILOGUE

In a survey that covers such a vast number of musical cultures it is appropriate that some attempt be made at generalizations. The search for musical categorizations can begin by turning to literate societies where specific theoretical explanations are found for many tonal and compositional principles. These principles cluster around three of the four major written music-theory systems of the modern world: the Arab-Persian, Indian, and Chinese. The fourth, the European, shares with the Near Eastern traditions certain historical roots in the Greco-Roman world. National music systems such as those of, for example, Uzbekistan, Japan, Sri Lanka, and the United States can be considered as satellite variations on the "big four." A fifth large unit may be the knobbed-gong culture of Southeast Asia, since it represents distinctive musical styles and instruments, though it did not possess extensive theoretical and historical written materials before the twentieth century. (Its early influences from the Buddhist, Hindu, and Moslem traditions also complicate the picture.)

Of the four large music cultures, three base their scale structures on a divisive principle. Only the Chinese uphold a cyclic technique through the use of the *lü* pipes, though the Indian system may have originated cyclically as well. On the basis of surviving sources from the four traditions, the Chinese and Indian systems contain more documentation concerning the ethical or extramusical implications of music. Such implications, of course, exist in the Arab-Persian and European systems and can be traced back not only to Greco-Roman roots but also to ancient Assyrian-Egyptian concepts. All four living traditions are closed theoretical systems; that is, they are complete in themselves and offer a thoroughly logical explanation of the particular characteristics of the music for which they were created. Throughout this book it has been emphasized that an appreciation of these logical but different systems is basic to an understanding of art music as a worldwide phenomenon.

Form seems to follow function in music as well as in architecture, as, for example, we have seen in the various religious musics studied. To attach extramusical values to specific instruments and elements of a tonal system is also a common tendency, and one important to the carriers of the culture that determined these values. One possible tool for those wishing to make comparative studies is musical cartography, in which maps are made of phenomena such as the locations of canonic disphony, a gong culture, or pitch-center preferences, or of the presence of a given type of musical instrument such as the *rebab* spike fiddle.[1] Some of these studies give us historical information about such matters as the spread of Islam, whereas others may indicate more general technological or physical similarities in conditions—for instance, the prevalence of bamboo or bronze instruments or the ecology of arctic regions.

If we turn now to view the multitudinous variety of musics mentioned in this survey plus the equally large number from other parts of the world, a fundamental question arises: are there any universal principles in music? Speaking always in the broadest terms, a few can be suggested. There does seem to be a basic need for musical tension and release, with all their melodic or rhythmic implications. Equally widespread are a need to mark off temporal lengths of music with distinct cadence sound, a tendency to find a tonal orientation or center in melodic music, an interest in creating a sense of forward progression by melodic, harmonic, or rhythmic stereotypes, and a principle of unity along with variety. Such things are necessary if music is to be perceived as moving logically and inexorably in a time continuum towards a recognizable

[1] Examples of such maps are seen in *The Historical Atlas of Music,* ed. Paul Collaer and Albert Linden (Cleveland: World Publishing Company, 1968).

ending. The use of some semiredundant patterns and progressions allows a knowledgeable listener to engage in prediction and anticipation (which is another way of saying he is really participating in or listening to the music).[2]

There are some musics in highly spiritual or functional situations and in parts of contemporary Western society that do not consider the generalizations given above as logical necessities. Their composers are sometimes able to create viable sonic events which seem to lie outside the neat concepts of the equally logical but different systems upon which most of this book is based. Ethnomusicologically speaking, however, they also fall within our generalizations. The logic of their "alogic" is found in their relation to the specific world view or function in which such sonic events occur. Their "value" is likewise seen in a cultural context. Thus, an answer to such a question as "Is it good music?" can only be made after a reply is given to yet a further question—"Good for what?" An instrumental variation piece played by a professional musician on the Korean *kayakeum* zither or on a Burmese harp and a song about water buffalo herds sung by a blind street musician playing a monochord in a Thailand village market are, in this sense, incomparable. They can really be evaluated best by members of the society that inspired them. They are of potentially equal value for a foreign listener only to the degree that he can understand their original cultural context, or, perhaps, relate them to some aspect of his own cultural or personal aesthetics.

Music is obviously as much a part of culture as a hoe or a potsherd. More than some aspects of culture, however, it has the ability to be emotionally moving and aesthetically pleasing. We have tried to show that when a carrier of a given culture becomes aware subliminally or consciously of the specific ways in which "his" music moves him, through some of the principles listed above, he begins to anticipate the events of a given piece. With this anticipation comes aesthetic pleasure. On occasions we have been able to give clues as to what to listen for in a given music, so that the reader might enjoy such musical experiences as well. However, our knowledge of world music is still rather narrow, and in many cases we can offer only the exotic surfaces of non-Western music—the sensuous titillation of a recording with a strange label and curious sounds. Intellectually, our message remains the same: These sounds, whatever they seem to a given listener, are *music* to someone, and as music they contain an inner logic that can be understood and admired—but only if one is inclined to listen to them on their own terms. It is not necessary to

[2] See further discussions of this principle in Leonard Meyer, *Emotion and Meaning in Music* (Chicago: Phoenix Press, 1956).

enjoy the music of every land, though understanding and exposure may certainly broaden one's musical tastes. What is necessary is that one recognize the value and tolerate the existence of these many systems of music.

Hedonistically speaking, new musical pleasures may have been gained from our study. Intellectually, many curious new facts may have been learned. These gains, however, are for naught without a new or reinforced sense of respect for man's musical inventiveness. The world is filled with logical but different systems in many other fields of human endeavor besides music. Perhaps a bit more understanding in music may contribute in a small way towards the great general need for better communication in other areas of international contact.

INDEX

A-ak, 177, 191
Aboriginals of Australia, (Fig. 1), 2–9, 208, 209
Abyat, 80
Accordion, 29, 33, 81, 85, 208
Acculturation:
in Borneo, 33–34
in Burma, 136
in Central Asia, 89–91
defined, 21
in Ethiopia, 56
in Japan, 206–7
in Madagascar, 53
in the Philippines, 31
in Polynesia, 21
in popular music, 81
in Southeast Asia, 118–19, 134–36
See also Influences
A'chiang, 177
Acoustics:
ancient Near Eastern, 82
Chinese, 146–49
classical Near Eastern, 71
for "split" tones, 144
See also Cyclic system, Divisive system, Music theory
Acrobats, 162, 166, 169, 191
Aden (map), 58
Adhan, 64
Adi tala, 104–5
Aerophone:
Africa, 53, 54
in ancient Near East, 81–82
Australian aboriginal, 3
Borneo, 33
Burma, 126–27
China, 150, 160, 162, 163
defined, 22–23
India, 108
Indonesia, 37
Japan, 186, 194, 199, 203, 204
Jewish, 85
Korea, 177, 180
Melanesia, 12, 15–17
Micronesia, 25
pan-Islamic, 61, 62
Polynesia, 22–23
Southeast Asia, 123, 125, 129–30
Tibet, 140–41
See also Accordion, Bugle, Clarinet, Double reed, Flutes, Free reed, Mouth organ, Panpipes, Quadruple reed, Trumpets
Aesthetics:
China, ancient, 146
China, modern, 169–70
Eskimo, 209
general view, 209, 215
India, 103, 107
Indonesia, 38, 43–45
Islam, 80
Japan, 197, 201, 203
Maori, 18–19
Micronesia, 25
New Guinea, 14
Southeast Asian scales, 121–22
Tibet, 139
Afghanistan, 88, 89, 92–93
Africa:
instrumental similarity with Ainu, 208
instrumental similarity in Southeast Asia, 132
Moslem music in black Africa, 53–57
northern traditions, *See* Ethiopia, Maghrib, Negro, North Africa
Agogic accents, 8
Agung, 30
Ahal, 59
Ainu, 208
Akhak kwebon (*Akhak kwebom*), 180
Akshara, 99, 100
Akshi-jo, 181
Alap (*Alapana*), 103, 104, 106
Alaska (map), 208–9
Alexandria, 70, 83
Al Farabi, 70, 89, 149
Algeria (map), 58, 59
Al Kindi, 70
America. *See* United States
Amsa, 98
Amzhad, 59, 63 (Fig. 15)
Analogy:
aboriginal and Western uses of melodies, 5
angklung music and Western bell-ringing, 38
Central Asian and European competitive songs, 91
Indian and Catholic chant, 94
Indian and Western senses of pitch, 97
Islamic music and calligraphy, 76
Japanese and Western dance suites, 186
Japanese *gagaku* and Western chamber music, 197
Kabuki and movie music, 204
medicine men techniques and Western psychology, 14
Sung China and Old London, 158

Note: Common alternate romanizations of many non-western terms are given in parentheses following the spellings used in the text. The word map will appear in parentheses if a term can be found on the map.

Analogy (*Cont.*)
T'ang China dances and football pageants, 155
Western and Indian music theory, 116
Western and Japanese lead sheets, 194
See also Comparisons
Analysis, musical:
basic information required, 7–9
of Chinese national anthem, 168
of Japanese *noh,* 200
of Shashmakom, 89
Soviet techniques, 91
Andalusia (map), Moorish classical music from, 69, 79
Anga, 100
Anghra, 93
Angklung, 37–38
Angkor Wat (map), 118, 135
Anhemitonic pentatonic, 33, 120, 134, 188, 190. *See also* Pentatonic
Animal symbolism. *See* Zoomorphism
Antara, 104
Antara ga, 97
Anthropology, preface, 14
Anticipation and prediction principle, 215
Antiphonal music, 10, 114, 142
Anudruta, 100
Anupallavi, 104
Arab music, 58 ff. *See also* Influence, Pan-Islamic music
Arab-Persian system, 69–76, 213, 214
Archeology, 69, 81–82
Archives, 2, 81, 91, 145, 156, 190
Argul. See *Yarul*
Arias, Chinese, 161–66, 168
Armenia (map), 84, 88
Arnhem Land (map), 2–6
Art music defined, 70. *See also* Classical music
Asabi, 71
Ashkinazi, 84
Ashirai, 186
Assyria, 82, 154, 214
Astrology and music, 146. *See also* Cosmology
Asymmetrical meter, 7
Atharva Veda, 94
Atlas Mountains, 59
Audava, 97
Audience and performance relation, 80, 103, 106
Australia (map):
aboriginals, Fig. 1, 2–9, 208, 209
Anglo-Europeans, 1–2
Avarta, 100
Avaz, 73, 74
Avicenna, 70, 89
Azan, 64
Azerbaijan (map, Azerbaidzhan), 88, 89
Babandil, 30
Babylon, 81, 191
Bachi, 191
Bachikawa, 191
Bagana, 56
Baghdad, 70
Baglama, 64
Bagpipe:
Near Eastern, 62
in Pakistan, 115
Bajo, 29
Balalaika, 90
Bali (map), 34, 48–49, 140
Ballads, Australian, 1–2. *See also* Narrative music
Ballet, 169. *See also* Dance
Bamboo instruments, 12, 15, 16, 25, 29, 33, 37, 126, 129, 134, 135, 146, 150, 186, 204
Ban. See Pan
Bands. *See* Ensembles
Bandurria, 29
Bangladesh (map), 114
Bangqiang. See Pang ch'iang
Bangzigiang. See Pang tzu ch'iang
Banku. See Pan ku
Banqiang (*Pan ch'iang*), 161
Banshiki, 190
Bansri, 108
Banziqiang. See Pan tzu ch'iang
Barung, 35, 39 (Ex. 2–1)
Barwal, 80
Bashkirs (map), 144
Bashraf, 80
Baya, 108, 109 (Fig. 28)
Bayin. See Pa yin
Bear cult, 208
Bedouin, 59 ff
Beethoven, L. 3, 209
Behavioral musicology, preface
Bells:
Burmese, 132
Chinese, 149, 152
Coptic substitution for, 56
Iranian, 66
Japanese *kabuki,* 204
Korean, 180
Tibetan, 140
Bendair, 61
Berbers, 59 ff
Beste, 79
Bharata, 95, 115
Bharata Natya-Sastra. See Natya Sastra
Bhatkhande, 99
Bian. See Pien
Bianqing. See Pien ch'ing
Bianzhong. See Pien chung
Biequ. See Pei ch'ü
Bin and *Bin sitar,* 110, 111 (Figs. 29 & 30)

Bird calls imitated on drums, 11
Bitonality in folk music, 142
Biwa, 191, 192 (Fig. 56), 195, 196 (Fig. 60), 197, 199, 202
Blasquinten. See Overblown fifths
Block flute, 23, 85, 130
Bo. See Po
Boat lute, 31
Bokhara (map), 89, 154
Bol, 100, 102
Bon religion in Tibet, 139
Bonang, 30, 36 (Fig. 11), 37, 39 (Ex. 2–1), 45
Book of Odes, 145
Book of Rites, 145
Borneo (map), 31, 32, 33–34, 53, 114, 129, 130, 183
Boru, 66
Bowed lute. *See* Lute, bowed
Bozug (bouzouki), 64
Bragha, 21
Breath rhythm, 197, 200
Brhaddesi, 95
Bronze drum, 135
Buddhism and Buddhist music:
 in Burma, 132
 in China, 123, 153, 154
 in India, 93
 in Indonesia, 34
 in Japan, 188, 189, 197, 199
 in Manchuria, 176
 in Southeast Asia, 134, 213
 in Sri Lanka, 115
 in Tibet, 139–41
Bugaku, 191, 195
Bugle, 140, 143
Buka, 44
Bull-roarer, 4
Bunraku, 202
Burma (map), 69, 120, 128, 131, 132, 136, 215
Buzzed lip aerophone, 3, 23, 66. *See also* Trumpets
Buzzing sounds in instruments, 53, 130, 159, 177

Cabalist music, 84
Cadence and cadence formula:
 aboriginal, 9
 Chinese, 165
 on gongs in Indonesia, 43
 Japanese, 187, 201
 masculine-feminine in Western music, 12
 as part of analysis, 8
 Persian, 73
 Tibetan, 141
Cai nhi, 128
Call and response, 10, 61, 133
Cambodia (map), 121, 123, 126, 128, 129, 135
Can. See Khaen
Cana, 79
Canada, Eskimos of, 208–9
Cane. *See* Bamboo
Canon, 10, 13 (Ex. 1–3), 14, 208
Canton (map), 160
Cantor, 84
Caodai, 134
Caranam, 104
Caroline Islands (map), 25
Cartography, musical, 10, 214
Caspian Sea (map), 88
Castanets, 133, 162, 167
Caturdandi-Prakasika, 99
Cavalry bands, 153
Celebes (map), 33
Celempung (tjelempung), 35
Central Africa, 54
Central Asia, 58, 69, 88–91, 153–54, 191
Centric melody, 133, 183, 184 (Ex. 7–4A)
Cents system, 20, 45, 46 (Ex. 2–2), 74, 119
Ceremonial music:
 aboriginal, 4
 China, 145
 India, 114
 Madagascar, 53
 Moslem, 79 (fn. 11), 127
 New Guinea and Papua, 12
 See also Confucian music, Liturgical music, Religious music, Ritual music, Sacred music
Ceylon (map), 93, 140. *See also* Sri Lanka
Chahar mezarb, 75
"Chain" melody, 141, 142 (Ex. 6–1)
Chakay, 31, 128, 129, 131 (Fig. 42), 132
Cham, 141
Chamber music:
 Chinese, 159
 Japanese, 204
 Korean, 181
 sound ideal, 197
 Sundanese, 37
 Vietnamese, 132
Chang, 69
Chang-an (map), 154, 155
Changko, 178 (Fig. 53), 180, 181, 182
Chants and chanting:
 China, 153
 Coptic, 56
 Eskimo, 208–9
 Hawaii, 23
 India, 94
 Islamic, 64
 Japan, 188

Chants and chanting (*Cont.*)
Jewish, 83, 84
Maori, 19–20
Ryukyu, 183
Southeast Asia, 133
Tibet, 139–41
Chap, 123
Chapey-thom, 129
Charanam, 104
Chasidism (Hasidism), 84
Cheng (*Zheng*), 150
Chevé notation, 168
Chi kuan (*ji guan*), 156
Ch'in dynasty, 152
Ch'in (*qin,* instrument), 150, 151 (Fig. 44), 152, 158–59
China:
Buddhism, 140, 189
commentaries about Java from, 34
instrument from ancient Near East, 82
instrument from Persia, 69
instrumental similarities in Borneo, 33
music of, 144–75
music theory system summarized, 213–14
See also Influence: China
Chinese pavilion, 66
Ching, 123
Ch'ing dynasty, 148, 160–61
Ch'ing (*qing*), 149, 173
Ching ch'ü (*jingqu*), 159, 173
Ching hsi (*jingxi*), 159, 161, 173
Chi nü (*ji nü*), 156, 173
Ch'in-shih-huang-ti, 152
Chiri-kara, 202
Chironomy, 82
Cho (*chō*), 190, 195
Cho songs, 130
Chopi, 53–54
Choral and Chorus singing:
China, 160, 167, 169, 170
Indonesia, 35
Islamic, 61, 76
Japan, 199, 205
Jewish, 85
Malaysia, 133
Manchuria, 176
Mongolia, 143
New Guinea, 10, 11
Oceania, 21
Soviet Central Asia, 91
Taiwan, 183
Tibet, 139
Chord. *See* Harmony
Chordophone:
Afghanistan, 92–93
Central Asia, 89, 90
China, 150–52, 155, 162–63
for comparative study, 31–33, 69
defined, 22
India, 108–113
Japan, 195–97, 202, 204
Java, 35, 37
Korea, 177–80
Madagascar, 53
pan-Islamic, 64–69
Oceania, 21–22
Ryukyu, 184–85
Southeast Asia, 128–29
Tibet, 141–42
See also Dulcimer, Guitar, Harp, Instruments, Lute, Lyre, Spike fiddle, Violin, Zither, Names of individual instruments
Chou dynasty, 145, 149
Christians and Christian music, 21, 29, 55, 56, 58, 140
Chromatic pitches in Chinese music theory, 148
Chu, 150
Chu Tsai-yü (Zhu zaiyu), 148
Ch'ü p'ai (*qu pai*), 158
Ci. See Tz'u
Cimbalon, 69
Circumboreal music, 209, 210
Clapper opera, 160 ff
Clappers, 81, 126, 132, 135, 162, 180, 195
Clarinet, 25, 53, 62, 81, 115, 130. *See also* Double clarinet
Classical music:
Arab, 59
Central Asia, 89
China, 152–55
defined, 70
India, 102–7
Indonesia, 37–38 ff
Japan, 188–204
Korea, 177–81
pan-Islamic, 67–80
Southeast Asia, 123–32
Western forms in Asia, 167–69, 206–7
See also Comparisons
Classification systems:
in Chinese court music, 152, 154, 155
in Chinese music periods, 145
in Chinese opera, 158, 160 ff
of instruments, 22
of instruments in China, 149–52
of music and non-music, 64, 66, 133
of polyphony, 10
of *raga,* 99
of schools of Islamic classical music, 70
of theory systems in the literate world, 213–14
Collectivization of music, 91, 169–70
Colotomic structure, 43, 123, 194, 195
Comma, 74
Communism and music, 91, 168–70
Comparative musicology, 208, 214
Comparative score, 105, 106, 143
Comparative studies, 215

Comparisons:
- aboriginal and Western functions of music, 3
- China and the ancient Near East, 150 (fn. 11)
- Chinese and European opera history, 160 (fn. 19), ff
- Chinese and Western science, 149
- Chinese and Western tone systems, 146
- Chinese opera and Indonesian and India forms, 166
- composers' roles, 169
- East Asian music theories, 181
- Eskimo and Western music, 209
- general, 213–15
- Gregorian and Buddhist chant, 188
- Improvisation in Indian music and jazz, 102
- Indian and Western music theory and performance, 103, 106, 116
- Indonesia and Africa, 53
- Indonesia and Tibet, 142
- Islamic and European medieval music theory, 70, 75
- Japanese and Western concert worlds, 203
- Japanese and Western neumes, 189
- Japanese *joruri* and Western opera, 202
- *kabuki* drums and Western harmony functions, 203
- Korean, pan-Islamic, and Flamenco singing, 182
- of musical instruments, 31
- *noh* and Western line setting and progression, 200–1
- origins of U.S. and Chinese national anthems, 167
- Southeast Asian and Western social dances, 136
- Vocal styles of Jewish and Christian youth, 85
- Western and Chinese music functions, 170
- Western and Chinese music history, 145
- Western and Chinese singers, 163
- Western harmony and Japanese drum patterns, 201
- Western orchestras and ancient Chinese ensembles, 152
- world tone systems, 190
- *See also* Analogy

Competitive songs, 91, 106, 133
Composer and composition:
- Chinese, ancient, 155
- Chinese, modern, 167, 169–70
- Central Asia, 91
- India, 107
- Indonesia, 38, 48
- Japanese ancient, 194
- Japanese modern, 206–7
- Japanese traditional, 203
- in Melanesia, 15
- role in society, 169
- Soviet, 91
- Western classical, 66
- Western contemporary, 215
- *See also* Beethoven, Erh, Foster, Kanami, Kineya, Miyagi, Mozart, Takemitsu, Tyagaraja, Rimsky-Korsakov, Yamada, Zeami

Composition committees, 169
Composite melody, 29, 38, 55
Concert:
- Indian, 103, 107
- Japanese, 203, 206–7
- pan-Islamic, 80

Conch-shell trumpet, 22, 141
Confucian music, 150, 152, 156, 170, 177, 180, 191
Confucius, 146
Conjunct melody, 8
Consonance and dissonance in melody, 122
Construction. *See* Instrument: construction
Contour, melodic, 8, 9, 47, 142
Controlled reed, 23
Coptic Christians, 55, 56, 83
Corroboree, 5
Cosmology and music, 82, 146, 149
Counterpoint. *See* Disphony
Court music:
- China, 152, 154–56
- Japan, 188–97
- Korea, 177–81
- Islamic, 69
- Southeast Asia, 126, 128, 133

Cueing device, 20
Cultural context of music, 209, 215
Cyclic system of tone generation, 146–47, 152
Cyclic time, 99
Cymbals:
- Burmese, 126, 132
- Chinese, 154, 162, 163, 164
- Indian, 114, 115
- Southeast Asia, 123
- Tibet, 140, 141

Dabakan, 30
Dabka (*debka*), 64
Daguci. See Ta ku tz'u
Dalang, 38
Damaru, 115, 140
Dambura and *Damburachi*, 92
Dan bau, 132
Danbigu. See Tanpi ku
Dance and dance music:

Dance and dance music (*Cont.*)
aboriginal, 2, 5
African, 53
Anglo-European in Australia, 1, 2
Berber, 59
Chinese, 152, 153, 155, 156, 169
Indian, 106, 114, 115
Indonesian, 38, 49
Islamic, 64, 66, 80, 81
Japanese, 186, 187, 194, 199, 202
Korean, 181, 183
Micronesian, 25
New Guinean, 12
Philippine, 29
Polynesian, 18, 23
pre-Islamic, 70
Ryukyuan, 184, 185
South American, 29, 81
Southeast Asian, 133, 135, 136
Tibetan, 141–42
trance, 66, 134
Western and Southeast Asian social dances compared, 136
Dance-drama. *See* Theater
Danci. See Tan tz'u
Dan day, 129, 133
Dan doc huyen, 132
Danmono, 204
Dan nguyet, 129
Dan ty ba, 129
Daoban. See Tao pan
Daramad, 80
Darbuka (*darabukka*), 62, 63 (Fig. 17)
Darwul, 66
Dastgah (*dastgah-ha*), 71, 72–74, 76
Dastgya, 89
Dbyangs and *Dbyangs-yig,* 139
Debayashi, 202
Debteras, 56
Degwa, 56
Demung, 35
Dervish music, 64
Descriptive music, 91, 155, 159, 169
Devadasi, 115
Dhol (*dholak*), 93, 108, 115
Dhrupad, 104
Diatonic, 148
Dich, 132
Diffusion, theory of, 30–33, 53, 128, 135
Dijeridoo (*digeridoo*), Figs, 1, 3, 5 (fn. 4), 209
Dikirbarat, 133
Disjunct melody, 8
Disphony, 10, 133, 208
Dissonance. *See* Consonance
Divisive rhythm, 102
Divisive system of tone generation, 71, 214
Dizi. See Ti tzu
Dodang sayang, 136
Doira, 89
Dombra, 90
Double clarinet, 81, 82, 89, 90. *See also Yarul*
Double reed aerophone:
Africa, 54
Central Asia, 89, 90
China, 162–63
India, 108, 114
Japan, 194
Korea, 177
Near East, 62, 77 (Fig. 24)
Tibet, 141
See also Quadruple reed aerophones
Dowel, 56
Dram-synan, 141, 155
Dream songs, 134
Dril-bu, 140
Drone, 3, 5, 21, 25, 33, 55, 62, 75, 81, 90, 103, 110, 113, 115, 129
Drums and drumming:
aboriginal, 4
Afghanistan, 93
Africa, 54–55
ancient Near East, 81
bronze, 135
Burma, 126
China, 157 (Fig. 50), 161, 162, 167
circumboreal (Eskimo), 209, 210 (Fig. 64)
Ethiopian Coptic, 56
India, 106, 107–8, 109 (Figs, 26, 27, 28), 114, 115
Indonesia, 37
Japan, 186, 194, 198 (Figs. 61, 62, 63)
Jewish, 85
Korea, 178 (Fig. 53), 180, 182
Mongolia, 143
Moslem and Infidel styles compared, 54
New Guinea, 11, 17 (Fig. 2)
Oceania, 22, 25
pan-Islamic, 59, 61
Philippines, 30
Ryukyu, 183
Southeast Asia, 123, 127, 129, 135, 136
Tibet, 140, 141
Tuareg, 59
Turkey, 66
Western, 53
See also Hourglass drum, Kettle drums, Membranophone
Drum circles, 108, 126
Drummer's calls, 200
Druse, 61 (Ex. 3–2)
Druta, 99, 100
Duana, 30
Duff, 61
Dulcimer, 69, 160
Dung-chen, 140
Durub, 75
Dutar, 90

Duun, 143

East Asia, 138–75
East Europe, 7, 64, 58
Ecology and music, 16, 25, 135, 209, 214
Edo period, 201–4
Education, music as a means of, 2, 3. *See also* Teaching
Egypt:
ancient, 31 (fn. 4), 154 (fn. 12), 191, 214
modern, 58, 61, 62, 71, 72
Elastic rhythm. See Breath rhythm
Electrophone, 22
Ellis, Alexander, 20
End-blown flute. *See* Flute, end-blown
Ensembles:
ancient Near Eastern, 81–82
Burmese, 126, 136
cafe, 62
Cambodian, 121 (Ex. 5–2)
Central Asian, 89, 91
Chinese, 152, 154–55, 158–66, 168–70
Chopi, 53
Indian, 114–15
Indonesian, 34–38, 48
Islamic, 66, 76, 81
Japanese, 194–95, 202, 207
Korean, 177, 180, 181
in Madagascar, 53
military bands in Turkey, 66
Mon, 128
Philippine, 29, 30
in Solomon Islands, 15
Southeast Asian, 123–36
Tibet, 140–41
See also Chamber music
Epics. *See* Narrative music
Equidistant intervals, 119
Erh, Nich, 167
Erh huang (*er huang*), 161, 163–66, 173
Erh hu (*er hu*), 158, 162, 173
Eskimo music, 208–9
Ethiopia (map), 55–57, 83, 84
"Ethnic" music, 170
Ethnochoreology, 29 (fn. 2)
Ethnomusicology, defined, 5
Europe, 150, 161, 213. *See also* Western music
Extramusical concepts in music, 12, 14, 43, 47, 71, 82, 94, 95, 98, 107, 139, 146, 149. *See also* Symbolism

Falasha Jews, 55, 84
Fang hsiang, 155
Farabi. *See* Al Farabi
Female music. *See* Women's music
Female symbolism in music, 12, 48, 99, 148
Festivals and festival music, 12, 145, 183, 186–87, 199
Fiddle. *See* Lute, bowed
Field collectors, 2, 14, 91
Film music, 114, 136
Finalis, 8, 190
Finger modes, 71
Fipple flute. *See* Block flute
Five Dynasty period, 156
Floating terms, 31, 93
Flutes and flute music:
defined, 23
end-blown, 24, 31, 61, 82, 128, 130, 134, 150, 159, 191, 192 (Fig. 56), 204
side-blown, 24, 105 (Ex. 4–6), 108, 115, 134, 150, 163, 177, 186, 191, 192 (Fig. 56), 194, 199, 202, 203
unspecified, 81, 93, 158
See also Block flute, Nose flute, Panpipe
Folk songs:
Armenia, 84
Australia, 2
China, 152, 154, 170
India, 114–15
Japan, 185–86, 187 (Ex. 7–7), 188
Jewish, 84
Korea, 182 (Ex. 7–3), 183
Mongol, 143
Okinawa, 185 (Ex. 7–5)
pan-Islam, 58–66
Southeast Asia, 134–35
Tibet, 142 (Ex. 6–1)
Form, 8–9, 20, 44, 79–80, 103–6, 200–3, 214
Formosa. *See* Taiwan
Formulas, melodic. *See* Stereotyped patterns
Foster, S., 205
Frame drum, 54, 61. *See also* Pan drum, Tambourine
Free reed aerophone, 23, 113, 160
Free rhythm, 7, 103
Frets, 67, 69, 71, 82, 110, 113
Functions of music. See Music, functions
Funerals and music, 25, 53, 66, 83, 134

Gabbang, 30
Gagaku, 188–97
Gagakuryo (*gagakuryō*), 191
Ga-grama, 96, 97
Gaita, 62
Gaku-daiko, 194
Gakusho yoroku (*Gakusho yōroku*), 190
Gamaka, 98, 152
Gambang kayu, 35, 39 (Ex. 2–1)
Gambia (map), 55
Gamelan, 34–51, 53, 119, 123, 126, 142, 161
Gandang, 30
Gandhara, 153

Gandharagrama, 96–97
Gandi, 140
Gangsa, 48
Gaogiang. *See Kao Ch'iang*
Gaozu (*Kao-tsu*), 155, 173
Gasba (*gasaba*), 61
Gat, 106
Gatra, 43, 47
Gaynat, 70
Gazel, 80
Geisha, 155
Gendang, 127, 133, 135
Gendang keling, 127 (Ex. 5–3)
Gendang nobat, 127
Gender (*gendér*), 35, 36 (Fig. 12), 37, 44, 47, 48, 123
Gendhing (*gending*), 38
Genibri, 64, 83
Genjoraku (*Genjōraku*), 194
Georgia (map), 88
Germany, 207
Gerusttone, 122 (fn. 4)
Gerong and *gerong bedayan*, 35, 39 (Ex. 2–1)
Goblet drum. *See* Pot drum
Gewel, 55
Geza, 204
Ghetto music, 83, 84
Ghitchak, 93
Gidayu-bushi (*gidayū-bushi*), 202, 204
Gishang, 182
Gitgit, 30
Glong that, 123
Go-in hakase, 189
Gong:
  flat, 29, 161, 163, 186, 194
  knobbed, 30, 33, 36 (Fig. 11), 37, 39 (Ex. 2–1), 46, 120, 123, 124 (Fig. 37), 126, 135, 204
  slit, 14
Gong. *See kung*
Gong cycle. *See Ketawang*
Gongan, 38–43
Gongnu. *See Kung nü*
Gophong, 141
Grajappi, 129, 132
Grama, 96–97
Graphic notation, 139
Greece, ancient music tradition, 56, 64, 69, 71, 74, 82, 83, 149, 171, 213–14
Greeks in Australia, 2
Greenland, 209
Griot, 55
Guan. *See kuan*
Guilds, musicians', 81, 186, 200, 203 (fn. 9), 206, 207
Guitar, 21, 25, 29, 31, 53, 85, 129, 132, 194, 208. *See also* Lute, plucked
Gulu, 46 (Ex. 2–3)
Gunbri, 64
Guru, 107
Gusheh (*gusheh-ha, gushé*), 73–74, 78 (Ex. 3–6)
Gusle, 143
Gyosan taikaishu (*Gyosan taikaishū*), 189

Ha, 200–1
Hadrah, 133
Haekeum, 177, 179 (Fig. 54)
Haka, 18, 19 (Ex. 1–4)
Halam, 53, 83
Halil, 85
Han dynasty, 146, 152, 153
Han, Tien, 167
Handclapping, 4, 18, 35, 59, 61 (Ex. 3–2), 186
Hare Krishna, 170
Harmonica, 33
Harmonics, 152
Harmonium, 113
Harmony:
  African, 54
  Borneo, 33
  Central Asian, 90 (Ex. 4–1)
  in China, 167, 169, 171
  compared to rhythmic devices, 163, 201, 203
  defined, 10
  Indian, 114
  in Islamic popular music, 81
  on Japanese *sho*, 194
  organal, 53, 90 (Ex. 4–1), 130, 133
  Southeast Asian, 129 (Ex. 5–4)
  Taiwan, 183
  Tibet, 139
  Western, 91, 136, 205
  Zionist, 85
  See also Homophony
Harp:
  Afghanistan, 92
  ancient Near East, 69, 82, 83
  Burma, 130, 131 (Fig. 41), 132
  China, 154, 155
  defined, 22
  Ethiopia, 56, 57 (Fig. 14)
  Japan, 191, 193 (Fig. 57)
Hasida, 55
Hasidism. *See* Chasidism
Hat a dao, 133
Hayari uta, 206
Hayashi, 186, 199, 202
Hebrew. *See* Jewish music
Heian period, 191, 195
Heightened speech, 18, 19 (Ex. 1–4), 25, 182
Heike-biwa, 197
Heptatonic scale, 97, 119, 158
Heterometer, 7, 141, 142 (Ex. 6–1)
Heterophony, 10, 33, 54, 55, 59, 60 (Ex. 3–1), 132, 133, 143, 163, 165, 167, 180–81, 194, 204

Hevehe ceremony, 12
Hexatonic, 8, 97, 119
Hichiriki, 194, 195
Himene, 21
Hinduism, 34, 93, 94–95, 122, 213
Hindustani music, 93 ff
Hira-gasy, 53
History through music sources, 2, 19, 81–83, 154, 197
Hne, 126, 127
Hocket, 48
Hogaku (*hōgaku*), 206, 207
Hokkaido (map), 208
Homayun, 73 (Ex. 3–4)
Homophony, 10, 25
Hong Kong (map), 169
Hoon, 180
Hora, 85
Horn. *See* Trumpet
Hornbostel, Erich von, 15, 21, 46
Hourglass drum, 11, 12, 22, 25, 54, 115, 135, 140, 178 (Fig. 53), 180, 191–92, 194, 198 (Figs. 61 & 62)
Hsiao (*xiao*), 159, 169, 173
Hsi ch'ü (*xiqu*), 159, 173
Hsi p'i (*xipi*), 161, 163–66, 173
Hsi wen (*xiwen*), 158, 173
Hsuan (*xuan*), 149, 173
Hsuan-Tsung (*Xuan Zong*), 154, 155, 173
Huang chung (*huangzhong*), 146, 147, 173
Huang-Ti (Huang Di), 146, 150, 173
Hu ch'in (*hu qin*), 128, 156, 157 (Fig. 47), 162, 173, 177, 180
Huda, 64
Hula, 23–24 (Ex. 1–5)
Hunan (map), 160, 161
Hurrian cuneiform, 82
Hu yüeh (*huyue*), 155, 173
Hyang-ak, 177
Hyderabad (map), 93
Hymns:
  Christian, 21, 122, 167
  Moslem, 55
  Vedic, 94–95
Hyojo (*hyōjō*), 190

Ibn Sina, 70, 89
Ichikotsu, 190
Idiophones:
  aboriginal, 4
  African, 53
  ancient Near East, 81–82
  Chinese, 150, 155, 162
  defined, 22
  Ethiopian, 56, 57 (Fig. 13)
  Indian, 108
  Indonesian, 33–37
  Japanese, 186, 194, 195, 204
  Korean, 179 (Fig. 55), 180
  Oceania, 14, 22, 25
  Philippines, 29, 30
  Southeast Asian, 123, 126, 132, 133
  Tibet, 140
  Tuareg, 59
  See also Bells, Bronze drum, Castanets, Clappers, Cymbals, Gongs, Stone instruments, Names of individual instruments
Ikuta school, 207
Ili ili, 22, 23
Imayo (*imayō*), 195
Improvisation, 76, 102, 106, 186
Imzhad, 59
In scale, 185, 188 (Ex. 7–8), 190
India (map) and Indians, 2, 31, 84, 93–117, 122, 213–14
Indonesia, 1, 31, 34–51, 53–54, 61, 123, 126, 142, 166, 180, 183, 185
Influences on other culture's music by that of:
  Asia, 191
  Buddhist chant, 188
  China, 29, 88, 89, 122, 128–29, 132–33, 135, 139, 143, 153–54, 176–77, 179–81, 183, 189 ff
  Christians, 21
  Gentiles, 83
  India, 129, 139, 153, 189
  Indonesia, 30, 33, 53–54
  Islam, 30, 54, 66, 122, 127, 143
  Japan, 183, 185
  Korea, 191, 199
  Latin America, 21, 29, 81
  Mongolia, 139, 156, 158
  Persia, 92
  Russia, 169, 176
  Southeast Asia, 191
  Spain, 29–30
  Tibet, 141
  the West, 34, 139, 204–8
Instruments:
  construction of,
    aerophones, 3, 15, 62, 123, 130, 150, 159
    chordophones, 22, 35, 67–69, 108–14, 128, 132, 143, 180
    idiophones, 4, 35, 123
    membranophones, 12, 22, 108, 115, 135, 140, 162–63
  decorations on, 14, 31, 126, 192 *See also* Zoomorphism
  playing method,
    aerophones, 3, 62, 126, 130
    chordophone, 21, 67–69, 110, 129, 132, 151, 177, 180, 184, 204
    idiophone, 22, 59, 180
    membranophone, 64, 108, 209
  For instruments from given areas *See* under the name of the area or

country
Instrumental music. See Chamber music, Ensembles
Intervals:
Central Asian, 91
Chinese, 146–48
counting of, 8
in *dastgah*, 73
on *dijeridoo*, 3
in Indian theory, 97
Islamic, 74
Japanese, 188
measurement of, 20
on panpipes, 15
in *pathet* system, 46
in Southeast Asian scales, 119–20
See also Scales, Tuning
Ipu, 22
Iqa'at, 75
Irama, 45
Iran (map), 58, 66. *See also* Persia
Iraq (map), 58, 72
Islam, 34, 54, 58–80, 127, 214. *See also* Influences
Isometer, 7, 23
Isorhythm, 7
Israel (map), 58, 83–85
Ist, 73
Italians in Australia, 2
Iterative form, 8
I yang and *I yang ch'iang* (*yiyang qiang*), 160, 173
Izawa, Shuji, 205

Jalatarang, 108
Jamisen, 184
Jangxiang. See fang hsiang
Janissary Band, 66
Japan (map), 140, 155–56, 160, 185–208
Japka, 182
Jati, 96, 97, 98
Java (map), 31, 32, 34–47, 123
Javali, 106
Jaws harp. See Jews' harp
Jazz, 102, 136
Jehol (map), 177
Jejo vaotavo, 53
Jenghiz Khan, 89, 158
Jewish music, 59, 83–85
Jews' harp, 16, 25, 29, 93, 208
Jhaptal, 100, 101 (Ex. 4–5)
Jiao (*Chiao*), 143 (Ex. 6–3)
Jingqu. See Ching ch'ü
Jingxi. See Ching hsi
Jinü. See Chi nü
Jiquan. See Chi kuan
Jiva svara, 98
Jo, 200–1
Joget, 136
Jordan (map), 58
Joruri (*jōruri*), 202–4
Jue (*Chueh*), 143 (Ex. 6–3)

Kabuki, 202–4
Kabul, 92
Kacapi (*kachapi*), 31, 32 (Fig. 7), 37, 129
Kagok, 181
Kagura-bue, 195
Kakali ni, 97
Kakegoe, 200
Kakko, 194
Kakui, 189
Kamanchay (*kamanja*), 67, 68 (Fig. 21), 180
Kamil, N. M., 89
Kanami, K., 199
Kandyan dance, 115
Kane, 186
Kangen, 191
Kanun (qanun), 69, 77 (Fig. 25), 113
Kao ch'iang (*gaoqiang*), 161, 173
Karnatak (*Karnatic*) music, 93 ff
Kasa, 181
Kasapi, 31
Kashgar (map), 154
Kashmir (map), 114
Katakali dance-drama, 114
Kathak, 115
Kaukaba, 89
Kawari, 13 (Ex. 1–3)
Kayakeum, 117, 178 (Fig. 51), 195, 215
Kazakhstan (map), 89, 91
Kebaro, 56
Kechapi vina, 31
Kedah, 127
Keman, 67, 68 (Fig. 22), 128
Kemanchay (*kemanche*), 64, 68 (Fig. 21)
Kempul, 37, 39–44 (Ex. 2–1, 2–2), 46
Kempyang, 43 (fn. 11)
Kendang, 37
Kenong, 37, 39–44 (Ex. 2–1, 2–2), 46
Kepatihan, 43
Kerala, 93
Kereshmah, 75
Ketawang, 43
Kethuk (*ketuk*), 37, 39–44 (Ex. 2–1, 2–2)
Kettle drums, 54, 55, 59, 62, 66, 89, 127
Khaen (*khen, can*), 33, 125 (Fig. 40), 129, 135, 136, 194
Khali, 100
Khana, 79
Khaneh, 66
Khil-khuur, 143
Khlui, 130
Khong (also *khong mong, wong yai,* or *wong lek*), 123, 124 (Fig. 37)
Khorezm notation, 89

Khotan (map), 153, 154
Khyal, 104
Kiangsi (map), 160
Kiangsu (map), 160
Kineya, Rokuzaemon, 203
Kirghiztan (map), 89–91
Kirtana, 104
Kitab al musiqi al kabin (book), 70
Kitara, 29
Knobbed gong culture, 213. *See also* Gong, knobbed
Koa flutes, 12
Komabue, 194
Koma Chikazane, 190
Komagaku, 191, 194, 195
Komungo, 177, 178 (Fig. 52)
Komuz, 90
Konghou. See K'ung hou
Konju (*Koinju*), 194
Koran, 64, 133
Korea (map), 150, 156, 160, 176–83, 191, 195, 208
Koto, 185, 195, 196 (Fig. 59), 204
Ko tsuzumi, 198 (Fig. 61), 199, 200
Krar, 56, 57 (Fig. 14)
Kriti, 104
Kroncong (*krontjong*), 38, 136
K'uai pan (*kuaiban*), 166, 173
Kuan (*guan*), 160, 173
Kublai Khan, 89, 158
Kucha (map), 153, 154
Kuchi, 92
Kudyapi, 31, 32 (Fig. 5), 129
Kugo, 191, 193 (Fig. 57)
Kulintang, 30
Kumaon tribe, 12
Kumitang, 29
K'un ch'ü (*kunqu*), 160, 163, 173
Kundiman, 29
Kung (*gong*), 148, 174, 181
K'ung hou (*kong hou*), 154, 174
Kung nü (*gong nü*), 155, 174
Kun tao (*kun dao*), 160, 174
K'unshan, 160
Kunst, Jaap, 43, 194
Kurobune (opera), 207
Kwena, 183
Kwitra, 69
Kyemon-jo, 181
Kyi waing, 126
Kyokunsho (kyōkunshō), 190
Kyu (*kyū*), 200–1

Laghu (*lagu*), 100
Lag-rnga, 140
Lakon, 135
Lamaism, 139–41, 143, 176
Laos (map), 118, 126, 128, 130
Laps, Lapland (map), 33, 208
Latin America. *See* Influences
Laud, 29
Lauta, 69
Laya, 99
Layali, 79
Lead sheets, 194
Lebanon (map), 58
Legend, Chinese, 146, 150
Lian ch'ü (*lianqu*), 161, 174
Libya (map), 58
Lima (Greek), 74
Lima (Javanese), 46–47
Ling Lun, 146
Lira, 64
Litany. *See* Chants and chanting
Lithophone. *See* Stone instruments
Liturgical music, 81, 84, 139–40. *See also* Ceremonial music, Ritual music
Liu shui (*liushui*), 166, 174
Li Yuan, 155
Lo (*luo*), 163, 174
Log drums, 4
Loochoo Islands, 183
Lü pipes, 146–48, 150, 152, 171, 214
Lundai, 92
Luo. See Lo
Lutar, 64
Lute:
  bowed, 30, 56, 59, 63 (Fig. 15), 64, 66, 67, 68 (Fig. 21, 22, 23), 93, 112, 113, 115, 128, 141, 143, 162, 177, 179 (Fig. 54)
  defined, 22
  plucked, 21, 29, 55, 64, 65 (Figs. 18, 19, 20), 67, 90, 92, 109–11 (Fig. 32), 129, 135, 140, 141, 151 (Fig. 45), 153, 155, 157 (Figs. 48, 50), 184, 195, 196 (Fig. 58), 197, 202
Lyre, 22, 56, 57 (Fig. 14), 68, 82

Mabi, Kibi, 190
Madagascar (map), 17 (Fig. 3), 53
Madhya, 99
Madhymangrama, 96
Madras (map), 93
Maghrib (*magrib, maghreb*), 58, 62, 69
Ma-grama, 96, 97, 119
Mahabharata, 38
Mahori, 128–29, 130, 133, 135
Mahur, 73
Makam, 71
Makom, 89
Malagasy (map), 53
Malaysia (map), 127, 133, 134, 136
Male-female analogies in music, 12, 48, 148
Mana, 18
Manchu, 177
Manchuria (map), 176–77, 191

Mandolin, 21, 29
Manipur, 115
Man pan (*manban*), 166, 174
Manyura, 46, 47
Maori, 18–20
Mao Tse-tung, 168
Maqam (pl. *magamat*), 71–72, 84, 190
Maqam phenomenon, 76
Marco Polo, 89, 143
Marginal survival, 29, 56, 79 (fn. 11), 141, 156, 169, 177, 191
Marshall Islands (map), 25
Marx. *See* Communism
Masenqo, 56
Mason, L. W., 205
Matanga, 95
Matra, 99, 100
Matsuri bayashi, 186
Mawalawiyah, 66
Ma'yong, 133, 134, 135
Mazim, 75
Meaning in music, 3, 25, 204, 215
Measures, defined, 7
Medical music, 14
Medieval European music, 70–71, 75, 100
Meiji period, 204–6
Melakarta, 96, 99
Melanesia (map), 1, 9–18, 208
Melismatic music, 9, 59, 60 (Ex. 3–1), 76, 78 (Ex. 3–6), 105, 127 (Ex. 5–3), 133, 143, 160, 176
Melodic formulas. *See* Stereotyped patterns
Melody, characteristics of, 7–9
Membranophones:
  Chinese, 150
  defined, 22, 23
  Eskimo, 209, 210 (Fig. 64)
  Indian, 107–9
  Japanese, 194, 199
  Oceanic, 12, 22, 25
  pan-Islamic, 61, 62, 63 (Fig. 17)
  Southeast Asian, 123, 129
  Tibetan, 140
  See also Drums
Mesopotamia, 81
Metabôle, 121 (fn. 2)
Metallophones, 35, 37, 123, 180
Meter, 7, 166. *See also* Heterometer, Isometer
Metronomic rhythm, 197
Mevlevi, 66
Micronesia (map), 1, 24–26
Microtones, 20, 74, 96
Mi gyaun, 31, 32 (Fig. 8), 128, 132
Mi-kagura, 195
Military music, 66, 136, 143, 152, 153, 162, 163, 205
Mimashi, 199
Ming dynasty, 158–59, 161, 167
Minorities, 92, 170
Minzoku geino (geinō), 187
Missionaries, 21, 205
Miyagi Michio, 207
Mnemonics, 5 (fn. 4), 75 (Ex. 3–5), 100, 102, 106, 115, 187, 195, 197, 203
Modernization of music, 38, 168, 204–8
Modes:
  Central Asian, 89
  Chinese, 148
  Indian, 96–99
  Indonesian, 46 (Ex. 2–3), 47
  Islamic, 72–75, 79
  Japanese, 188, 190
  Korean, 181
  in pentatonic scales, 121
  rhythmic, 30, 75
  Southeast Asia, 120
Modulation, 79, 121, 203
Moeities, 2
Moghul Empire, 93, 95, 115
Mohammed, 66
Mon, 31, 128, 132
Mongolia and Mongols, 88, 143–44, 162, 176
Monochord, 21, 131 (Fig. 43), 132, 215
Monophony, 10, 11, 18, 54, 81
Moon guitar. See *Yueh ch'in*
Moors, 59, 79
Morocco (map), 58, 59, 67
Moro-moro, 29
Moros, 30
Moslem music. *See* Pan-Islamic music
Mouth organ. *See* Harmonica, *Khaen, Saing, Sheng, Sho*
Mouth to mouth chanting, 208
Mozambique (map), 53–54
Mozart, W. A., 66, 199, 209
Mridanga, 106–9 (Fig. 26), 115
Mudang, 183
Mudras, 189
Mukkuri, 208
Multisonance, 10 (fn. 6)
Murcchana, 96, 97
Muruts, 33
Music analysis, rudiments of, 7–9
Music as a non-international universal, 3, 209
Music, defined, 4
Music, function of, 3, 14, 25, 37, 134, 139, 205
Music teaching. *See* Teaching
Music, theory:
  books, 70, 89, 95, 122, 148, 180, 189 190
  Central Asian, 89
  Chinese, 146–49, 156
  four basic systems of, 213–14
  Indian, 95–102, 116
  Islamic, 69–76
  Japanese, 189–90, 199–201
  Java, 38–47

Korean, 180–81
in non-literate societies, 12
Persian, 71–75
Southeast Asian, 119–23
Musical bow, 183
Muwashshah, 79
Mysore, 93
Mythology. *See* Legend

Nabab, 64
Nada, 94, 95, 96
Nadasvaram, 108
Nafir, 66
Nafiri, 127
Nagarah, 143
Nagasvara (*nagasura*), 108
Nagauta, 202
Naghmah, 71, 73
Nagora, 89
Nagpur, 114
Nai. See Nay
Nakara, 66
Nan ch'ü (*nanqu*), 158, 174
Nan hsi (*nanxi*), 158, 174
Nanqu. See Nan ch'ü
Nanxi. See Nan hsi
Naqqara, 62, 67
Nara period, 191
Narrative music:
African, 55, 60
Ainu, 208
Central Asian, 91
Chinese, 166–67
Islamic, 55, 60
Japanese, 197, 202, 203–4
Korean, 181, 182
Mongolian, 143
Southeast Asian, 133
Nasal breathing, 3, 127, 129
National anthem of China, 167, 168 (Ex. 6–5)
Nationalism in music:
Central Asian, 91
Chinese, 169–70
Israel, 85
Japanese, 207, 208
South Asian, 115
Southeast Asian, 126, 136
Natori, 203 (fn. 9)
Natya-Sastra, 95, 97, 115
Nawba, 79
Nay, 31 (fn. 4), 61, 67, 82, 89
Near East, 58–87, 213. *See also* Islam, Pan-Islamic music
Neffar, 66
Negro and negro music, 10, 54, 55, 59, 70
Nei chiao fang (*nei jiao fang*), 155, 174
Nem, 46 (Ex. 2–3), 47
Nenggara, 127
Nepal (map), 141
Netori, 197
Neumes, 139, 189
Neutral tones, 119, 120
New Guinea (map), 4, 9–18
New York, 83, 169
New Zealand (map), 18–20, 25
Ney. See Nay
Ngodo, 53
Nieh Erh, 167
Nigun, 84
Nile River, 62, 83
Nobat, 79 (fn. 11), 127
Noh (*nō*), 199–201, 202, 203
Nokan (*nōkan*), 199
Nonsense syllables, 184
Nong-ak, 183
Norai, 181
North Africa, 52, 58, 59, 64, 67, 69, 79. *See also* Maghrib
North Asia, 208
Nose flute, 16, 17 (Fig. 2), 22, 25, 29, 134
Notation:
ancient Near Eastern, 82
Central Asian, 89
Chinese, 152, 158–59, 168
Ethiopian, 56
Indonesian, 43
Japanese, 190, 194, 195
Korean, 180
limitations of, 85
methods, 20
Tibetan, 139–40
types defined, 139–40
Notes, frequency of, 8
Nuba, 79
Nurestan, 69, 92
Nuru, 183

O, 179 (Fig. 55), 180
Oboe. *See* Double reed aerophone
Ocarina, 145, 149
Occupational music, 187
Oceania (map), 1–27, 169, 183, 184
Octavina, 29
Odaiko (*ōdaiko*), 186 (Ex. 7–6), 204
Ohe hano ihu, 22
Oirats (map), 144
O-kagura (*ō-kagura*), 195
Okinawa. *See* Ryukyu
Oli, 23 (Ex. 1–5)
Oman, 58
Omoro, 183
Onomatopoeia, 5 (fn. 4), 37
Opera:
Chinese, 158–66, 169, 177
in Japan, 207

Opera (*Cont.*)
Western compared to Chinese, 163–64
Oral tradition, 2, 19, 38, 115, 119, 180, 195, 197
Orchestra. *See* Ensembles
Organ, 113, 130
Organal harmony. *See* Harmony, organal
Ornaments, 54, 98, 122, 152, 186. *See also* Melismatic music
Oro, 20
Osaka, 202
O'shak, 71
Oshiki (*ōshiki*), 190
Ostinato, 4, 33, 103, 141, 187 (Ex. 7–7)
O tsuzumi (*ō tsuzumi*), 198 (Fig. 62), 199, 200
Ottoman Empire, 69, 70
Outadokoro, 191
Outer Mongolia. *See* Mongolia
Overblown fifths, 46, 147–48
Ownership in music, 15

Pahu, 22
P'ai hsiao (*pai ziao*), 148, 150, 174
Pak, 180, 195
Pakhawaj, 115
Pakistan (map), 93, 115
Palestine, 58
Pallavi, 104, 106
pan (*ban*), 162, 166, 174
Pan drum, 176, 209, 210 (Fig. 64)
Panembung, 35
Panerus and *Panerusan,* 35, 39 (Ex. 2–1)
Pang ch'iang (*bangqiang*), 160, 161, 174
Panghyung, 180
Pan-Islamic music, 58–81, 182
Pan ku (*ban ku*), 157 (Fig. 50), 162, 174 (also *tan-pi ku*)
Panpipes, 12, 14, 15, 134, 148, 150
Pansori, 181–82
Pan tzu ch'iang (*banzi qiang*), 160, 174
Papua (map), 12
Paraphony, 10 (fn. 7)
Parlando-rubato, 7, 143, 185
Part-books, 195
Pashtun (Pathan), 92
Patere, 19
Pathet (*patet*), 44, 46 (Ex. 2–3), 47
Pa yin (*ba yin*), 149, 174
Pear Garden, 155
Pei ch'ü (*beiqu*), 158, 174
Peking (instrument), 35, 39 (Ex. 2–1), 44
Peking opera, 159, 161–66, 168
Pelog, 45–47
Pentatonic scale, 8, 13, 33, 97, 120–22, 134, 146–48 (Ex. 6–3), 165 (fn. 21), 168, 181, 185, 188 (Ex. 7–8), 189, 190
Percussion. *See* Idiophone, Membranophone, and specific percussion instruments
Performance practice:
in analysis, 7, 10
in *angklung* ensemble, 37–38
Chinese, 152, 154–55, 161 ff
Indian, 102–3
Indonesian, 35
Islamic, 61, 76–80
Japanese, 197
Korean, 177, 181–82
loud and soft style in ensembles, 37, 123–29
Oceania, 9, 12, 18, 21, 23, 25
Philippine, 29–30
Southeast Asian, 123–29
See also, Ensembles, Instruments, playing method
Persia, 62, 67–69, 72-75, 89, 92, 191, 213–14
Pesindhen (*persindhén*), 35, 39 (Ex. 2–1)
Pesrev, 80
Phach, 133
Philippines (map), 1, 28–33, 50, 183, 184
Philosophy. *See* Aesthetics
Phin nam tao, 132
Physics of music, 15. *See also* Acoustics
Piano, 69, 136
Piba. See P'ip'a
Pien, 148, 165 (fn. 21)
Pien ch'ing (*bianqing*), 149, 174
Pien chung (*bianzhong*), 149, 174
P'i huang (*pihuang*), 160, 161, 174
Pillar tones, 122
Pi nai, 123, 124 (Fig. 38)
P'ip'a (*pipa,* also *piba*), 151 (Fig. 45), 153, 155, 158–60, 162, 167, 174
Pi phat, 123, 126, 128, 135
Piri, 177
Pi saw, 130
Pitch, 97, 146–47, 152
Pitch center, 8
Piyutim, 84
Plato, 82
Po (*lo*), 163, 174
Poetry and poems, in:
Afghanistan, 92
ancient Egypt, 83
China, 145, 154, 156, 158, 163
Ethiopia, 56
India, 115
Islam, 60, 66, 76, 79
Japan, 195, 197, 199
Korea, 181
Oceania, 9, 18, 25
Vietnam, 133
See also Text
Pokok, 48
Political music, in:
Central Asia, 91
China, 167–70
Israel, 85
Japan, 205
Mongolia, 143

Polygenesis, theory of, 30
Polynesia (map), 1, 18–24
Polyphonic stratification, 38, 126
Polyphony, 10, 11 (Ex. 1–2), 21
Popular music:
  Afghanistan, 92
  Characteristics of, 206
  Chinese, 169, 170
  Indian, 114
  Indonesian, 38
  Islamic, 80–81
  Japanese, 194, 195, 202, 206
  Jewish, 85
  Southeast Asian, 136
Portuguese songs, 38, 136
Pot drum, 63 (Fig. 17). *See also* Darbuka, Duff, Tombak
Praise songs, 55, 56, 64, 133
Precentor, 11
Prediction. *See* Anticipation
Processional music, 127 (Ex. 5–3). *See also* Ceremonial music
Progessive form, 9
Puccini, G., 207
Puk, 182
Pungi, 114
Pungnyu, 181
Puppet theater:
  Chinese, 166, 177
  Indonesian, 38, 49
  Japanese, 202, 204
  Southeast Asian, 136
Puteri, 134
Pwe, 126
Pwo Karen, 134
Pyonchong, 180
Pyong-jo, 181
Pyongkyong, 180
Pythagoras, 82, 149

Qanun, 69, 77 (Fig. 25)
Qasida (qasidah), 66, 79
Qin. See Ch'in
Qing. See Ch'ing
Quadruple reed aerophones, 123, 124 (Fig. 39), 126, 127, 136
Qupai. See Ch'ü p'ai

Rabab, 67, 68 (Fig. 23), 93. *See also* Rebab
Radif, 76
Raga (rag, ragam), 96–99, 102 ff, 105 (Ex. 4–6), 106 ff, 110, 122, 190
Ragamala, 104 (fn. 15)
Rag-dung, 140
Ragini, 99
Ramadan, 59, 66
Ramal maia, 71, 72 (Ex. 3–3)
Rama pria raga, 104 (Ex. 4–6)
Ramayana, 38
Ranat (ek, ek lek, thong, thum, thum lek), 123, 124 (Fig. 36)
Range, 3, 8, 9, 94, 105, 123
Ranj, 98
Rappa-bushi, 206
Rasa, 98
Rast panjgah, 73 (Ex. 3–4)
Rattle, 16
Rebab, 30, 35, 36 (Fig. 9), 37, 39 (Ex. 2–1), 44, 47, 53, 64, 128, 133, 136, 214
Rebana, 133
Rebec, 30, 64
Recitative, in Chinese opera, 163
Reciting tones, 20, 98
Reconstructed folk music, 91, 169, 170
Recorder. *See* Block flute
Reed aerophones. *See* Double reed, Free reed, Quadruple reed, single reed
Reed pipes, 81, 82
Rekkukara, 208
Religious music, 30, 104, 133–34, 183, 195, 205, 214. *See also* Sacred music
Remel, 75 (Ex. 3–5)
Responsorial singing, 10, 18, 81, 114
Resultant melody or rhythm, 29, 38, 49 (Ex. 2–4)
Reverting form, 9
Reyong, 48
Rgya-gling, 141
Rhythm:
  in analysis, 7
  Chinese, 165–66
  Hawaiian, 23
  Indian, 106–7
  Indonesia, 43–45, 49
  Islamic, 74–75
  Japanese, 186–87, 200–1, 203
  modes, 30, 75 (Ex. 3–5), 130
  Negro and Moslem compared, 54
  patterns, 75, 81, 197, 200–1, 203
  sticks, Fig. 1, 4
Rig Veda, 94
Rimsky-Korsakov, N., 144, 170
Ritchak, 93
Ritsu scale, 188 (Ex. 7–8), 189–90
Ritual music, 141, 150, 170, 177, 180, 187. *See also* Ceremonial music, Liturgical music
Rnga-chung, 140
Rodat, 133
Roei, 195
Rol-mo, 140
Roman tradition, 56, 59, 83, 84, 153, 213–14
Romanization policies:
  Chinese, 147 (fn. 10)
  in general, preface
  for Indian languages, 98 (fn. 8)
  for Indonesian, 35 (fn. 7)
  for Tibetan, 140 (fn. 4)
Romanzas, 83
Rondalla, 29
Ronggeng, 136
Rote learning, 20, 82, 187. *See also* Oral

tradition
Russia, 84, 176. *See also* Soviet Union
Ryo (*ryō*), 188 (Ex. 7–8), 189–90
Ryukoka (*ryūkoka*), 206
Ryukyu Islands (map), 1, 183–85
Ryuteki (*ryūteki*), 194

Sa, 98, 103
Sachs, C., 21
Sacred music:
Indian, 94
Islamic, 64, 66
Japanese, 195
Oceania, 3, 5, 12, 18–19
Southeast Asia, 133–34
Tibetan, 139–41
See also Ceremonial Music, Chants, Liturgical music
Sadjagrama, 96
Safi al-Din al Mummin, 70
Sa-grama, 96, 97
Sahara desert, 54–55
Saibara, 195
Saibari, 195
Sailendra dynasty, 34
Saing (*saing waing*), 126, 180
Saing wang ah-pwe (ensemble), 126
Salamanca, 69
Sam, 100, 107
Samai, 80
Samarkand (map), 69, 154
Sama Veda, 94
Samisen, 187, 202
Sampurna, 97
Samvadi, 98
San ch'ü (*sanqu*), 158
Sanga, 47
Sangati, 106
Sangita-Ratnakara, 95
San hsien (*san xian*), 157 (Fig. 48), 159 ff, 167, 174, 184
Sankyoku, 204
San no tsuzumi, 194
Sanshin, 184, 185
Sanskrit spellings, 98 (fn. 9)
Santur, 69, 160
Sanxian. See San hsien
Sapeh, 31, 33
Saptaka, 96
Sarangadeva, 95
Sarangi, 112 (Fig. 33), 113, 115
Sarinda, 112 (Fig. 34), 113
Sarki, 79
Sarod, 112 (Fig. 35), 113, 115
Saron, 35, 36 (Fig. 10), 37, 39 (Ex. 2–1), 47, 123
Sato-kagura, 195
Satsuma biwa, 199
Saudi Arabia (map), 58
Saw (*saw duang, sam sai*), 128
Saxophone, 136
Say pha, 133
Saz, 64
Scales:
in analysis, 8
in Borneo, 33
in the cents system, 20, 46 (Ex. 2–3)
Chinese, 147–48
Indian, 96–99
Indonesian, 45–47
Islamic, 71–74
Japanese, 185, 188 (Ex. 7–8), 189
Korean, 181
in New Guinea, 13
Southeast Asian, 119–23
Tibetan, 141
tritonic, 23
world views, 214
See also Anhemitonic, Heptatonic, Hexatonic, Modes Pentatonic, Tuning, Tone systems
School music in Japan, 205
Schools:
national, 70, 91, 108, 132, 205
stylistic, 70
of Tibetan chant, 139
See also Guilds
Scrappers, 4
Se, 150
Secret music, 5, 139, 186, 189
Secular music, 5, 55, 61–64, 83–85, 106, 133 ff, 141–42, 158 ff, 187 ff. *See also* Popular music
Segi, 126
Sehtar, 67
Selampit, 133
Senegal, 55
Seoul, 180
Sephardic Jews, 59, 83
Serenade, 21, 130
Serunai, 127, 133
Setar, 90
Shadava, 97
Shahed, 73
Shahnai, 108
Shair, 70
Shakalin Islands (map), 208
Shakubyoshi (*shakubyōshi*), 195
Shakuhachi, 204
Shamanism, 70, 134, 139, 141, 143, 144, 176, 183, 208
Shamisen, 145, 187–88, 196 (Fig. 58), 199, 202–4
Shang dynasty, 144
Shashmakom, 89
Sheng, 33, 130, 150, 151 (Fig. 46), 163, 174, 194
Shensi (map), 160
Shibuji. See Shih pu chi
Shih (*shi*), 158, 174
Shih pu chi (*shibuji*), 154, 174

Shingon sect (Buddhist), 189
Shin-hogaku (*shin-hōgaku*), 207
Shinto, 188, 195, 199
Sho (*shō*), 33, 194, 195
Shoko (*shōko*), 194
Shomu, Emperor, 190
Shomyo (*shōmyō*), 188
Shomyo yojinshu (*Shōmyō yojunshū*), 189
Shoso-in (Shōsōin), 190–93
Shriners, 66
Shur, 73 (Ex. 3–4)
Si (cymbals), 126, 132
Sib, 31 (fn. 4), 61, 82
Siberia (map), 88, 144, 176, 208, 209
Sijo, 181
Sikkim (map), 141
Sil-snyan, 140
Singapore (map), 169
Singing. *See* Vocal music
Single reed aerophone, 25, 53, 62, 81, 115, 130
Sing-sing, 14
Sistrums, 56, 57 (Fig. 13), 82, 83
Sitar, 110, 111 (Fig. 32), 113, 115
Siter, 35
Sitting music, 155
Six dynasties period, 153
"Slack" guitar, 21
Slendro, 39 (Ex. 2–1), 45, 46 (Ex. 2–2), 47
Slentem, 35, 39 (Ex. 2–1)
Slit gong, 14
Socialist realism. *See* Communism
Sociology, 169
Sojo (*sōjō*), 190
Sollukattu, 102
Solmization, 96, 97, 106, 115
Solomon Islands (map), 15
Sona, 162, 163
Sornay-zurna type, 123
Sorogan, 47
South America. *See* Dance, South America, Influences, Latin America
Southeast Asia, 66, 118–36, 213
Soviet Union, 88–91. *See also* Russia
Spain, 29, 59, 69, 70, 79, 83, 182
Spike fiddle, 56, 59, 64, 67, 128. *See also Rebab*
"Split" tone, 139, 144
Sralay, 123
Sri Lanka (map), 93, 115, 213
Sruti, 74, 95–97
Sruti box, 113
Standing music, 155
Stereotyped patterns:
  melodic, 47, 73, 98, 158, 161, 163–66, 189, 195, 204
  rhythmic, 75, 99–100, 103, 166, 200–1, 203, 204
Sthayi, 104
Stone instruments, 22, 120, 145, 149, 153, 180
Stratified polyphony, 30, 38, 126
Stringed instruments. *See* Chordophones
Strophic form, 9, 143
Sudan (map), 55, 62
Suddha jati, 97
Sufi, 64, 79
Sui dynasty, 154
Suites, 53, 79–80, 89, 186
Suji, 108
Suling, 31, 35, 37, 44, 61
Sulu, 30
Sumantran, 140
Sumeria, 81
Sunda, 37, 55, 62
Sung dynasty, 152, 156, 158, 177
Suona. See Sona
Sur, 97
Surna, 141
Surnay, 62
Sur-petti, 113
Su yueh (*suyue*), 155, 174
Suzuki, Shinichi, 207
Svar, 97
Svara, 96
Svaramandala, 113
"Swallowed" reeds, 23, 62, 126
Sweden, 208
Switzerland, 141
Syllabic music setting, 9, 160
Symbolism, 14, 71, 148, 204. *See also* Cosmology, Zoomorphism
Syria (map), 58
Szechwan (map), 160, 161
Szu hu (*sihu*), 162, 175

Taar, 61
Tabl, 62
Tabala, 55
Tabla, 108, 109 (Fig. 27), 115
Tabla tarang, 108
Tablature, 89, 139, 140
Tabu (taboo), 18
Tabu (instrument accessory), 35
Tact, 7, 100
Tadjikstan (map), 89
Taekeum, 177
Tagalog, 29
Taigensho (Taigenshō), 190
Taiko, 186, 198 (Fig. 63), 199, 203
Taishiki, 190
Taiwan (map), 169, 170, 183
Takebue, 186, 203
Takemitsu, Toru, 208
Takemoto, Gidayu, 202
Ta ku (*dagu*), 167, 175
Ta ku tz'u (*daguci*), 167, 175
Tala, 99–102, 104–6, 166
Talam, 115, 132

Talea, 100
Tambourine, 59, 61, 89, 93, 133, 136
Tambur (*tanbur*), 65 (Fig. 19), 67, 89, 90, 92, 110
Tambura, 103, 113, 115
Tamerlaine, 89
Tan tz'u (*danci*), 167, 175
Tanchi, 189
Tang-ak, 177
T'ang dynasty, 148, 154–56
Tao pan (*daoban*), 166, 175
Tapone, 123
Taqsim (*taksim*), 79, 80
Tar, 65 (Fig. 20), 67
Tarana, 104
Tatum, Art, 209
Tawshih, 79
Tchai, 106–7
Teaching and teachers:
  aboriginal use of music in, 2
  ancient China, 155
  ancient Near East, 82
  Ethiopian, 56
  Indian, 102, 107
  Indonesian, 48
  Japanese, 187, 197, 200, 203, 205–7
  Maori, 19
  Southeast Asian, 119
Tempered tuning. *See* Tuning, tempered
Tempo, 7, 99
Tempo giusto, 7, 143
Temporal cycle, 43–44 (Ex. 2–2)
Tendai sect (Buddhist), 189
Tendi, 59
Ten Kingdom period, 156
Terraced contour, 13
Tetrachords, 71, 99
Teukkyeng, 180
Text:
  aboriginal, 5
  Chinese, 145, 152, 161–170
  Indian, 94, 115
  Indonesian, 38
  Japanese, 195, 199, 205
  Korean, 181
  syllable relation to melody, 9
  See also Poetry
Thailand music, 31, 118, 123 ff, 134, 135
Thap, 129
That, 96, 99
Theater and theater music:
  Chinese, 153, 156, 158–66
  Indian, 114–15
  Indonesian, 49
  Japanese, 197–204
  Southeast Asian, 119, 126, 135–36
  Tibetan, 141
Theka, 100
Theory and practice differences, 74, 122
Theories. *See* Diffusion, Music, Theory, Overblown fifths, Polygenesis
Thod-dam, 140
Thom, 129
"Throat" tone, 139, 144
Through-composed, 203
Ti and *ti tzu* (*di, dizi*), 150, 163, 175
Tibet (map), 115, 123, 138–42, 154, 155, 170, 189
Ti-fang hsi (*difangxi*), 159, 175
Tiled melody, 13
Tillana, 104
Timbula, 53
Timbuktu (map), 59
Time markers, 37, 43–44, 162, 165, 194
Tingkling, 29
Ti tzu (*dizi*), 150, 160, 175
Tjelempung (*celempung*), 35
Todai-ji, 190
Togaku (*tōgaku*), 191, 194, 195
Tokhara (map), 153
Tokugawa period, 201–4
Tokyo, 202
Tombak, 63 (Fig. 17), 64, 67, 129
Tone center, 190
Tone quality:
  in Afghanistan, 92
  Ainu, 208
  Chinese, 163
  of *dijeridoo,* 3
  of *gender,* 35
  Indian, 114
  Japanese, 185, 202
  Jewish, 83–85
  Korean, 182
  of Moslem Negroes, 54
  in popular music, 81
  in Southeast Asian folk music, 134
Tone systems:
  Chinese, 147–48
  Indian, 96–99
  Indonesian, 45–47
  Islamic, 71–74
  Japanese, 185, 188–89
  Korean, 181
  Maori, 18
  Southeast Asian, 119–23
  Tibetan, 141
  world views, 214
Tonkori, 148
Toyohara, Sumiaki, 190
Tranh, 132
Transcriptions, preface, 5, 20, 190
Triads, 21, 141–42
Tribes and tribal music, 2–3, 12, 28–29, 114, 118, 134, 143, 174, 183
Triputa tala, 105
Tritonic scale, 23
Tro, 128
Trombone, Turkish, 66
Trompong, 48
Trumpets, 15–16, 22, 25, 114, 127, 134,

Trumpets (*Cont.*)
136, 140–41, 153
Tsa chü (*zaju*), 158, 175
Tsenatsil, 56, 57 (Fig. 13)
Tsuzumi, 198–201, 203
Tuareg, 59, 60 (Ex. 3–1)
Tube zither, 16, 29, 53, 110
Tunggalan, 30
Tuning:
of instrument, 45, 48, 130, 143, 162
paste, 108, 123
tempered, 81, 91, 119, 148
Tunisia (map), 58, 59
Turfan (map), 153, 154
Turkey (map), 58, 62, 67, 75, 79, 80, 90
Turkish crescent, 66
Turkmenistan (map), 89
Tuvinians (map), 144
Tyagaraja, 104–7
Ty ba, 132
Tz'u (*ci*), 158, 175

Ud, 65 (Fig. 18), 67, 69, 71, 79
U-jo, 181–82
Ukeke, 21, 22
Ukelele, 21, 22, 25
Uke mitsuji, 200–1
Uliger, 143
Uliuli, 22
Ululation, 144. *See also* Yodel
Umui, 183, 184 (Ex. 7–4)
United States, 16, 66, 213
Universals in music, 214–15
University of Auckland, and University of Hawaii, 25
University of Paris, 70
Ur, 81
'Ushshaq, 71
Usul, 75
Utai, 199
Uzbekistan (map), 89, 213

Vadi, 98
Vaji, 69, 92
Valiha, 16, 17 (Fig. 3), 53
Value judgments of music, 215
Variation form, 159, 204
Veda, 94, 194
Venkatamakhi, 99
Venu, 108
Vibhaga, 100
Vietnam (map), 120, 128, 129, 133, 134
Vikrta, 97
Vilambita, 99
Vina, 108, 110, 111 (Fig. 31), 115, 129
Violin, Western, 53, 64, 67, 115, 128, 136, 162, 207. *See also* Lute, bowed
Vocal music:
aboriginal, 2, 5
Afghanistan, 92
Ainu, 208
Borneo, 33–34
Central Asian, 91
Chinese, 160–67
Indian, 94, 104, 105, 106, 114
Indonesian, 35
Islamic, 59, 80
Japanese, 185, 195, 197–200, 202–5, 206–7
Korean, 181–83
Mongolian, 143–44
Oceanic, 10, 14, 18–20, 23–25
Philippine, 29, 30
Southeast Asian, 130, 134–36
Voice quality. *See* Tone quality

Wa, 132
Wagner, R., 207
Wagon, 195
Waiata, 19
Wai chiao fang (*wai jiao fang*), 155, 175
Wa let kyong, 126
Wang san-ak, 177
Watashimono, 190
Wayang kulit, 38. *See also* Puppet theater
Wedding songs, 62, 66
Weighted scale, 6 (Ex. 1–1), 8
Wela, 44
Wen wu (*wenwu*), 152, 175
Western music:
cadences, 12
in China, 167–70
in Israel, 84
in Japan, 205–8
in popular music, 81
in Southeast Asia, 136
as one of four major systems, 214–15
See also Analogy, Comparisons, Influences, Violin
Whakaeke, 18
Wolofs, 55, 83
Women's music:
in the ancient Near East, 82
in China, 155, 156, 163
Indian, 115
Islamic, 62
Japanese, 202
Korean, 182
Thai, 134
Tuareg, 59
Wood blocks, 162
Word painting, 203
Wu sheng (*wusheng*), 147, 175
Wu-ti, 152
Wu wu (*wuwu*), 152, 175

Xiao. See Hsiao

Xipi. See Hsi p'i
Xiqu. See Hsi ch'u
Xiwen. See Hsi wen
Xuan. See Hsuan
Xuan zong. See Hsuan-tsung
Xylophones, 16, 30, 33, 53, 123, 124 (Fig. 36), 135, 136

Ya gwin, 126
Yajur Veda, 94
Yakuts (map), 208
Yamada, Kosaku (Koscak), 207
Yang, 148, 175
Yang ch'in (*yangqin*), 69, 160, 175
Yang-yig, 139
Yao pan (*yaoban*), 166, 175
Yarul, 62, 63 (Fig. 16), 83
Ya yueh (*yayue*), 152, 155, 175
Yellow Bell, 146
Yemen (map), 58, 83, 84 (Ex. 3–7)
Yen yueh (*yenyue*), 152, 175, 191
Yiddish music, 85
Yin, 148, 175
Yiyangqiang. See I yang ch'iang
Yo (*yō*), 185, 188 (Ex. 7–8)
Yodaya, 130
Yodel, 59, 144
Yogaku (*yōgaku*), 206
Yokthe pwe, 136
Yokyoku (*yōkyoku*), 199
Yü (*yu*), 150, 175, 179 (Fig. 55)
Yuanban. See Yuan pan
Yüan ch'ü (*yuan qu*), 158, 159, 175
Yuan dynasty, 158
Yuan pan (*yuan ban*), 166, 175
Yuanqu. See Yüan ch'ü
Yueh ch'in (*yueqin*), 129, 157 (Fig. 49), 159, 160, 162, 163, 175
Yueh fu (*yuefu*), 152, 175
Yueqin. See Yueh ch'in
Yugoslavia, 143
Yukar, 208

Zaju. See Tsa chü
Zamr, 62
Zarbi, 75
Zarzuela, 30
Zat pwe, 136
Zeami, Motokiyo, 199
Zheng. See Cheng
Zhi (*Chih*), 143 (Ex. 6–3)
Zhu. See Chu
Zhu zaiyu. See Chu Tsai-yü
Zikibarat, 133
Zil, 66
Ziryab, 70
Zither:
- Ainu, 208
- Chinese, 150, 151 (Fig. 44), 160
- defined, 22
- Indian, 113
- Indonesian, 31, 35
- Japanese, 185, 195, 196 (Fig. 59), 204
- Korean, 177, 178 (Fig. 51, 52)
- in Madagascar, 53
- Southeast Asian, 132–33
- *See also* Dulcimer

Zoomorphism:
- in dance, 2, 187
- on instruments, 11, 31, 32 (Fig. 8), 128, 135, 143, 150, 179 (Fig. 55), 180

Zorna, 62
Zukra, 62
Zurna, 62, 66, 77 (Fig. 24), 81, 89